MAKEITALIFEOFADVENTURE.COM

**LIVE WITHOUT FEAR!
DISCOVER WHERE YOUR
ADVENTURES WILL TAKE YOU!**

• • • •

SCOTT MACWHERTER

LIFE OF ADVENTURE BOOKS

Melbourne, Australia

Copyright © 2025 Scott MacWherter | makeitalifeofadventure.com

All rights reserved. No part or any portion of this book may be reproduced in any form, mechanical, or digital, or transmitted without the prior written permission of the author, except for the use of brief quotations in a book review.

This book is presented solely for educational and entertainment purposes. It is the intent of the author to provide general knowledge and helpful information on the subjects discussed to assist readers in their quest for greater understanding and utilization of the ideas, thoughts and principles presented. The advice and strategies contained herein may not be suitable for your situation. While all best efforts have been used in preparing this book, the author makes no representations or warranties of any kind and assumes no liabilities of any kind with respect to the accuracy or completeness of the contents, and specifically disclaims any implied warranties of merchantability or fitness of use for a particular purpose. The author shall not be held liable or responsible to any person or entity with respect to any loss or damage, incidental or consequential, caused or alleged to have been caused, directly or indirectly, by the information contained herein.

LEGAL DISCLAIMERS: The information and recommendations contained are for informational purposes only. This book is not meant to be used, nor should it be used, to diagnose or treat any medical or psychological condition. For diagnosis or treatment of any condition, medical or psychological, please consult with a physician. Some of the contents of this book will be confronting and triggering for certain readers. Please proceed with caution. Many of the activities described in this book have inherent risks. Some are incredibly dangerous! Neither the publisher nor the author is liable for any physical, psychological, emotional, or financial damages resulting from injury or death. Some of the activities are strenuous. Please consult with a physician before engaging in any activity recommended in this book. Please take personal responsibility for your actions.

For information about this title or to order other books
and/or electronic media, contact the publisher:
Life of Adventure Books
makeitalifeofadventure.com

Cover and interior design by The Book Cover Whisperer:
OpenBookDesign.biz

Library of Congress Control Number: 0000000000

978-1-7638407-0-6 Paperback
978-1-7638407-1-3 eBook

Printed in the United States of America

FIRST EDITION

• • • •

In loving memory of my father and mother, Charles and Clara MacWherter. I am not sure how they survived me and my brother and sister as long as they did. To my lovely wife, Narelle, and amazing daughter, Zoe. Thank you for being in my life.

CONTENTS

Chapter 1: What is a Life of Adventure?
1

Chapter 2: The Tao of Risk
18

Chapter 3: Your Brain on Adrenaline
51

Chapter 4: The Fear That Lies Within
80

Chapter 5: Finding Courage
113

Chapter 6: Creating the Expeditionary Mindset
155

Chapter 7: The Power of the Great Outdoors
180

Chapter 8: Reigniting the Passion of Childhood Dreams
203

Chapter 9: Be a Traveler
231

Chapter 10: Living with Urgency
251

Endnotes
273

Chapter 1:

What is a Life of Adventure?

Security is mostly a superstition...
Life is a daring, bold adventure or it is nothing.
— HELEN KELLER

I sat in the car's passenger seat and quietly surveyed the landscape of my new home country. The area we were driving through was flat grassland—farm country. It was hot, and everything was brown, for it was high summer, and there was a drought. The scenery was not quite as arid or desolate as the outback, but still, it felt like a dry, lonely place. We periodically passed large farms and cattle stations. I noticed many of the stations had windmill water wells for their cattle, a very stereotypical image representing all things Australia. We occasionally saw cows, sheep, and even a mob of kangaroos resting beneath an isolated clump of trees.

The sea of dead grass appeared endless, but we weren't that far from several mountain ranges, temperate rainforests, or even the beach where we were heading on the last leg of our holiday. The beach would be a nice rest from almost a month of constant traveling. It would be the last refuge of vacation before my wife and I had to face reality and do those annoying things that needed to be done, like finding jobs and a permanent place to live. It was hard for me to believe this wasn't like the handful of times I had visited Australia before. This was home now.

The prior six months had been anything but dull. For my daughter's seventh birthday, we visited a beautiful resort and swam with dolphins. After that, things went fast, and life got weird. The plan seemed simple enough. Fix up the house and sell it. Rent a recreational vehicle and drive it from Florida to California. Fly to Melbourne, Australia, where we would then live.

We hadn't counted on the fact that we would get caught in one of the biggest hurricanes in recorded history. As soon as we recovered from that and got the house up for sale, we had a serial killer stalking the neighborhood. I probably don't have to tell you how quickly that can change a seller's market into a buyer's market.

Still, we managed to take an RV across America. We had plenty of exploits along the way, including a dispute about water rights between me and a very large and thirsty elk in our campsite at the Grand Canyon. I lost this dispute and ended up running for my life! The elk was giving full chase. Although being chased by an elk wasn't much fun for me, it was hilarious to my daughter and some neighboring campers who witnessed the whole thing.

The drive across the continental US went fast, and before I knew it we were on an airplane to the other end of the world. Now I was driving through the Australian countryside—one adventure ending and another just beginning.

Before you read any further, I must tell you this is a personal development book of sorts, but it's unlike your typical motivational book that promises you world domination if you just keep psyching yourself up. Nor is it one of the countless self-help books that try to build self-esteem through an "I'm okay, you're okay, everything will be all right if you just stay positive" kind of philosophy.

Instead, it is based loosely on the adventure recreation model found in experiential learning circles. The idea is that you participate in activities that you find personally challenging and engaging, generate significant meaning, and allow you to set personal goals.

This is personal development by doing things you find difficult to do. If they are thrilling, that adds a layer of fun and makes the challenges a little more palatable, but easy is not what we are going for. The possibility of failure and real-world consequences accelerates the process. It allows you to build character by overcoming adversity. This, in turn, helps you create a truly positive mental attitude built on a solid foundation of incremental success.

The tools in this book will help prepare you for whatever life throws at you and even allow you to have a little fun with the things that once might have frightened you to death.

I would say overall, I have lived an adventurous life, although there are plenty of people who are a lot more adventurous than I am. I am not even the most adventurous person I know, but hopefully, I have enough experience to give you some ideas on how to become more adventurous yourself.

I have always had a powerful thirst for adventure. When I was a little kid, I was always the first to tromp off into the woods. I was usually the first to climb the unclimbable tree. I was the one to sneak into an old, abandoned house that was "haunted" before the other kids decided it was safe enough to explore.

This carried over into young adulthood. Immediately after graduating high school, I joined the Marines. When my service was completed, I wasn't back home long before I got the itch to go again. So I traveled the world working aboard luxury cruise ships as a massage therapist.

I have had the fortune to travel all over the world, and I have done some cool things and seen some amazing sights. But I would not have been able to do them without developing the concepts, mindsets, and principles found in this book.

I use personal stories to explain many of the principles. I tried to balance out the "I have been here and done that" stories that on their own could be interpreted as egotistical with all the feelings of trepidation and self-doubt I experienced immediately before or during. It is important to note I am not one of those superhuman extreme-sports athletes. I am just a normal person who likes to push my boundaries a little. I have also included some stories where I performed as a counterexample of how you should behave and added what I hope is some good old self-deprecating humor. I have included some mistakes to show how making mistakes can be important to the growth process (if they don't kill you).

So what is the life of adventure? What is an adventure, for that matter? The word can mean many different things to people. Some will define adventure as nothing less than a grand expedition that requires you to put your very life in peril.[1] While that certainly is adventure, I disagree with that definition. I don't think you have to put your life in danger at all.

Because there are so many possibilities about what adventure can mean, let's redefine that word so it has a more personal meaning for us. But before I can define it properly, let me first state what it is not. Adventure is not a scorecard. It is not about how many times you have climbed Everest. It's not even whether you have gone mountain climbing, snorkeled with piranhas in the Amazon, raced sled dogs in the Antarctic, bungy jumped from a helicopter over a volcano, or any other thing people associate with adventure. Adventure is not a contest. It is a personal experience.

Adventure is anything you do outside of your safe space or daily routine. This is especially true if it propels you toward what you want in life or teaches you a life lesson. Or maybe it's just fun.

We all have limits to what we can do. The thing is, most of these limits are self-imposed. We usually reach a limit of what we are willing to do long before we get remotely close to the limit of what we are capable of. With this book I want to help you push some of those self-imposed limits—and push them in a way that makes them expand. You want things to be challenging but in a way that makes you feel good. You want to find your own personal edge.

The important thing is to not focus on what other people are doing or the level they are willing to take things to but to work on your own barriers and limitations. Just because someone else has pushed it further doesn't mean an experience isn't adventurous for you. If you check your ego, adventurous undertakings can be truly transformative. On the other side of that, some things you think are no big deal may be colossal triumphs for someone else.

Before we get into the *how* of being more adventurous, I want to get into some of the reasons *why* you could be more adventurous. The *how* is always much easier if you have a compelling *why*. What can living adventurously do for you? There are many benefits. Below I list nine. Of course, this list isn't all-inclusive, but it's at least a good start.

1. **It instills confidence that can be transferred to other areas of your life.**

Most of your adventures require you to learn and integrate new skills. Whenever you learn a new skill, it gives you a great feeling. "Hey, I have accomplished something new!" The *how* of the fact learning makes you feel good is discussed in later chapters, and it involves some pretty interesting chemicals in the brain.

As you accomplish new things, you build confidence. This is particularly true for a skill you think you have no aptitude for. In other words, the harder you find learning at the beginning, the bigger the sense of accomplishment when you reach a milestone. I have found tying knots extremely difficult since I was a kid in Boy Scouts. It was something that frustrated me to no end, so I would just give up. When I managed to learn the retraced figure eight, a knot that has been responsible for saving my life, I felt incredibly proud. Now I am going back and learning some of the basic knots I struggled with as a boy. Whenever I get frustrated at trying to learn something new, I think of how I can do a retraced figure eight. It reminds me that I can learn things I initially found difficult. As an added benefit I also get a little perspective. When I am trying something new, even if I get it wrong, it probably won't lead to me falling to my death like messing up a figure eight can do.

Confidence is transferable. When you accomplish something difficult or seemingly impossible, you can have a fresh outlook. Now you can create a new belief: the belief that you can accomplish other things that you once didn't think were possible.

I remember when my daughter was learning how to ride a bike. I had taken it for granted for so long that I forgot all the steps involved in riding a bike until I had to teach it. For some time she just wasn't getting it, and after a couple of tumbles, she didn't even want to try. She said it was impossible and demanded I put the training wheels back on her bicycle. I convinced her to keep trying. Then finally it clicked. She got it and could ride all by herself! She beamed with pride and wanted to ride everywhere. Now whenever she is struggling with homework or anything else, and she wants to give up, I simply remind her how she thought learning to ride a bike was impossible. The boost of confidence allows her to dig in deeper and keep going.

Even if a lot of technical learning is not required, just doing something you didn't feel comfortable with can create a sense of massive accomplishment! If someone who is afraid of heights climbed an extremely high tower or went zip-lining, they may find it a lot easier afterward to ask someone out on a date or go for that promotion at work.

I am sure you can see how accomplishing new things increases self-confidence. Self-confidence is your belief in your abilities. Stacking a multitude of self-confidence builders like blocks in a metaphorical pyramid increases self-esteem. Self-esteem is your overall appreciation of yourself. Self-confidence and self-esteem together are the gateway to achievement.

They are probably also the two biggest factors in measuring overall life satisfaction.

There are countless stories about at-risk youth participating in adventure camps like Outward Bound[2] where they learn to take pride in themselves. These are kids who may have had terrible home lives. Some come from abusive homes. They have been getting into trouble. Many have already served time in juvenile detention. Most are on the brink. If something isn't done, they are probably heading for a life of crime and addiction.

Once they have completed the course, these youths see themselves in a different light. When they return to the real world, grades improve, behavior becomes better, and there is often a positive domino effect in their lives. Sometimes a three-week canoe trip or a backpacking course is just what a troubled teen needs to build enough confidence to change the course of their life forever! If an expedition like this can have such a profound effect on troubled teens, what do you think trying something new can do for someone like you?

2. It increases your mental flexibility and problem-solving skills.

No matter how well-prepared you are, the unexpected is bound to happen. Adventuring requires you to solve problems. How do you get from point A to point B? What happens when the path you expected to take is blocked? You took a wrong trail. A critical piece of equipment is broken. The GPS fell into the water. You misplaced your headlamp. It's getting dark, and you can't see. You capsized, and now you must flip this canoe over, drain the water, and find a way to retrieve your paddle that is floating down the river. The possible variations to any given scenario are as endless as the choices you can make. The key is finding the right choice when the unexpected happens.

Even more important, if you make the wrong choice or a series of wrong choices, how do you course correct without going into full-blown panic mode? If you messed up badly and are in danger, how do you get to safety? As you get used to the roadblocks along the way, you tend to think of them less as problems and more as challenges. Then it is much easier to get out of victim mode—"Why does this always happen to me?"—and into puzzle-solving mode: "There is a solution here. I just have to find it." This mindset infuses into the rest of your life, and that's important, because in life the unexpected is bound to happen, no matter what.

One time I was hiking with my family—my wife, Narelle, and our then ten-year-old, Zoe—in an area that had been ravaged by bushfires a few years before. The forest was coming back nicely, but there were a lot of large dead trees that had either recently fallen or were going to fall within the next couple of years. Giant dead trees that are still standing are referred to as widow-makers by the hiking community, so we were a little nervous to be around so many.

Well, after the halfway point, sure enough, we came upon a large mountain ash that had fallen down the length of the trail. On one side of where our hiking trail should have been was a deep ravine, and on the other was an upward incline so sharp it basically amounted to being a wall. The fallen tree was big—about 150 feet (fifty meters) long, with a diameter of about six feet (two meters). Rather than hike another two hours back, we decided to use the tree as the trail. We had to use the roots to climb up, but we walked along the length of the tree and then climbed down the branches on the other side. Even though my wife was more than a little nervous with the drop-off to one side, I held her hand as we walked along the length of the trunk, and she did well. This was a pretty literal example of the saying by Roman emperor and stoic philosopher Marcus Aurelius: "What stands in the way becomes the way."[3]

Psychologists suggest that having the mental flexibility to adjust to uncertainty, novelty, and change is perhaps the most important mental skill you can develop as a human. I know some of my best results have come when I was able to adapt on the fly. Some of the worst times in my life happened when I failed to adapt or didn't want to accept change and deal with it. Mental flexibility can easily be summed up with this simple we use in the Marines: "Improvise, adapt, and overcome!"

3. It gives you the ability to step outside your comfort zone and face your fears.

Conquering your fears is both a benefit and a large part of the process of becoming an adventurer. Most of the things you might call adventure are based on this concept. It's an important one, and I devote a large part of this book to it. I address what fear-induced adrenaline does to the body, methods to deal with fear and anxieties, and how to use them as tools for self-development instead of the enemy most people think they are. Don't worry. I drill deep down into the term *comfort zone*.

4. It allows you to live in the moment.

Do you ever want to turn off the voice in your head? We all have them. I don't know about you, but mine has been known to be exasperating sometimes. For most people, often the voice acts as an inner critic, and it can seriously throw off your game when it's yapping away. People spend a great deal of time thinking about the past, rehashing times when they felt someone slighted them or things didn't go as planned. The other thing is planning and possibly worrying about the future. For most of us, there is almost constant chatter inside our heads, reliving things that have already happened or worrying about things that haven't happened yet and might not ever.

Psychologists, athletes, Zen masters, yogis, martial artists, extreme sports aficionados, and even performers talk about an ability to shut off or tune out all this internal noise. This quieting of the mind, often called a flow state, is living in the moment—a meditative or Zen state. It is when your internal dialogue is turned off and you are truly in the present. This meditative state is one of the healthiest mental states to be in and a possible path to spirituality and enlightenment. Some people spend their whole lives trying to find this flow state, but when you are fully immersed in something joyful yet challenging and maybe even a little scary, a flow state is also one of the easiest states to find yourself in.

I have had some experience sitting in a half-lotus position doing formal meditation. But for me, stillness of the mind is best generated by movement of the body. Even a nice long hike in the woods can quiet the mind. If nothing else, your conscious mind will be preoccupied with not tripping over the next root or slipping on the next rock, and that can be just the touch of Zen you need. This is called a walking meditation and it still counts as meditation. It is a whole lot more fun than twisting your legs into a pretzel and trying to let go of your thoughts. It doesn't matter if it's rock climbing or climbing a tree—you can find stillness in action.

5. It increases your fitness.

Adventuring often involves varying levels of physical exercise. Entire books are devoted to the numerous benefits of exercising, and you no doubt already know exercise is important for your overall health. Trying to describe all the health benefits would require a book dedicated to that.

Let's face it. Working out in the gym gets boring. So many things can give you a great workout without the monotony. I admit I used to be a gym rat. Somehow I thought the layers of muscle I was packing on were some kind of armor. After two hernia operations and a major surgery on my shoulder, I changed my mind. I began to think more about functional strength, which seems to be getting popular these days.

Different types of adventure exercise your body in different ways. The SAID principle in fitness says if you constantly do the same exercises, you will get good only at those exercises. SAID stands for Specific Adaptation to Imposed Demands. So now I concentrate on functionality as opposed to pure strength. I must admit I can't think of one time when I needed to bench-press three hundred pounds (136 kilograms). I have, however, needed to scale an eight-foot (2.5-meter) fence when I locked my keys in the house, and the only way to get in was through the back door, which I had left unlocked. Doing types of exercise involved in exploratory activities develops more functional fitness that may serve you in a pinch.

You may be captivated by nature while getting your workout or having so much fun that you don't even realize you're getting the exercise your body needs. There's no reason fitness can't be fun.

6. It reduces stress levels and increases your sense of happiness and well-being.

We all want to be happy, don't we? Everyone wants to reduce the level of stress they feel.

Adventuring can certainly be the answer.

The body naturally produces a host of chemicals responsible for mood regulation. These are sometimes more effective and certainly a lot safer than most of the medications produced pharmaceutically.

As counterintuitive as it appears, doing something super exciting can have a relaxing effect. You'll learn about how the chemicals released in your body when you do something thrilling calm you down in chapter 3. Chapter 7 explains how the mere act of being outdoors can lead to feelings of euphoria.

7. It can help you make more money.

That's right. Adventurers make more money! Okay, that is not necessarily true. I'm not going to say an adventurous mindset is the key to wealth, because that would be ridiculous. I am not rich yet. Plenty of adventurers out there are making barely enough to survive, keeping just enough money to eat and do the things they enjoy. Doing more with fewer resources is a method of being adventurous. Some adventurers delight in doing just enough to get by or living off the grid completely, having little to do with society, let alone building wealth. However, there are plenty of examples of adventurers who make a ton of money.

These days you are as likely to read an article about an adventure athlete in *Forbes* as to read about one in *Outside Magazine*. Enough entrepreneurs and high-level business professionals have some kind of extreme sport as a hobby that there appears to be a correlation.

Take, for example, my favorite billionaire, Richard Branson, the founder of Virgin Records, Virgin Airlines, and Virgin Galactic. He has had some enormous business accomplishments. To achieve these, he has taken on an enormous amount of risk. He is also known for taking very big risks with his personal safety, including an ill-fated attempt to achieve the fastest Atlantic crossing by boat. He ended up capsizing and had to be rescued by helicopter. He also was almost killed when attempting to cross the Atlantic in a hot-air balloon. Now he is even an astronaut. He is one of the richest men in the world, but he also knows how to really be alive—sometimes at the risk of nearly dying.[4]

A lesser-known billionaire adventure businessman is Yvon Chouinard. When his family moved to southern California, he got into falconry, which led him to rock climbing. Because climbing gear was too expensive, he learned the craft of blacksmithing. He then started selling climbing gear he made himself from the back of his car. He concentrated on high quality as if his life depended on it. He used his own equipment, so it did. He created a company specializing in climbing gear. This was the beginning of the outdoor company Black Diamond.

From there he went on to create another outdoor gear and clothing company, Patagonia, with annual sales of over $300 million. He built this company by taking many risks in both his personal life and business. He is a great person to study because he built an empire using a high level of ethics rarely seen in business today. From everything I have read and seen about him, he maintains a certain humility, constantly referring to himself and all his friends as *dirtbags*.

At one point I did a community television show. It wasn't a big deal. It was a simple talking-heads show. The cool thing about it was I was able to interview dozens of successful entrepreneurs, business leaders, and performance coaches. The one thing they all said was the biggest key to success was the ability to step out and take calculated risks. Many of them considered the businesses they built as adventures in themselves, and some had very interesting stories of travel and exploration.

I had similar conversations with some of my high-end clients on ships. I had the privilege of working for a couple of exclusive cruise lines, and while a few of the passengers came from old money, the vast majority I talked to started from humble beginnings and built vast business empires. Although it is no guarantee, the path of adventure can lead to wealth! Most independent, wealthy people I've talked to say the same thing—learning to take risks was the biggest key to their success. Adventuring, by definition, is taking risks, so that must mean there is some kind of correlation.

8. It makes you sexier!

It's true. First, it is a well-known fact that confidence is an attractor. I have already mentioned learning to do new, challenging things will lead to increased confidence; therefore it makes sense that increased confidence also increases your desirability.

A willingness to get out of your comfort zone and overcome the fear of rejection can enable someone to be willing to make the first move more often. Have you ever seen two people who were obviously attracted to each other but were both so afraid that neither one was willing to take the initiative? Maybe it has happened to you. For those who never ask, the answer is no 100 percent of the time.

Being physically fit is an obvious attractor. Athleticism also increases stamina. Less stress, more endorphins, and other feel-good hormones can combat erectile dysfunction.

Probably the biggest connection between adventure and sexuality has to do with the adrenal response. Have you ever wondered why young couples like to see scary movies? All that excitement makes them . . . well, excited!

When adrenaline is fired into the system, oxygen, and glucose are increased in the skeletal muscles. Your senses are heightened. This is a similar response to sexual arousal. It doesn't take much to shift between the two forms of excitement. A lot of research suggests adrenaline increases sex drive.

Is there any wonder why physiological arousal and sexual arousal share many characteristics? When you think about it, the drive to procreate is the second most powerful drive in nature, second only to the drive for self-preservation, which is the reason for the adrenal response mechanism. Doing adventurous things arouses your sensory system, and that can also arouse your sexuality.

Numerous scientific studies correlate increased arousal and attraction because of adrenal stimulation going back to the 1960s. In one such experiment in 1974, an attractive female research assistant was placed at the end of two bridges.[5] All the test subjects were male. One bridge was sturdy. This was the bridge the control group would cross. The other bridge was much more adventurous—it was a swinging suspension bridge that was considerably higher. The swinging bridge was designed to induce fear, creating an adrenal response in the test subjects.

After crossing the bridge, the test subjects were given an ambiguous picture by the female research assistant and told to write a brief background story explaining the picture. The researcher gave the subjects her phone number and told them to call her if they had any questions about the experiment.

The test subjects who had gone over the scary suspension bridge not only wrote stories about the picture that were more sexually explicit in content but also were more likely to call the researcher. Many of them asked her out on a date.

A 2003 experiment was held on a roller coaster at an amusement park.[6] In this experiment men and women subjects were asked to rate the attractiveness of a person in a picture. The control group rated the person in the picture before the roller-coaster ride. The other group rated the person immediately after riding the intense coaster. As you can guess, the people who took the thrill ride first rated the person in the picture much higher. Simply put, intense experiences contribute to increased sex drive.

Now you single guys reading this, before you decide to take all your first dates big-wave surfing or helicopter snowboarding, understand many other factors are involved in attraction. It is not a simple formula, but adrenaline may be a piece of the puzzle—possibly a very big piece of the puzzle. Getting some adventure in your life may be the answer to that age-old question of how to get more *lovin* in your life.

9. It teaches you about yourself.

The words *know thyself* are inscribed at the Temple of Apollo in Delphi, Greece. The saying is attributed to Plato, Socrates, and other prominent philosophers of the time.

We all wear different masks around different people. You can be a confident professional to some people, a wild party animal to others, perhaps the jokester to someone, the quiet neighbor to another. You can change masks so many times you may not know who you really are anymore. Sometimes people lose themselves to the identities they carry. People's roles as parents, spouses, children, employees, bosses, students, friends, and partners can overshadow the person underneath. You need to be shown you are more than what you do most of the time. The identities you assume are not the complete picture of who you are.

There is nothing like a good adventure to peel back the layers under which we hide our true selves. It is one thing to muse about what you think you would do in any given situation but another thing entirely to cast yourself into an experience directly.

Only then you can truly reflect on doing. Where did your boundaries really lie? Did you thrive when challenged? What areas were you weak in and needed improvement? Where did you shine? Lessons you learn about yourself in your adventurous undertakings can be refined and applied to everyday life. Introspection is an important part of a life well lived, but you must put the iron in the fire before you can truly test the mettle, so to speak.

Placing yourself in an unfamiliar environment, doing things you are not used to doing, regularly allows you to see flaws in your character that you might not otherwise notice. A good adventure challenges you not only physically but also mentally and emotionally. This allows you to develop yourself in all three areas simultaneously and holistically.

This probably just scratches the surface, but these are a few of the reasons why *you want to have adventure in your life*. If nothing else, having a strong thirst for adventure will keep life interesting. Again, it doesn't have to be an epic expedition to the ends of the earth to be an adventure.

As I said before, this is a personal development book. Each chapter contains one or more exercises for you to complete. Please do them. They are designed to build on each other, and I can attest they have made a dramatic difference in my life. They can in yours too, but only if you do them. If you decide to take up the mantle of exploration, a few years from now you will look back and be glad you did.

EXERCISE

Write down your own reasons for wanting to be more adventurous.
How do you think living adventurously can improve your life?
What would life be like if you lived more adventurously?
What aspects of life do you think you could be more adventurous in?

Chapter 2:

The Tao of Risk

*It seems to be a law of nature, inflexible and inexorable,
that those who will not risk cannot win.*
— John Paul Jones

Tao (pronounced *dow*) is a Chinese word that means *the way* or *the path*. Risk in its simplest terms is the possibility of something bad happening.[1] Regardless of how remote that possibility is, there is a chance. So the Tao of risk is the path of, or the way of, risk. Tao can also be translated as the doctrine or philosophy of. This chapter is the doctrine of walking the path of risk. If you, like me, want to have a richer and more rewarding life, you're going to have to take risks. This chapter will give you some concepts on how to take risks while reducing some of the dangers involved in taking them.

A more precise explanation of risk might be this: exposure to the possibility of some sort of loss or undesired consequence. This could be financial, physical, or even psychological. Understanding the concept of risk is important, because it is risk and how we relate to it that drives most of our decision-making, not only consciously but sometimes at a level underneath or, maybe more accurately, above our conscious threshold. How you handle risks, both real and imagined, is largely responsible for your world and what happens in it. Your relationship with risk largely determines how life turns out, maybe even how long it lasts. So it is an important study.

Your body naturally craves adventure. It is an innate part of your DNA. You have a built-in goal-striving, risk-taking mechanism that is as old as the lizard part of your brain. In the animal world, risk is as unavoidable as it is potentially beneficial. Environmental hazards are everywhere. Grazers and smaller animals are under constant threat of being eaten, but they must find food or they will die. Even the top-of-the-food-chain alpha predators are at risk from others of their own species as they compete for territory, water, food, and mates.

When humans were hunter-gatherers, it was the group willing to take the risk and slay the woolly mammoth that had the greatest chance of eating and passing their genes on to the next generation. The ones who were afraid to take risks starved. Risk-taking used as an adaptive behavior by our ancestors is why we are here. Although not everyone feels it on the same level, the need to take risks is hardwired into your neurology.

Sometimes something goes wrong, and that natural drive for risk becomes risky behavior in a negative sense. Please don't confuse the willingness to take risks with recklessness. While recklessness is a willingness to take risk, it is vastly different from positive, calculated risk-taking.

Sometimes certain psychological factors combine to make a person overly risk averse. But the hardwiring is still there. Taking calculated risks is an advantageous behavior. Learning when and how to take risks for the right reasons is a skill set just like any other. It needs to be developed.

Although the implementation will be vastly different, the same basic principles apply to all risk, whether you are out deep in the wilderness, in business, investing, or even in your day-to-day life. The principles of risk are universal.

Almost all innovation, regardless of whether it is in the field of science, the arts, or business development, is created by risk-takers. Everything new under the sun was invented by someone who took a risk and would have had to deal with the consequences had it not worked out. All advancement is achieved by taking risks. This concept of adventure is the paradigm you use to teach yourself when and how to take risks for your benefit.

Every aspect of your life gives you a chance to advance by taking risks—everything from asking for a raise at work (you risk being rejected), to starting your own business (you risk failing), to driving anywhere (you risk an accident). Even in dating—especially in dating—you have the initial risk of rejection. Then if something comes of it, you risk getting your heart broken, and if you have a conscience, like most people, you have the risk you may have to break someone else's heart. If you are too afraid to ask, you may never know what might have been.

Matters of the heart were my first real lessons in taking risks. In my senior year of high school, I liked this girl in my speech class a lot. I was extremely shy and had some serious self-esteem issues. I did have a couple of girlfriends, but they were girls who went after me. I think they simply mistook my shyness for the sort of aloofness that teenage girls find a challenge. When they found out I wasn't the challenge they thought I would be, it was over quickly.

Anyway, I wanted to ask this girl out all year, but I could never work up the nerve. The internal dialogue in my mind kept saying things like "Why would a girl like that be interested in a guy like me?" and "What if she figures out what a weirdo I am?" I was so afraid of rejection. I wasn't willing to take the risk. On the last day of school, we got our yearbooks and were signing each other's books. She and I exchanged books, and even then I couldn't work up the nerve to tell her how I felt. She could, however. Well, she didn't tell me, but she wrote it in my yearbook.

When I read what she had written, I gasped: "I have been waiting all year for you to ask me out," and she included her phone number. How could

I have been so afraid? I was angry at myself for not having the nerve to ask her for a date before that.

I went on one date with her. It was nice, but it was far too late for anything to come of it. By then the next evolution on my path was already laid out. The following morning I left for Parris Island and Marine boot camp. We wrote to each other for a while, but I never saw her again. It was a valuable lesson in the cost of not taking a risk.

Uncertainty is a fact of life. The idea of total safety is an illusion. I have been almost killed a couple of times when I thought I was in the safest part of a situation. Even when you lie in your bed, you are not 100 percent safe. I read about a man who was asleep when a giant sinkhole opened under him, and just like that he and his bed were gone. How crazy is that? If there is risk everywhere anyway, you might as well start using it to your advantage.

There are many different types of risk, but the risk that most often springs to mind is the risk to life and safety. Some of the other types of risk that are worth considering are financial risk, risk to health and well-being (that includes mental health), and risk to the environment. Of course, there are a ton of subcategories: market risk, liquidity risk, operational risk, and the like, which all belong in the broader category of financial risk.

What about the lesser kinds of risks, like a risk to your pride or ego? We tend to think of these less consciously, but they are very big drivers for many people. Sometimes people cling to a self-image they have constructed so tightly that it gets in the way.

Any time there is risk, there is the potential to experience fear, which is what the next two chapters are all about. Solid, real-world risks are easier to quantify and objectively evaluate. You know a financial risk can drain your bank account. You know you can be hurt or killed by taking a physical risk. But your mental constructs are internal and prejudiced anyway. If your ego or pride or something in your mental model of the world is threatened, you may experience fear and not know why or not recognize it as fear. You might not recognize the risk could be to a mental model of how you think things ought to be instead of a real-world tangible risk.

Fear of rejection, of being laughed at or ridiculed, of appearing foolish, or of failure can normally be attributed as a risk to your ego or pride. Sometimes the real-world risk is negligible, and the upside is very high. But if your pride is on the line, you may hesitate and avoid the minimal real-world risk to protect your mental idea of yourself. My failure to ask the girl out until it was too late in high school was a small example of this, but people often miss big opportunities with little real downside to protect their egos.

Sometimes people tilt the other way on the scale. They forgo everything else to protect their pride. Sometimes they double down on a bad decision when deep inside they know they have made a big mistake. The risks can become looming, insurmountable dangers, but they still refuse to see the forest through the trees. They are willing to continue down a reckless path with enormous risks and a closing window of possible success, all in the name of protecting their foolish pride.

This has led to the financial downfall of many would-be entrepreneurs and investors. In outdoor adventure settings, this phenomenon has led to grievous injuries and sometimes death. When world leaders do this, it can lead to war and countless lives lost. I am sure you can think of examples of times when people were blinded by their egos. Learning to manage risk includes learning to manage yourself. Sometimes this requires learning things about yourself that on some level you may not want to know.

There are three basic ways to handle risk. All three are useful in different situations. The first is risk avoidance—avoiding the risk altogether. Imagine a trickling stream turning into a raging river after torrential rainfall from an earlier monsoon. You don't have a boat or even rope and carabineers to make a safe river crossing, so if you can't find a suitable place to cross, maybe it is not a good idea to even try. Even trying to drive through floodwaters in an SUV is a big no-no. It's usually best to avoid it.

Risk avoidance is good when the risk is big or the magnitude of a negative outcome is extreme. Is your potential date throwing out red flags? Maybe the date is better to avoid altogether.

A lottery ticket has a huge potential upside. It also has a very low chance of success, so in that sense the risk is very high. However, the negative outcome is negligible, so the magnitude of the risk is very small. What's five bucks, after all? But if you are betting the farm on a million-to-one odds, and you see it's going to come down to luck (by luck I mean factors outside your control), maybe it is better to avoid the risk altogether, even if the potential upside is incredibly tempting. Draining your life savings to invest in your second cousin's business that you don't understand because they say "it's the opportunity of a lifetime" is a good example of a time to use risk avoidance.

While risk avoidance can be useful, it should not be something you are in the habit of doing all—or even most—of the time. Why? Because it's risky! Yes, there is an inherent risk in not taking risks. In fact, not taking risks is sometimes such a big risk that there is a special name for it. It is called the risk of opportunity loss. Most of the biggest opportunities in life require taking risks.

With most risks, there is a potential reward. It may be something big, like wealth, or fame, or owning the business you always wanted. It may even be intangible, like the sheer thrill of it. The adrenaline rush and accompanying feel-good hormones are worth the risk in many sports and thrill rides. Maybe it's the sense of accomplishment. Maybe it's that you learn something.

Maybe there is an external or internal reward you didn't see beforehand, even if you fail to accomplish your goal. Maybe a failure will lead to an even better opportunity. With each failure, if something new is learned or some insight is gained, the metric of risk skews more in your favor the next time. Maybe the intangible of the risk is gaining the ability to step out and take a risk. When a big opportunity with some risk attached comes along later, you are already used to taking risks, so you are primed and ready for it.

The biggest opportunity cost of always using avoidance to deal with risk is it stunts personal growth and may limit your chance to lead a more fulfilling life. One of the consequences of opportunity loss that cuts the deepest is regret. Some regrets are quickly forgotten, and some are kept for life.

The other downside of not taking risks is the possibility of a degrading status quo. The one unchanging fact about the world is it is always changing. Sometimes changes are slow and almost imperceptible, and sometimes they are radical and disruptive. A classic example of this is a large company that is considered a leader in an industry. It has an established way of doing business that has always worked, so it doesn't take risks or try anything new. Often these businesses are considered too big to fail. Then along comes a nimble new start-up that is willing to take big risks and completely change the way things are done. By the time the big company realizes its business model is no longer working, the nails in the coffin are almost all hammered in.

Another more dire example is refugees from a war-torn region. They take tremendous risks, setting out across hostile territory, often with little more than the clothes on their backs and a tiny sliver of hope for a better future. As risky as this is, nine times out of ten, these people are better off than those who stayed behind.

The second way to handle risk is the opposite of avoidance: throw caution to the wind and just go for it—dive right in without checking how deep the water is. Now, this is a good strategy and even a good habit when the risks are low or all in your head. This avoids overthinking and analysis paralysis.

Sometimes this is what you need in social situations—asking for dates, cold calling, and asking your superiors for what you need. Cutting through red tape is something you need to dive into and keep going until you get it done. Do it without thinking. Just go for it. Get used to hearing *no* and keep on diving right in. Sometimes you will wear them down. Sometimes, it's a numbers game, and sometimes, the fact that no doesn't bother you can lead to more yeses.

Whenever you ask anybody for anything, you stand the chance of rejection. They might say no. In some instances, they might even be rude about it. The risk of rejection is real; however, any further meaning you attach to it is your own psychological BS. The risk to your measure of self-worth if you are rejected is purely subjective and, therefore, not a real risk. It is a perceived risk. That's why sometimes it's good to dive right in and go for it.

Uncertain if diving in or avoidance is the best course of action? This is why it is good to break down the risk even more. Again, the risk is the chance of something bad happening. This is the possibility of a negative outcome. That can be broken into two more metrics: the first is the likelihood of something bad happening, and the second is the magnitude or severity of the negative outcome. At the low end of the magnitude scale are the subjective feelings of self-worth affected by rejection or perceived failing, usually caused by not meeting your own preconceived expectations for yourself.

Hazards are things in the environment that cause risk. At the higher end of the magnitude scale, we normally use the term *danger* to describe hazards that can have catastrophic negative outcomes. If the risk is physical, this usually means something that can cause death or a permanent disability. In finance, catastrophic is something that can take all your money or, worse, put you into a level of debt from which there appears to be no escape. Both the likelihood and potential magnitude of the risk involved should be weighed when considering any endeavor.

The reason it's good to break down risk is this: diving right in is good for low-magnitude risks. But this is not a good strategy to use if the risks are high and the possible consequences catastrophic.

Here's another high school story as an example. In my senior year, I was enrolled in the US Marine Corps Delayed Entry Program (DEP). With DEP, you sign a contract for military enlistment before you graduate from high school. It was counted as part of my commitment to the reserves after I did my regular enlistment. I had weekly meetings with the recruiters and did physical training like push-ups, sit-ups, and mountain climbers, followed by a run. Then every couple of months, we had a picnic. One of these picnics was held at a park on a beautiful spring-fed river.

Well, we found this place where a giant oak tree overhung the river. There was a fork in the branches over the edge of one of the springs. It was about a thirty-foot drop into the water, so we were all taking a bit of a risk jumping into the spring from the fork in the tree.

One of the recruiters saw what we were doing and, not to be outdone, decided to up the ante. He climbed up the tree and, without pausing to glance down, did a perfect swan dive straight into the water. If it had been a competition dive in an Olympic swimming pool, it would have been a nearly perfect score. He went straight in—no splash at all.

When he floated to the top, he was face down. At first, we thought he was playing a joke, but as he started floating down the river, still face down, we knew something was seriously wrong. The other recruiters quickly jumped in and rescued him. They were able to get him breathing on his own, but he had missed the spring and broken his neck on a rock at the bottom of the river. He seemed somewhat conscious, but we couldn't tell for sure because he couldn't speak. We took turns holding him while he floated face up until the paramedics arrived. We didn't want to take the risk of bringing him up on the riverbank because we were afraid we might damage his spinal cord even more. It was horrific. Just like that, a man in the prime of his life was rendered a quadriplegic.

Had he gone feetfirst, the worst he would have suffered was a broken ankle. Had he pushed off the tree like the rest of us before he went into his dive, he probably would have cleared the riverbed, landed in the deep part of the spring, and been perfectly fine. This horrible accident was a lesson for me about how bad things can go if I don't take time to evaluate the risks. He dove right in without looking and paid an immense price for it. When you take bigger risks, it is a good idea to follow the advice of General George Patton: "Take calculated risks. That is quite different from being rash."[2]

The third way to deal with risk is through a process called risk management. This way is optimal if conditions allow. Risk management isn't usually a sexy topic. If you start throwing around terms like *risk assessment* and *risk mitigation* at a party, people's eyes glaze over as their thoughts turn to expensive lawyers, lengthy insurance contracts, and the strange, complicated world of hedge funds. It can be a cool study, though. As you learn to take risks, especially big risks, learning to manage the risk of negative outcomes becomes extremely important.

The first part of risk management is assessment or analysis. Know the risk! Again, both the likelihood and magnitude of the risk should be considered. It is a good idea to research what the risks are and the steps you can take to reduce your exposure. Risk is called that for a reason. It's risky. The world is a risky place. People really do fall off mountains and get eaten by predators. There are accidents. Businesses really do fail, and investment deals do go wrong. People sometimes lose all their money and end up deeply in debt. Relationships fall apart. There is crime in the world. Natural disasters happen. Wars break out. Pandemic is no longer just a reference to a bad movie. Bad stuff happens. That doesn't mean you should hide out in a bunker, but it does mean you should take the responsibility to know what you are getting yourself into no matter what you are doing.

If you already know what to look for and what your options are should something go wrong, you are in a much better place to course correct or bail out. This is just as true whether you are starting a business, taking up a new sport, or going for a hike in the woods. What are the risks, and what steps can you take to minimize them? Do as much research as you can.

You may still be forced to use one of the first two strategies if you are in a time crunch or find out the information you have is wrong or the situation has changed significantly. Even if you must make a snap decision to go for it or avoid it because you will not have all the facts in time, it is better than walking in completely blind, not even knowing what you don't know.

Safety procedures and protocols are involved with everything from mountain climbing to walking across the street. Some are incredibly involved and require a lot of time and preparation, like acclimating yourself to higher altitudes for mountaineering. Others are simple and seem more like common sense, such as swimming with a buddy. Aaron Ralston, the famous mountain climber who had to amputate his own arm after getting stuck under a boulder, said he would still have his arm if he had left a note telling somebody where he was going.[3] Tell somebody where you are going—that is about as simple a precaution as you can get and a good habit for managing risks in personal safety.

After assessing the risk, there are five strategies to use to manage it. The first I already covered in the basic strategies: *risk avoidance*. Risk avoidance is easier once you have all the facts. Being well informed also reduces your chances of feeling the regret of opportunity loss. If you choose avoidance with good reason, it will help you learn how to handle risk rather than if you just said, "Nope, not doing that," before you found out anything about it. The other four strategies are *risk reduction*, *risk mitigation*, *risk transfer*, and *risk acceptance*.

Risk reduction is reducing the chances of a bad thing happening. This can be as simple as remembering to look both ways before you cross the street. It can also be as complicated as a team of wilderness first responders trying to figure out how to rescue skiers trapped in an avalanche with a blizzard moving in. There is a time crunch to rescue the victims, but also they don't want any of the rescuers trapped or killed themselves. Risk reduction is anything you can do to avoid something bad from happening while moving forward and taking the risk of that negative event occurring. Learn what hazards you are likely to encounter and how to avoid or navigate them.

The next strategy in risk management is *mitigation*. Some risks are beyond your control. You can't stop the bad thing from happening. If you can't prevent it completely, the next best option is damage control. Your cars seatbelt is a form of risk mitigation. It won't prevent a car accident. But it might save your life if you are in one. Things that fall into the category of risk mitigation are tools, techniques, procedures, and equipment to reduce the effect should a negative event occur.

For instance, when white-water rafting, it is almost impossible to completely prevent the possibility of someone being thrown from the raft.[4] However, if all participants were required to wear helmets and life jackets, if someone was thrown from the raft, the chance of them banging their head on a rock, becoming unconscious, and drowning would be considerably reduced.

Narelle learned the fact that people get thrown from rafts during a white-water briefing about five minutes before we were to board our raft. I could see the panic rising in her flushed face as the instructor casually explained that not only was getting dumped into the river a possibility, but also it happened quite often. When the instructor was done, she asked me coldly, "Did you know how easy it is to get thrown from the raft?"

Internally I was saying to myself, "Oh, man, I probably should have told her about that. I'm in trouble." That is not the answer I went with, though. The answer I went with was, "Yeah, hon. I thought everybody knew that. That's what makes rafting *sooooo* much fun!" I laid on the enthusiasm as thick as I could. It certainly looked as if she was going to back out for a minute and possibly kill me, but then she dug down, held back her fear, and had a great time rafting.

Another example of risk mitigation is in basic rock climbing or top roping, as it is called in the climbing world. The risk of a negative event is a fall. In rock climbing, falling is a given. It is not a matter of *if* you are going to fall but *when*. So for this reason there is a ton of safety gear and procedures around wearing a safety harness and having a good belay system in place. That way you don't even try to significantly reduce the risk of falling. But you mitigate the risk, so when you do fall, no matter how high up you are, you fall only a couple of feet instead of plummeting all the way down the side of the cliff. That is assuming the person on belay is paying attention, as they should be.

Generally, when you take a fall top roping, you are not even hurt—maybe a small scrape or bruise here and there. Unless you're using an auto belay in a rock climbing gym, you don't even have to start over at the bottom. You just hang by your harness slightly below where you fell. Then, when you have rested and caught your breath, you just grab the rock and start climbing again. The act of falling off the side of a cliff, which by all rights should be deadly, can instead be kind of fun.

So to be clear, risk reduction is taking steps to reduce the chance of a negative event happening, and risk mitigation is reducing or eliminating the negative effects if it does.

Here are some other examples. Suppose you are hiking through bear country. Not having sweets with you, like chocolate bars and chewing gum, reduces your chance of a bear being attracted to the smell. When camping, if you are in a place where there are bears, always put all food and anything that might smell even remotely sweet in a bear hang. This includes things that you might not think of, like deodorant and toothpaste.

A bear hang is a sack tied to a rope. The rope is then thrown over the middle of a big branch high enough that the bear can't reach it. You also want to make sure it's not too close to the trunk, because bears can climb, and you don't want one shimmying up the trunk and grabbing the bag. Then you tie it off so the bear can't undo the rope. Last, you must make your bear bag site far enough away from camp so that any curious bears attracted to the bag don't wander into your tent. Yes, it's a pain making a bear hang every night and taking it down every morning, but it's a good way of reducing the risk of waking up to a big furry visitor tearing through your tent in the middle of the night.

Wearing a bell is another good idea for risk reduction. Most bear attacks are triggered when the bear is surprised. If bears can hear you coming, they may stay clear, and this reduces your risk of encountering them. You are still in bear country, you still might run into a bear, but you have taken steps to cut that chance considerably.

The first couple of cruise ships I worked on were stationed in the inside passage of Alaska. This was prime grizzly country. Once I got all the whale watching and sea kayaking out of my system, my favorite thing to do when I wasn't working was hike. When we first arrived in late May, there was still a lot of snow on the ground, and when that melted, at first everything was kind of barren. You could see for miles, so stumbling into a grizzly wasn't much of a concern at the beginning of the summer. But that area of Alaska is mostly temperate rainforest. The summers are short and wet, so the foliage grows incredibly fast. By midsummer, areas that had been completely barren when we first arrived were so thick with plants that had grown over our heads that the trail system might as well have been an impenetrable hedge maze. We could be five feet from a seven-hundred-pound (three-hundred-kilogram) grizzly bear and not even know it.

This possibility was driven home on a hike at Exit Glacier, just outside the town of Seward. Back then there was no fancy visitors' center like there is now, and it wasn't roped off, so you could just walk up to the front of the ice floe. We walked into caves with tons of ice above us. In hindsight going into a cave with tons of ice overhead that could collapse any minute might not have been the best of ideas. But that's risk for you. After exploring the front of the glacier, we hiked four miles (six kilometers) up to the ice field that feeds it.

When we got to the top, one of my friends pulled out his binoculars. We looked and saw some people exploring the mouth of the glacier, where we had been two hours before. Then one of us noticed a large bear about forty feet away from them. From our high vantage point, we could see both the bear and the group of people. But the trail between them zigzagged. Clumps of large bushes and giant ice boulders that had fallen from the glacier obstructed the group's view of the trail ahead.

The people couldn't see the bear, and the bear was busy foraging, completely oblivious to them. Then the bear started moseying toward them, getting closer. We were miles away and thousands of feet up, so there is no way they could hear a yelled warning. We could only helplessly watch the whole thing unfold and hope for the best. The bear kept getting closer and closer. Finally, at about the ten-foot mark, the bear stopped, sniffed the air, and wandered off into the bushes. I don't think the people ever knew he was there.

We had to wonder if the bear had been as close to us when we were at the bottom of the glacier. How many times had something like that happened to us and we didn't even know it? After that when we were hiking, we kept the conversation very loud. If I was hiking alone in a maze of undergrowth, I would sing—very badly. I don't know if it was just the noise or because my singing voice is so awful, but I never ran smack-dab into a bear and got mauled, so my risk-reduction plan must have worked.

But what if you are up there looking for bears? They are deceitfully cute but very dangerous. You know this and still want that perfect selfie of you with a brown bear. Then this is *risk acceptance.* You are aware of how perilous this can be. You are knowingly willing to take that chance and accept the risk. Risk acceptance is like just going for it but a more informed version. Hug that bear for me, would you?

Unfortunately, whether or not I want to, I belong to the group of people who believe if you are not bleeding, you are not really trying, so I have had my share of injuries. Most of the time it's my own fault, and I know exactly what I did wrong. I accept the risk and the responsibility for my pain and rehabilitation if needed.

Risk mitigation for a bear encounter would be having a ready can of bear-away spray. This is a giant can of pepper spray designed for bears. If you encounter a bear and it decides to attack, a negative event has already been triggered. If you successfully deploy your bear repellent, you may escape uninjured or at least with non-life-threatening injuries. In that case, you successfully mitigated the risk of a bear attack.

Before you go out, you should do some risk assessment. Have there been recent bear sightings or attacks in the area you are going to? If you have done five to ten minutes of research on the risk of bear encounters, you probably know that in 90 percent of bear encounters when bear spray is used there is no injury to the person or the bear,[5] so it is a very good form of risk mitigation.

The downside of bear spray is it is effective only as a close-range form of mitigation. You must spray the bear in the face for it to work. Sometimes bear spray is labeled bear repellent. It is not like insect repellent, though. If you spray yourself ahead of time to reduce the risk of a bear encounter because the label says bear repellent, it may have the opposite effect and attract bears. Yes, this is something they know, because people have made that mistake.

Then there is *risk transference*. When you buy insurance, you are paying to transfer some of a certain risk—usually financial risk—from you or your property to the insurance company. Normally, risk transference is done through things like insurance, but it can get personal. If a person who is engaged in a high-risk business venture takes on partners, it is usually to spread the financial risk among them. The partners are normally sophisticated enough to know they are taking on risks in exchange for potential future profit. If things do go bad, and they feel their partner oversold the potential upside or underreported the potential risks, they will lawyer up, and things will get ugly.

When you participate in dangerous sports or take an adventure tour, and operators make you sign a liability waiver, they have just transferred a big risk back to you! Read these waivers carefully. Some of them have clauses that say you or your heirs will not hold the operators liable even if you are injured or killed by gross negligence on their part. You can still accept the risk if you want. You don't get to play if you don't sign, but if you read it first, at least you know what you are getting into.

In the bear scenario, if you carry a twelve-gauge shotgun instead of a can of bear spray, you are now transferring some of your incurred risk onto the bear. Not all the risk gets transferred, though. Bears occasionally get the drop on well-armed hunters and kill or maim them. If the bear attacks or gets too close, and you shoot it, you have just made the bear suffer the consequence of the risk you took traveling in a bear habitat.

These techniques don't always have to be static. They can be fluid. You brought the shotgun for risk transfer, but a bear is getting too close, so you fire a warning shot to frighten it off. If it works, that could be considered risk reduction or mitigation, depending on how close the bear is and what he's doing when you fire the shot.

That covers some of the basic principles of risk management. My best example of risk management in an adventure setting was how Outward Bound handled my asthma. Their professionalism and attention to detail was bar none. I guess this is why they are considered the gold standard of adventure education.

I decided to do an adult hiking, backcountry camping, and rock-climbing course with Outward Bound North Carolina. I called and said I wanted to book the trip. After she took my credit card details and ran my deposit, the woman on the phone said, "I just have a few medical questions to ask before we get the go-ahead."

"Okay," I replied awkwardly. I thought it would have been better if she had asked the medical questions before she took my money.

"Do you have a heart condition?" she asked first.

"Nope, I am good to go," I said. All right, first question down, and I'm batting a thousand. I was derailed on question two, however.

"Do you have asthma, emphysema, or any other pulmonary diseases or issues?"

"I have asthma, but it's well controlled," I answered, trying to muster as much false self-confidence in my tone as I could.

Two years prior, my asthma was not well controlled, and at the time my doctor had not been entirely confident I would survive the pollen season, but I decided to leave that out of the conversation. My asthma doctor was a very gruff man from South America. He really knew his stuff, but he had no bedside manner. If he thought I wasn't following his directions closely enough, he yelled at me with all the dramatic emphasis of a Telemundo character. "Scott, I am an asthma doctor, and I have had only two other patients as bad as you. Neither one of them are here anymore, so listen to me very carefully and do what I say, or you are going to die!" That was a typical conversation with him, so I was a little nervous about my asthma.

After I answered the asthma question, there was silence on the phone—not a brief pause, but a long, uncomfortable silence. "Hello, are you still there?" I finally asked.

"Yes" was the quick answer, then silence again.

"Is that a problem?" I asked, trying to get some kind of response and wondering if I could get my deposit back.

"That is a pretty big red flag!" she finally answered.

Okay, should I go ahead and ask for the deposit back? was my next thought. As if she had read my mind and decided she didn't want to give me a refund, she began to speak. "Asthma doesn't necessarily exclude you from the course, but there are going to be a lot of additional hoops to jump through before you can be medically cleared."

That is when the first of three waves of panic about my trip hit me. She then carefully explained that I would need a doctor to sign a waiver, giving me permission. The doctor had to have an asthma action plan for me. We would be in the wilderness, so you couldn't just call an ambulance if something went wrong. The asthma action plan was what to do if I had an asthma attack and we were hours away from a suitable evacuation site.

The doctor had to test my lung capacity and oxygen saturation ratio—once before I submitted my paperwork and again the day before we left. I was also required to purchase special traveler's insurance with a rider, so the insurance would pay if I needed to be evacuated to a hospital by helicopter.

That night I couldn't sleep. I had some serious self-doubts. I had to face the fact that I was no longer the twenty-year-old Marine I used to be—the guy who had no problem hiking twenty-plus miles with a sixty-pound pack and body armor. No, I wasn't that guy anymore. Instead, I was a middle-aged asthmatic with a bit of a spare tire and sore joints. Still, this was something I felt I had to do if I could.

I knew my asthma doctor would never okay this. Not in a million years. So I picked the doctor at my general practice office with the most easygoing personality. It was like choosing a university class because you heard the professor was soft when it came to grading. I think I actually told the receptionist when I made the appointment, "Yeah, he's cool. I'll take him."

Even though I wasn't sure I would make it, I jumped through all the hoops Outward Bound asked of me. The day before I left for North Carolina I passed my final breathing test. That is when my anxiety turned into excitement. Before we began hiking, our instructors went through all our gear to make sure we had everything. For me, this included a maintenance inhaler, two emergency inhalers in case I lost one, and a bottle of high-dosage prednisone if I needed it.

The instructor's medical kit included a wilderness oximeter to test my oxygen levels in the field if need be. Everything went fine, but we were certainly prepared if it didn't. In the beginning, all the extra precautions really frightened me, because they forced me to face a truth I had been trying to avoid: that asthma is dangerous, and I could die from it. But once I faced that truth, the extra measures of safety from the asthma action plan gave me confidence that I could still do something challenging and have a great time doing it.

Having an emergency action plan when you take on serious risks is one of the smartest things you can do. With a good action plan, you take all the emotion out of decision-making at a time when emotions tend to run high. That way you are unlikely to make a poor, rushed decision or, possibly worse, panic and make no decision at all when you need to!

Having a plan in place cuts down reaction time, which may be critical in an emergency. The decision on what to do has been made before the event that triggers it. There is no critical time being wasted thinking about it. All you must do is implement the plan.

Action plans should be as simple as possible. *This* happens, and we do *that*. If it is a serious emergency, almost everyone involved will be in an adrenalized state. I go into this in detail in the next chapter, but for now, just know when you are in an adrenalized state, you are stronger and faster but possibly less coordinated and may not be in full control of your mental faculties. Simple is better.

Action plans are normally written down in detail, but they don't have to be if they are simple enough. Everyone involved in implementing it should know the plan inside and out and be on board with it. You must have a total buy-in to the plan, or it won't work. You need to know this in advance. When bad things are happening is no time to find out someone isn't going to follow the plan because they didn't think it was a good idea in the first place. Let people point out possible flaws in the plan. Hash them out and revise the plan until you are sure it is the best possible course of action.

When you board a commercial airline the flight attendants take a few minutes to explain how to put on your oxygen mask and life vest. Then they point out the locations of the emergency exits. That is them letting you in on the small part of their emergency action plan that they want you to help implement if an emergency arises. People who listen to this briefing and read the safety brochure have a much higher chance of survival in an airline disaster.[6]

Emergency action plans can be used in business and personal lives as well. Most business and real estate contracts are detailed maps for assessing and managing risk. They have quite a few contingencies built into them. Contingencies are action plans put into place automatically once a risk has been identified.

You can have action plans for just about anything that can go wrong in life. Is the area you live in potentially prone to a certain type of natural disaster? What's your action plan? Do you think you might be laid off from work? You need an action plan. Think that weird mole on your back might be cancer? What's your action plan if it is? Are your kids having trouble in school? Form an action plan. Do you think society as we know it is about to collapse? Then you need a good action plan. If you can worry about it, you can form an action plan. Having a feasible action plan is also a great way to proactively reduce that worry.

There is a sliding scale from the very risk adverse to the extreme risk takers. If you are going to become more of a risk taker, you are going to need good action plans. As you might have guessed from the title of this book, I tend to lean toward the high-risk side of the scale. I have never gone completely past the tipping point into full-on adrenaline addiction, but there was a time in my life when I was beginning to slide in that direction. I had a close call, and I was at a crossroads. I could continue to push the limits and become all-consumed by an adrenaline sport or pull back to safety. Luckily, I met Narelle when I did, or I might have slipped over that mental edge. She is very good at keeping the delicate balance between "Okay, I have to let him do this crazy thing he wants to do," and when to put her foot down and say, "No, you are absolutely not doing that!"

I have also been known to use gray areas to circumvent the rules in this regard. Like the time when I decided to try hang gliding without telling my wife first. It seemed easier that way. When I got back, I accidentally left the brochure about it on the kitchen countertop, so I was busted.

The conversation started with, "Honey, did you go hang gliding today?"

I was still mentally high from hang gliding, so I wasn't ready for someone harshing my buzz, let alone having any kind of reasonable argument prepared to defend myself. I can't lie to my wife, so I blurted out the very Homer Simpson–style double negative answer: "Well, I didn't *not* go hang gliding."

She raised her voice a little. "You promised not to do that!"

Thinking as rationally as I could, I said, "No, I specifically promised not to go skydiving. Hang gliding is completely different." And so the argument went. She of course won, and the loophole was closed, with me promising not to do anything she would consider dangerous without discussing it with her first.

This brings us to our next topic: risk ecology. Relax, I am not going to talk about global warming. In this context, I am not using ecology to describe the natural environment. At its most basic level, ecology is the study of how life-forms interrelate within a system. In human ecology, you study how systems affect a person and how they can affect the system.[7] One such system that is very important is the family unit. The risks you take and the outcomes you generate affect the others within the system.

For example, take two people who are considering the very unforgiving sport of BASE jumping. BASE jumping is jumping off a fixed object, like a building, tower, high bridge, or the side of a mountain, with a parachute.

One of these people is single and unattached. The other is a parent of two young children. Even though they are contemplating the same act, the risk for these two people is different because the ecology is different. The fatality rate of BASE jumping is forty-three times higher than that of traditional skydiving, so the parent must consider how the possibility of their untimely death will affect the children before they make the decision if BASE jumping is the sport for them. That is the ecology of risk.

Zoe was six when I went hang gliding, and a couple of people on the outside viewed this as completely reckless and gave me a lot of flak. Because I didn't talk about it with anyone beforehand, everybody thought it was just a spur-of-the-moment decision on my part. It wasn't. I had investigated the hang-gliding company quite a bit. It had an impeccable safety record. Despite having taken thousands of people on tandem flights, it had zero fatalities and not even a serious injury reported.

Another hang-gliding center closer to where we lived didn't have the perfect safety record, so I took a pass on it. Yes, it wasn't completely risk-free, but for piloting an engineless aircraft five thousand feet (1,500 meters) above the ground, this was as safe as I could get.

Those of us with families need to consider these things. That doesn't mean we can't have any fun. I can't function without some small element of danger in my life from time to time. That is just part of my makeup. It is like getting enough sleep or getting the vitamins I need. I am listless and irritable without it. I do, however, always consult with my wife first on these things now . . . well, most of the time, except for the gyrocopter.

A different example of risk ecology might be the CEO of a large corporation. The company is a system made up of interdependent individuals. The risk the CEO takes with the business and the outcomes they generate affect not only the bottom line of the business but also all employees. That in turn affects the families of these people. If there are shareholders, it affects them too. And of course suppliers and customers are affected by the company's decisions as well. If the company is big enough, those decisions can have repercussions throughout the economy.

I have a few more concepts that will help create a bridge between this chapter and the next two. The first is risk tolerance,[8] which is the maximum risk you can handle. This may depend on things like skill sets, resources, psychology, and even physiology.

From the psychological perspective, risk tolerance is the absolute maximum amount of risk you are willing to take and for how long you are willing to take it. Your risk tolerance will vary from situation to situation. You may have a higher tolerance in one area of your life than others. My risk tolerance is much higher when it comes to physical danger than financial risk.

Not long after I got married, I decided to become an equities swing trader as a side project. A swing trader is like a day trader but instead of holding the stocks for less than a day, you hold on for a couple of days. Like most trading, the idea is to buy low and sell high. With swing trading, you work with small price changes over a couple of days called swings, hence the name *swing trade*.

The one cardinal rule of swing trading is to never hold your position over a weekend. A lot of geopolitical events happen over weekends that can wreak havoc on the stock market.

This was a wild time in the stock market. It was less than a year after the collapse of the World Trade Center and the end of the first tech boom. Stocks that were once fifty to sixty dollars per share were trading around ten to fifteen. It seemed like the perfect time to begin.

At first I spent months researching trading. I read what I could online, and I purchased books on trading and investing in general. I got books from the library on both the fundamentals of investing and technical investing. Some were simple and straightforward, while others were eight hundred pages long and seemed like you needed a master's degree in economics just to be able to grasp what they were talking about. But I read them all cover to cover. As I read, I started paper trading. Paper trading is when you have a trading account, but you use pretend money. It is a safe way to learn the ropes of trading. The one thing paper trading can't teach you is how to keep from panicking when you have your own money on the line.

After several months of paper trading, I finally decided I kind of, sort of knew what I was doing. I decided to begin in earnest. I was young and newly married. We had just spent thousands of dollars emigrating Narelle from Australia to America. We didn't have a lot of money saved, but I had it in my head that I wanted to be a trader, so to cover the commission of trades and make a profit, I would have to use all of it. I reluctantly drained our savings account of everything except enough money to keep the account open. I opened a real trading account and began.

After six months of trading, I was performing well. Not so well that I could quit my day job, but that was starting to look like a possibility. I was using mostly action plans of stops and calls, so buy and sell orders were done by the price movement instead of manually making the order. When the price of a stock dropped to my predesignated buy price, the order was executed. While I owned the stock, I had two orders—one to sell and cut my losses if it dropped further and one to sell if it rose to the point where I would make an acceptable profit.

The idea was to keep my emotions out of the decision-making process as much as possible. There was just one problem. I was not a natural trader who loved the thrill of it. I was scared shitless all day every day that I was going to lose my shirt in the stock market. I constantly had knots in my stomach, and I was afraid I might be developing an ulcer. I was losing a lot of sleep at night.

Looking back now I think part of my reason for wanting to be a speculative investor was a form of rebellion against my father. He was of Scottish heritage and had grown up in the 1930s Depression. To say he was a frugal man was an understatement. He didn't believe in investing in the stock market at all, let alone popping in and out with everything you owned based on a highly technical guess.

The thing I didn't realize was that my father had instilled his beliefs and values about money way deeper in my psyche than I could ever dig out without the help of a therapist. Still, I sucked it up and pushed forward with the fear. I spent six months out of my financial comfort zone, but I was still as frightened with each trade as I was on the first one. I needed a break from this, or I would snap.

On a long holiday weekend, Narelle and I decided to rent a cabin in the Smoky Mountains. I had a buy order in, because that's what you do as a trader, but I didn't think the stock would drop to my buy price, so I wasn't as worried as I usually was. Friday we packed, and I took one last look at the financial news after the close of the markets. Sure enough, my stock had not dropped quite enough. It was hovering a few cents above my buy price, all clear. This was before everyone had smartphones, so everything was done by email. The stock ticker clearly told me my stock never made it to my buy price. No need to check my email again. It was time to drive to the mountains and take a much-needed break from the grind.

We got back late Monday night. Before going to bed, I made the mistake of checking my email. My eyes grew to the size of saucers. Late in the afternoon on Friday, all the money I had except what I'd kept to pay that month's bills had been converted into shares of the ultimate Mickey Mouse operation. We now owned a tiny piece of the Disney Corporation (stock ticker DIS). Somehow the price had dipped to my buy price on the trading platform without it going reported.

I had violated the golden rule of swing trading—owning a stock over the weekend, and a long holiday weekend at that. I panicked and immediately put in the order to sell. This wouldn't happen, though, until the markets opened in the morning. I didn't know any of the fear management strategies you will learn about in chapter 4 at the time, so I spent the rest of the night staring at the ceiling, thinking about such unlikely events as a nighttime terrorist attack in Orlando within the next six hours.

The next morning, when my shares were safely converted into cash, I closed my trading account and deposited the money into our savings account. That night, for the first time in half a year, I slept like a baby. I simply did not have the risk tolerance to be an equities trader. I never traded again. I made a little money, but most importantly I learned a bit about myself. It just wasn't worth it to me to take those kinds of financial risks, and that's all right.

That brings me to the next concept of this chapter, and it is a very important one. *Risk is cumulative.* It is imperative to remember that repeated or prolonged exposure to any given risk increases the level of risk. If you are building a tolerance to a particular type of risk, you should never mistake becoming used to the danger for it lessening. It is easy to get complacent with risk management, but just because something bad hasn't happened yet doesn't mean it won't. In the case of my stock trading, even though I was making money, the longer I did it, the greater chance I had of something going drastically wrong.

Repeated exposure can be explained with the lottery ticket from earlier in the chapter. If you spend five dollars on a lottery ticket, it's no big deal, right? So why not buy more lottery tickets? A lot more! You shouldn't, because that increases the risk. If you go crazy and buy ten thousand lottery tickets, you have only increased your odds of becoming a multimillionaire marginally, but you have magnified the magnitude of losing by ten thousand times. Your chance of winning goes from one in three hundred million to ten thousand in three hundred million, or one in thirty thousand. Those are still slim odds. You are, however, 100 percent going to be out fifty grand! That is repeated exposure.

If a sport or activity has a 1 percent chance of an accident that causes serious injury, and you engage in it fifty times, you are as likely to have a serious injury as not.

Prolonged exposure can be explained by the odd fact that more people die in the summer each year from hypothermia than in the winter.[9] Some of this is explained by the simple fact that people are less prepared in the summer for wetter, cooler conditions. Water is an incredible conductor of heat, so if you are out in the rain for an extended period without shelter or rain gear, even if it's not that cold, you could find yourself in serious trouble.

A lot of summertime drownings are caused by immersion hyperthermia. Let's say you and your buddy are out on a hot day, and there is not a cloud in the sky. You decide to go to the lake and take a swim. It's freezing cold but invigorating. Then let's say your buddy dares you to swim out to the middle of the lake and back. It is a deep lake, but you are a good swimmer, so you take them up on the challenge.

Unfortunately, that cold has a cumulative effect. What was invigorating at first becomes debilitating. Every minute you are in it you stand an increased chance of your core temperature dropping to the point where your peripheral muscles stop working and then you drown. That is an ever-increasing risk due to prolonged exposure.

To drive these concepts home, I want to share a real case study that gives a clear picture of both sustained and repeated exposure, a complete lack of risk management, and a false sense of invulnerability built over time. Since I used the bear analogy a few times in this chapter, let's stick with that.

You may have heard about the curious case of Timothy Treadwell.[10] He was the subject of several documentaries. Every summer for thirteen years Timothy traveled to the Katmai coast of Alaska to live among the area's grizzly bear population. He took a lot of amazing footage of bears close-up and even interacted with a few of them. He did some good work in educating the public about bears.

Whether it was true or the anthropomorphizing fantasy of someone losing touch, Timothy believed the bears were his friends, and he felt more comfortable around them than he did people. You could safely say he had about the highest risk tolerance to the dangers of grizzly bears of any human on the planet, ever. This was not a good thing.

Timothy had both repeated and extended exposure to dangerous predators and did not use even basic risk management strategies. He relied solely on his knowledge of the temperament of bears. Timothy was cited multiple times by park rangers for violations, including having food in his tent. He even reduced his risk management assets. He carried bear spray in the early years. After an incident where he successfully deployed it, Timothy complained that he didn't like that it caused the bear pain, so he just stopped carrying it.

Then his luck finally gave out. The evening before they were to be picked up by seaplane, Timothy and his girlfriend were killed and partially eaten by a bear. The video camera was rolling, but the lens cap was still on, so there is only audio of their last horrifying moments alive. Park rangers and wilderness guides who had run across him over the years believed his death was inevitable. This was a tragic story of someone who managed to defy the odds for thirteen years, which is amazing. But in the end, he tempted fate too many times.

The reason I tell this story is so you remember just because something hasn't happened doesn't mean it can't. Risk is cumulative. Not understanding this concept has crushed businesses, livelihoods, and sometimes entire markets. In the wilderness, it has cost lives.

Having said that, most of us don't do things in a vacuum. Repeatedly taking risks or being exposed to risk for an extended period does not have to be a recipe for failure. The key is making sure you never get complacent. As you go along, you should periodically reevaluate and refine emergency action plans. Safety drills need to be repeated every so often. Skill sets should continually be improving. Check gear every time you use it. Be on the lookout for changing conditions. Always work on improving the odds.

One of the biggest teaching events that should never be discounted is the near miss. The near miss or close call is when something really bad almost happens but doesn't. Maybe the negative event was avoided or mitigated by a strategy or safety equipment, maybe someone intervened on your behalf, or maybe you were rescued by a Good Samaritan. Maybe it was dumb luck that saved you. Whichever way, it can be a teachable moment. It might be just the thing you need to show you the weaknesses in your risk management strategy. Maybe a near miss will make you realize you don't have the tolerance to face that particular risk again. Maybe you will find it exciting and be hungry for more. That's when you need to do a little self-examining.

Learn what you can about what went wrong and what you can do to keep it from happening again. All adventure programs and most industrial workplaces now require incident reports to be filled out after a near miss. Usually valuable information is gained from these. Sometimes a new safety procedure needs to be created. Often, the procedures are already there, but there is complacency about following them. Many serious accidents and fatalities are avoidable if lessons are drawn from near misses that preceded them. Never underestimate the teaching value of a near miss. Consider a close call a gift. Learn from it.

This brings me to the final concept of this chapter, challenge by choice. It is one of the best ideas to come out of the adventure education industry. The important thing is that you pick the risk level that is acceptable to you. You challenge your own comfort levels. No risk-taking should be mandated or forced by anyone. There should be no feeling of coercion, and you retain the right to quit anytime you want (assuming you can withdraw from the situation without causing additional risk to yourself or anyone else). Challenge by choice puts personal responsibility into the process of how you deal with risks. You are responsible for the outcomes you generate. If something goes wrong, you are responsible for the decisions you make. You don't want to sound like a ten-year-old who gets into trouble and defensively argues, "Well, they made me do it."

Personal responsibility makes the triumphs your own as well. If you tackle a challenge that has an inherent risk, you did that! If you tackle one of your fears, no one can say, "See, aren't you glad I made you do that?" You did it!

EXERCISE

We have all been told since we were little not to talk to strangers. Well, as an exercise in learning to take risks, I want you to talk to strangers.

It's simple. You are going to loiter around a mall or, if it is a nice day, a park. Choose an area that has high foot traffic. You are going to walk up to people and try to start conversations. It doesn't have to be about anything specific, and there should be no ulterior motive. You are not trying to get a date or sell them anything. Just see if you can get people to engage you in conversation.

Once you get them talking, see how long you can carry on a conversation and not be imposing. If they look like they are getting uncomfortable or impatient, casually end the conversation and break away. When that person has left the area, see if you can strike up a conversation with someone else. You might be surprised once you get past their initial defenses just how friendly people can be.

It sounds simple, but unless you are a true extrovert or have a lot of experience in cold calling, you will probably find this exercise uncomfortable at first. There is the risk of rejection. At first some people will assume anyone who approaches them in public and tries to start a conversation is either trying to sell them something or a stalker. Be prepared to be brushed off. If you can't get in, move on to the next one. Be nice and polite, and don't be creepy. If someone disrespects you, don't take it personally.

It doesn't matter how many people blow you off; there is no way to fail this exercise except by giving up before you have any conversations. Have fun with it. Once you get used to rejection and get into a rhythm, it is a very fun exercise. Remember, you are not trying to get a date or sell anything, so that should take the pressure off.

Yes, you can have someone in the area for safety if you want. But they need to pretend they don't know you. No double-teaming people. You must start conversations by yourself.

That's it. Start conversations, have fun, and make notes of any observations.

Chapter 3:

Your Brain on Adrenaline

> The edge . . . There is no honest way to explain it because the only people who really know where it is are the ones who have gone over.
> —Hunter S. Thompson

I hadn't slept in over seventy-two hours. Sleep deprivation, among other things, had led to a series of mistakes on my part. I was now completely lost, driving a Humvee with no headlights around in the dark. I really should have tested the lights when I checked the vehicle out of the motor pool. My assistant driver, who was supposed to be navigating for me, had long since passed out in the passenger seat. I was completely delirious. Through the fog in my brain, I could hear the drone of giant C-130 aircraft circling above. It was a monotonous tone, seeming to lull me further into my daze.

I had driven the dirt roads of a makeshift city within a city for the better part of the afternoon. The sun had set, and now I'd driven the dirt roads in the dark for over an hour. All of a sudden, I was on asphalt. "Oh, this must finally be the main road they were talking about." I drove on for a bit. I looked to my side and in my delirium said to myself, "Oh, cool, there are little blue lights on the sides of the road. That's trippy."

Then I was suddenly awake and alert. The brain fog completely vanished. I didn't realize it at the time, but that was my brain producing norepinephrine because of the novelty of my situation. That is what alerted me that something was seriously wrong. There should not be little blue lights on the sides of the road. Little blue lights light up a runway, so planes can see where to land.

I realized what I had done, and that's exactly when the sound of the Hercules aircraft became quite loud. The aircraft's headlights were shining like some kind of nighttime sun, illuminating the space in the truck with a light so intense it was blinding. In my sleep-deprived delirium, I had driven a vehicle with no working lights down the middle of an active runway.

Then the full dose of adrenaline hit. We were about to be pancaked by a 155,000-pound (70,000-kilogram) cargo plane! In C-130s the pilots sit high, and they approach with their noses up, so I doubt they would have seen us before they mowed over our vehicle. I took a sharp left and floored the accelerator. We flew off the side of the runway in the nick of time. The two-foot drop off the side bounced my A-driver awake. Then I hit the brakes and skidded to a stop before we crashed into an armored personnel carrier. Had I not had the adrenaline rush, there is no way my exhausted body would have gotten us off the runway in time. That night I was so tired I slept through a mortar attack.

A large portion of this book is devoted to pushing past fears to do the things you want. To do this, it is important to understand the effects of fear, anger, difficult physical challenges, and incredible excitement on the body. This is the science of adrenaline—or the physiology of adventure, if you prefer.

Of all the chapters in this book, this and the next one have the most science, so please bear with me, because having a basic understanding is important. Understanding your adrenal response is the first step in managing and controlling it. Controlling the system in your body that is largely responsible for reactionary impulses is quite an achievement and an important part of self-mastery. Plus a properly managed adrenaline rush can be super fun!

As the name implies, the autonomic nervous[1] system is the part of your nervous system that controls things automatically. For the most part, it is involuntary and works without conscious control. Things like your heart rate and digestion are controlled by the autonomic nervous system. Yes, Shaolin monks and yogis can control them consciously, and so can you to some degree, but most people are not aware of many of these processes.

For functional purposes, we can divide the autonomic nervous system into two systems. The first is the parasympathetic system. It tells your body to relax. This is the rest-and-digest part of the nervous system. When the parasympathetic nervous system is on, your body works to maintain homeostasis, which is a balanced, tranquil state. Homeostasis is when your body is in its "just chilling" mode. If you are lying on a beach on the Caribbean island of St. Thomas, chances are your parasympathetic nervous system is in charge.

The other part of your autonomic nervous system is your sympathetic nervous system. The sympathetic nervous system is the body's involuntary, rapid response to danger, stress, excitement, or intense physical exertion. If you decide to go parasailing at that beach in St. Thomas, the sympathetic part of your nervous system will probably take over, especially if the guy driving the boat that is towing you pulls you dangerously close to a rocky outcropping. Yes, I'm speaking from experience.

When you do things like fast-rope out of a helicopter, are chased by an enraged elk, or are faced with an armed assailant, your body reacts with what is called the *acute stress response.*[2] This is more commonly known as the *fight-or-flight* or more aptly the *fight, flight, or freeze* response.

Instinctually your body is preparing for physical combat, to run away from danger, or in some cases to freeze, so you are not noticed and therefore not attacked. The acute stress response is governed by the sympathetic nervous system.

Scientists have mapped the part of the brain that controls the body's stress response. This is the limbic system.[3] It's the part of the brain that governs survival and is responsible for activating the sympathetic nervous system. The parts of the limbic system we are concerned with here are the amygdala, hypothalamus, nucleus accumbens, and hippocampus. Although not technically part of the limbic structure, arguably the prefrontal cortex can also be included.

The main part of this system is the amygdala. That is where the fight, flight, or freeze decision is made. The amygdala is an almond-shaped set of neurons in the brain's temporal lobe. It plays a big part in processing intense emotions. Excitement, aggression, and fear are all processed in the amygdala. When the fight-or-flight response is triggered, it is the amygdala that makes the decision to fire it.

It is essential to know you usually don't have a conscious choice about the initial firing of the sympathetic response. Your amygdala may decide that for you, because in an emergency the conscious process is too slow.

Your limbic system is constantly processing sensory information—sight, hearing, smell, taste, and touch. When you have a flinch or jump response to a sudden stimulus, that is the amygdala activating motor neurons to protect you before you can mentally process what the stimulus is.

Have you ever reflexively jumped out of the way of something or managed to shield your face from an errant football, Frisbee, or another high-velocity object flying at you from seemingly out of nowhere? That is this process at work. The acoustic startle reflex is the auditory version of this, which is triggered by a sudden noise above about eighty decibels.

Whenever you are startled, you get that flinch reflex to protect yourself as well as a rush of adrenaline. It is automatic.

Depending on the stimulus that triggers the response, you might not get the conscious choice of whether the urge is fight or flight or freeze. Your amygdala may select that for you, at least initially. I have had it surprise me a few times, but here is probably the best example. In Florida we were members of the local zoo, which had prekindergarten classes called Zoo School. It was an amazing experience.

We enrolled Zoe in Zoo School when she was three. One day I picked her up from class and decided to go through the main zoo. It was late in the day, the zoo was getting near closing, and it was almost feeding time for the predators. We were watching the panther pace back and forth in her enclosure, waiting for her food. We watched this big strong cat for quite some time because she was usually asleep when we came by. I admired how strong and muscular she was. The claws and teeth were every bit as impressive as lions' or tigers'.

Then something weird happened. Zoe turned to me and said, "Daddy, let's go see the otters," and she turned her back to the cat and started running in the opposite direction. This triggered the panther's hunting instinct. In the wild, big cats like to hunt baby animals because they're usually an easy meal. A generation or two of cats having a sedentary life in a zoo is not going to win against millions of years of evolution. The panther started running back and forth and jumping up at the cage, trying to get out and give chase to my child, who was oblivious to the whole thing, running in the direction of the otter enclosure.

I almost lost it. Seeing the cat's predatory instinct to go after my three-year-old instantly fired my parental protective instinct. My sympathetic nervous system engaged, and the adrenal surge activated, even though consciously I knew 100 percent that the cat was safely behind bars. Fight mode fired off before I had even processed why.

Instantly I had an intense feeling of white-hot rage! My heart started racing, my hands began to sweat, and without thinking about it I started looking for a stick or rock on the ground big enough to strike the cat. I was ready to kill or be killed, if only for a second.

Panthers, known as mountain lions in most of America, have been known to kill full-size adults. I wouldn't want to fight one, but in that moment, I was in total battle mode. In protecting the young, flight is not an option, so unconsciously the fight response was selected for me. Even though my rational human brain was saying, "The panther is in its enclosure. Everything is all right," my primitive brain was taking sensory information from the cat, bypassing my higher brain and drawing its own conclusion. The caveman in me was saying, "Predator wants to eat my offspring equals fight to the death!"

It took a few seconds for my cognitive thinking brain to take back over. I stood there for a moment, calming myself down. When I realized my daughter was almost out of my line of sight, I took off after her, completely amazed that my body could react so strongly to a danger that wasn't even real. Whether the danger is real, imagined, or somewhere in between, it can still trigger a hard adrenal response, and you may not get the choice of what form it takes.

In fight or flight, the first thing that happens is your amygdala receives sensory data that it interprets as some kind of danger.[4] It then sends a signal to the hypothalamus, which acts as a command center. When the amygdala sends a distress signal to the hypothalamus it hits the accelerator on everything else. This then sends signals through the endocrine system, which is the system in your body that makes hormones, and it goes into overdrive. This floods the brain and nervous system with chemicals designed to optimize your chances of survival.

The term *hormone* can be deceptive, because most people think of hormones as slow acting, moving only as fast as the blood flows. Anyone who has cared for an active toddler knows that when you go into fight-or-flight, it's instant. If the toddler has somehow figured out how to open the baby gate in the kitchen and is reaching for the carving knife on the counter, you can be across the room faster than you probably thought was possible.

This is because many of the chemicals involved are not just hormones but also neurotransmitters. A neurotransmitter is a chemical messenger that communicates between the nerve cells. An electrical impulse is sent down a nerve cell and is converted to a chemical to communicate with the next nerve cell, where it is reconverted into an electrical impulse, and so on.

Nerve signals travel at speeds up to 120 meters[5] per second or 270 miles per hour. That's fast. Because many of the specialized hormones mentioned in this chapter act as neurotransmitters once they are released into the body, they act with the speed of the nervous system. If there is danger, you can't wait around for the blood to take the chemicals necessary for immediate action through the bloodstream.

Adrenaline, known scientifically as epinephrine, is normally the first chemical fired into the system. Your body is chemically preparing itself for battle or to make a quick escape. The heart beats faster. Adrenaline is a bronchodilator, meaning it opens the tiny air passages in the lungs, so you can get more air. Oxygen and glucose are increased in the brain and skeletal muscles. All nonessential body functions like digestion are suppressed. This adrenaline surge makes you considerably stronger and faster for a short time. If anything in this world can give you superpowers, it's adrenaline! I am sure you have heard stories of great physical strength like lifting a car off someone trapped beneath it. That kind of strength comes from the adrenal surge.

With the adrenaline surge, your senses become more acute. Your eyes dilate to let in more light, and your vision becomes clearer. You hear more. Your mind usually becomes clearer, particularly regarding things involving your immediate survival. I normally get a tingling feeling in my neck.

The adrenal glands are located just above the kidneys, and they must be important because we have two of them. These glands make a couple of other chemicals. Noradrenaline (norepinephrine) is also dumped into the system with adrenaline and acts very much like adrenaline. It helps increase heart rate and blood sugar levels for energy and muscle strength. In addition to aiding in the things regular adrenaline does, noradrenaline narrows the blood vessels, increasing blood pressure to pump fresh blood to the places that need it faster.

Most noradrenaline is made in the adrenal gland. However, it is also made in the brain stem, and whenever you are in a situation that differs from what you are used to, it may be fired directly into the brain. This makes you more alert before you have even realized there is danger. That was what happened right before I realized I was on the runway.

If you are caught off guard, it will be adrenaline that hits the system first. But if you are in a situation that tells you there may be danger here but it's uncertain, the noradrenaline will already be pumping through the system to keep you alert before the full adrenaline rush kicks in.

Another chemical made in the adrenal glands is a steroid called cortisol. Cortisol is a corticoid steroid as opposed to an anabolic steroid. It won't make your muscles bigger. A corticoid steroid suppresses the immune response. Inflammation is your body's primary immune response. Among other things, inflammation creates swelling in injury-affected areas.

Inflammation allows your body to repair itself, but it slows you down when in a fight or trying to escape. If you were chased by a wild panther and he bites your leg, breaking bone and tearing flesh, inflammation or swelling would help slow the bleeding, splint the bone, and help with the muscle repair.

That's great, but you must get away from the panther first, and that same inflammation is going to slow you down. The cortisol stops the inflammation temporarily. You also want to reduce inflammation in the lungs to allow better airflow. This gives more much-needed oxygen to the muscles involved in the battle or retreat.

Once the adrenal response has been activated, your prefrontal cortex consciously assesses the threat level. The prefrontal cortex is what we commonly refer to as our thinking brain or conscious mind. At this point, if there is still a threat, you can continue to pump more adrenaline or calm down if it's safe. Only when the prefrontal cortex is activated will you be able to make conscious choices about your situation. Here is where you can gain some kind of control over the adrenal response. If you decide the threat has subsided and your brain agrees with you, the prefrontal cortex will tell the hippocampus, and it will deactivate the amygdala's stress response.

The great thing is when you learn to control this fight-or-flight response, it can be beneficial. You can use the rush as a source of power to draw on. The first step in using this power is to learn how to quickly recognize when your amygdala has hijacked control. Then you can begin to apply the thinking brain to the situation as opposed to just reacting.

After the initial dump of adrenaline, another set of chemicals is injected into the system: endorphins, your body's natural painkillers. These chemicals are opiate-like in nature, meaning they have a similar effect on your body as morphine, oxycodone, and other painkillers derived from the poppy plant. Doctors have suggested that molecule for molecule, the body's natural endorphins are more powerful than morphine.[6]

Endorphins are fired in a fight-or-flight situation, so the body can carry on fighting or escaping after it has been damaged or would be too exhausted to otherwise do so. If that mountain lion bit your leg, the pain might be too unbearable to keep fighting or making a run for it, but the endorphins are there to keep you going. After the fight is over, the reduction of pain helps calm you down as well.

These endorphins and a relatively newly discovered type of

neurotransmitter called endocannabinoids cause what is known as a runner's high—an intense euphoric feeling caused by an adrenaline rush and intense physical exercise. Anandamide[7] is the most well known of these. The word *anandamide* is taken from the Sanskrit word for bliss, which is *ananda.*

Whereas endorphins are the body's natural opiates, anandamide affects the body in a similar manner to tetrahydrocannabinol (THC), the active ingredient in marijuana. In fact, anandamide may have remained undiscovered if it had not been for research into medicinal uses for cannabis and how cannabinoid receptor sites in the central nervous system work. In layperson's terms, researchers were trying to figure out how weed affects the brain. The scientists understood we probably didn't evolve receptor sites in our nervous system for illicit drug use and went on to discover that we naturally produce chemicals in our body that have the same effects.

The biggest injection of anandamide comes with intense physical exertion. If you need to use that adrenaline rush physically, the high that comes with it can be incredible, and it's a lot healthier than any externally induced buzz. *High on your own supply* isn't just a catchy phrase, it's real.

After the endorphins and anandamide, if you see the situation is under control and there is no longer a call to have the gas pedal to the floor, another type of chemical is released into the system called serotonin. This is also a well-known contributor to feelings of well-being. Known as the "happiness hormone," serotonin is important to your sense of contentment—so much so that most antidepressant drugs prescribed today are designed to elevate or maintain serotonin levels in the body. The rise in serotonin after the adrenaline response is part of how adventurous activities make you feel good.

The final chemical I will talk about is another powerful hormone/neurotransmitter called dopamine. Dopamine has some characteristics like serotonin but is a bit different. They are both powerful feel-good hormones, but serotonin's job is to calm you down and return everything to homeostasis. Dopamine, by contrast, is designed for motivation, learning, future survival, and propagation of the species. Dopamine is your brain's reward system for a job well done. It's also to ensure you do it again next time (positive reinforcement).

After going through a scary situation that fires your adrenal response, your brain says, "Okay, you had me going there. I was scared. That's why I shot you full of adrenaline, but you didn't get us killed. Good job. Here's some dopamine." Next time you are presented with a similar situation, your brain will say, "Well, you didn't get us killed last time, so do whatever you did before. Here's a little dopamine. If you keep us alive again, I promise there is more at the end." Dopamine doesn't just feel good, it intensifies memories of things that feel good, and being alive after your sympathetic nervous system decided you were in danger feels pretty good. Damn good, actually!

Biologically, dopamine is intended to help you learn things that will keep you living. Of course, this is an oversimplified explanation, but that is dopamine in a nutshell, at least in how it relates to the adrenal response. The dopamine feed taught our hunter-gatherer ancestors to take risks to improve their chances of survival.

That is what happens when an adrenal response is activated—a lot of powerful chemicals are released into the blood and nervous system in quick succession. Since this cocktail of hormones also acts as neurotransmitters, it can make for some intense altered states of consciousness without having to introduce a foreign substance to the body.

Some of the effects of this natural rush are similar to the effects of hallucinogens. One of the most common altered states of perception is *tachypsychia*, or changing the perception of time. Usually this change is the slowing down of perceived time. If you have had the misfortune of being in an accident or managed to avoid one you could see coming, you have probably experienced adrenal-induced tachypsychia. Everything just seems to move in *sloooooow* motion.

From a psychological perspective, for many of the sensations reported by people who participate in adventure sports or have a job where they are faced with life-and-death situations, the intense adrenal rush they describe fits in with the characteristics of what Mihaly Csikszentmihalyi described as flow states,[8] or what Abraham Maslow expressed as peak experiences. These are profound experiences in which a person feels ecstasy, happiness, overwhelming joy, and a sense of wonder. Many people who have experienced a powerful adrenal rush believe it helped them achieve a heightened state of awareness.

In a flow state, sensory acuity and focus can be brought to levels that seem supernatural.[9] Proximity wingsuit fliers talk about being able to see almost every minute detail of the rock formations they are screaming past at over two hundred miles per hour. Free climbers or rock climbers who climb without safety equipment talk about being able to feel changes in rock and intuitively know what route to take, even though they have never done it before. Big wave surfers can feel what the wave is going to do before it does. They often feel they have melded with the environment and are one with the wave.

The first times I experienced these fluid, profound moments I was among trees. As a young boy I could not throw or catch a ball to save my life but get me up a tree and I was the master. When I was growing up, we had an enormous, sprawling grandfather oak in our backyard. I practically lived in that tree. I was in the tree so much that I became an expert in climbing it. The branches spread far, and some of them were close to a foot thick. I got to the point where I could walk along the branches like they were balance beams, only my balance beams were fifteen to twenty feet in the air. Walking along these branches was where I found my bliss. It required a high level of concentration to keep from falling, and with that level of focus, there was simply no room in my mind for the awkward self-consciousness I normally felt on the ground. Small adrenaline rushes were frequent as I jumped from branch to branch, not always sure if I was going to stick the landing. Whenever I got the chance, I was up a tree, climbing to a peak experience.

Maslow described peak experiences as "exciting, oceanic, deeply moving, exhilarating, elevating experiences that generate an advanced form of perceiving reality and are even mystic and magical in their effect upon the experimenter."[10]

Being adrenalized is not the only way to find flow states or have peak experiences. Artists, musicians, and writers can sometimes slip into a flow state without having to traverse the edge of the extreme. They are lost in their work, and everything else seems to disappear. Because of the increased demands in intense situations, it is just easier to find the flow when there is an element of danger.

As Steven Kotler put it in *The Rise of Superman: Decoding the Science of Ultimate Human Performance*, anyone can achieve a flow state, but extreme athletes can drop into "the zone" more readily than the rest of us because "when you're pushing the limits of human performance the choice is stark: it's flow or die."[11]

Maslow is best known for his pyramid-shaped hierarchy of needs with the concept of self-actualization being at the top. He believed peak experiences were an important part of becoming self-actualized. Maslow described self-actualized people as being at their highest self or having unlocked their full potential and having a sense of transcendence. Self-transcendence is a feeling of being beyond the constraints of your body and connected to others, the world, and even the universe. It is this transcendence where the lines between physics, psychology, and mysticism tend to blur.

Some people believe the surge of adrenaline and endorphins generated from the fight-or-flight response is an intense spiritual experience.

Transcendence is a word adventure athletes use a lot. Many people who have been in life-and-death situations or are engaged in extreme sports report similar sensations to having mystical or religious experiences.

It is no wonder many rites of passage and shamanic rituals require elements of courage, focus, endurance, and in some cases a high level of pain tolerance. Some ancient rituals resemble modern-day adrenaline sports. At least two modern-day adventure sports that I can think of are derived directly from Indigenous rituals.

Modern bungee jumping[12] was developed by members of the Oxford University Dangerous Sports Club after watching a documentary on land diving on Pentecost Island in Vanuatu. Land diving is a ritual where young men jump off a tall wooden tower with vines attached to their ankles. Unlike bungee jumping, land divers are expected to hit the ground. The vines are there to keep them from hitting the ground so hard it kills or permanently disables them. This works well most of the time. With bungee jumping, you jump off a bridge or tower with a giant elastic rope attached to your ankles or waist. The elastic stretch and subsequent bounce reduce the shock of being stopped by the rope, so you don't hit the ground. It is very scary but also fun!

Surfing also has its roots in the ancient rituals of Polynesian culture.[13] Anthropologists believe surfing has held cultural and spiritual significance in Hawaii dating back at least 1,500 years. In ancient times the best surfing spots were reserved for royalty. Surfing and spiritual practices tied to it inundated every aspect of island life. Even today, big wave riders in many ways sound more like Zen masters than athletes. For them, riding waves is the ultimate spiritual experience.

Luckily we don't have to push ourselves quite as far as extreme athletes to get to those peak experiences. As far as your sympathetic nervous system is concerned, perceived danger can count just as much as actual risk to life and limb.

Perceived danger or perceived risk is your subjective appraisal of the danger of the current situation. Real risk is the actual, inherent danger in each moment. It can go both ways. In some instances you can be in a lot more danger than you realize. But normally when I talk about perceived danger or perceived risk, I'm talking about a danger primarily in your imagination or getting sensory feedback that makes you think you're in much more danger than you're actually in. The senses and the amygdala can be deceived—and therein lies the magic.

Your senses can pick up signals of danger even though you consciously know there is no danger—like with my panther experience. The amygdala may pick up on sensory cues and fire off the adrenal spike despite what your higher-thinking mind is saying. Anybody who is afraid of heights when they look through a window of a high building even though they are safe inside knows this.

The amygdala is a primitive part of the brain that predates your ability to reason, so it doesn't understand safety features like high-impact glass windows or that the harness you wear on a zip line is going to keep you safe. It knows only that a fall from that high up can kill you, so it better pump you full of adrenaline.

Remember, the amygdala processes information much faster than the prefrontal cortex, so you will probably react before you can even say, "That's nothing to be afraid of." Imagine a butterfly is floating behind you, and you turn around. You might flinch and throw your hands up to protect your face. The perception is that something is dangerously close to your face. Then the prefrontal cortex takes over and tells you it's only a butterfly. After that comes the serotonin to calm you down.

Sometimes managing the perceived danger is a battle of will. On many advanced high-rope courses, there is an element called the leap of faith as the exit from the course. You are hooked into a cable belay system with your climbing harness. You stand on a platform usually about thirty feet (nine meters) up, and you jump off, going into free fall for a couple of seconds before the belay kicks in, slowing you to a gentle landing.

Now, I have done a lot of jumping-from-high-up activities, but even I get hit with the freeze on the leap of faith more often than not. Almost every time I jump from one of these platforms I get an adrenal rush, and my body wants to fight me. This is my amygdala's self-preservation system trying to override my conscious brain.

I have physically gone to jump and then been frozen in place, unable to take that last step. I have to mentally push myself to do it, because it is simply not a natural act. It is a big confidence builder once you work up the nerve to jump, but it can be a challenge doing that.

At the subconscious level, you may perceive all kinds of things that aren't dangerous as threats. If someone has a fear of heights, riding in a glass elevator can be one of the most adrenaline-producing things they have ever done. Giving a speech in public, performing onstage, or making a sales call can produce an adrenal response. These things aren't physically dangerous, but the amygdala may process them as if they were.

The fact that your sensory input can make things appear to be more dangerous than they are can cause strife, but it also gives you a chance to confront mental barriers and challenges, enabling you to grow without having to take it to the razor's edge of life and death like our ancestors did. Most of the things people fear can be confronted while maintaining a level of relative safety.

Sometimes a lack of sensory information also causes an adrenal spike. Any time you have heard a noise in the dark and freaked out a little, that's why. Your brain puts that noise in the category of danger until you get enough sensory information to prove it is not. "Whew, it's just a raccoon trying to break into my garbage cans. I can relax now."

One of the basic exercises in adventure education takes advantage of the fact that a lack of sensory input causes the fight-or-flight response.

The trust fall, also called the trust lean, is used widely by corporate team-building retreats, sports teams, Scouts, church youth groups, and sleepaway camps.

There is a good chance at some point in your life you have done trust falls. The idea is one person stands in front of the group with their back to the others. They lean back on their heels until they fall backward. The team members act as spotters, catching the person. Sometimes this is done from a height like a park bench or tree stump to kick up the perceived danger. You can't see behind you and don't really know if you'll be caught until you are. Nobody wants to crack the back of their skull on the deck, so this can cause a pretty intense adrenal rush.

The jury is out on how much trust it builds within a team, but it is a great exercise for forcing yourself to do something that innately causes an adrenaline spike. If you have never done it before, I recommend you get with some close friends and give it a try. Just make sure you don't pick sadistic jerks who might let you fall as friends. As simple as this exercise is, if not done properly you can be seriously injured.

Of course, there is also the rock 'n' roll extreme version of the trust fall: the stage dive to crowd surf. I have been injured by this, so I do not recommend it. I have received injuries as both the stage diver and one of the people tasked with catching them. I have also witnessed this go extremely bad and people being wheeled out of a concert on gurneys by paramedics. Yes, even listening to music can be an adrenal sport, but that was my younger days when my body healed much faster.

Returning to our process of adrenal response, after the adrenaline rush, when the body has pumped in endorphins, cannabinoids, and maybe a little dopamine and serotonin, it begins to calm down. Once again the parasympathetic nervous system takes over, and the body returns to homeostasis. If you have expended a lot of energy, you can feel drained, and it is time to rest. If you are on that beach in St. Thomas, maybe it's time to stroll up to the bar and order a Bushwacker. That's the island's signature drink. Be careful of those too. They sneak up on you.

That about covers the basics of the adrenal response and why it happens. Next I want to talk about what can go wrong with this system.

THE DARK SIDE OF THE ADRENAL RESPONSE

So far I have mostly talked about the positive aspects of an adrenal rush. Earlier I explained some of the benefits of an adrenal spike, such as enhanced strength, speed, clarity of mind, and the cascade of feel-good hormones. The potential for incredible peak experiences is produced by, or at least enhanced by, the fight-or-flight response. But there is also a downside.

First, in some extreme cases, if you are not used to an adrenaline dump, it can make you nauseous.[14] Many public speakers, actors, stage performers, and pop and rock stars have reported they were so afraid their first couple of performances they got physically sick the first few times they went onstage. Extreme nausea from stage fright is such a common problem that some venues have airsickness bags placed in strategic locations around the edges of the stage so performers can dump the contents of their stomachs without leaving too much of a mess. Because, of course, the show must go on.

The same is true of heart-pounding adventure sports. In a tandem skydive, the novice jumper is physically attached to the instructor. A harness mounts the instructor to the student's back. When I was getting ready for my first tandem skydive, my instructor explained that the adrenaline dump can make you sick to your stomach. Then he kept telling me how to lean my head to the side, so if I spewed, I would not hit him in the face with it. He repeated himself enough times and with enough imperative that I figured it must be a common problem with first-time jumpers.

When someone is new to skydiving, it is recommended that they do one or two tandem jumps before being allowed to jump without an instructor attached. On jump three, you are not attached to anyone, but you jump with two instructors for safety. This brings me to the next couple of potential pitfalls of the adrenal spike. One of the reasons for doing tandem jumps is because the first couple of times the adrenaline of free fall can cause a freeze, and you might not be able to pull the rip cord and deploy the chute in time.

Another reason is the possibility of performance degradation. Adrenaline increases your heart rate. This is good up to a point. Blood is pumped to the muscles more rapidly, which can increase the speed of your reaction time, but too much overloads your nervous system and instead makes it harder to execute tasks.[15]

In my first tandem skydive, the instructor told me that when we got to the right altitude, I would be pulling the rip cord and deploying the parachute. When it was time to pull, I missed the rip cord twice, and the instructor had to pull it for me. I was just too adrenalized to be coordinated enough to make the grab.

Experts say this adrenaline-altered heart rate increases your ability to perform up to about 145 beats per minute (bpm). Optimal performance lies on average between 115 and 145 bpm. With an adrenal-induced heartbeat of 145 to 175 bpm, you start to lose complex motor skills. Things like being able to put your key in a lock, tying knots, or pulling a rip cord or pilot chute on a parachute become extremely difficult.

Above 175 bpm, you can perform only gross motor movements. You can't do anything that requires complexity. You might get tunnel vision and auditory exclusion where you can't hear anything, and your ability to think begins to break down. At this level, the animal brain takes over. This is where someone would be considered hysterical. In instances of violence, people are likely to freeze, attack with wild arm swings, or run away as fast as possible. They lose coordination, so they are likely to trip. The girl in the horror movie running from the killer and falling every couple of seconds probably isn't too far off the mark of how many people would respond in that situation. Sometimes they just lie down in a submissive posture. They may lose bladder and bowel control. And with an adrenaline-induced heartbeat of 175 bpm or more, anybody with an underlying heart condition is at serious risk of a heart attack. It truly is possible to scare someone to death.

Another thing about the adrenaline rush is if it is a full dump, you get only about a minute of improved performance before you experience exhaustion. If you maintain elevated adrenal levels for too long, this fatigue becomes parasympathetic backlash, which can, in turn, begin to worsen performance significantly as well as inhibit cognitive function, thus reducing your decision-making ability. These are some of the negatives of adrenaline in the short term. But what about long-term effects?

Another negative aspect of the adrenal response is stress. Technically, stress happens any time the sympathetic nervous system is fired. But it is supposed to be the acute stress response. Acute means intense but for a short period. Chronic stress is what people are talking about when they refer to bad stress. Chronic means long-lasting, and it's not good.

The human body is effective at handling acute stress, but chronic stress? Not so much. The way the autonomic nervous system is designed, your body creates adrenaline and all the other chemicals that go with it to address a threat, deal with it, then calm down and heal. This is a throwback to the lizard part of the brain, which served well when our ancestors were fighting off saber-toothed tigers and enemy tribes on a regular basis. The system works best for dealing with a quick, immediate threat and then releasing and returning to a relaxed homeostatic state.

Unfortunately, we have not evolved a better system to deal with the new threats of modern society, so the old-world sympathetic nervous system is activated, and we feel stress. Prolonged stress is not what the system was designed for, and if it goes for too long, it can cause serious damage to your health.

With the stress of modern life, the perceived threat cannot always be dealt with the way we were designed to deal with it. If you are caught in a traffic jam, someone cuts you off, or your boss is breathing down your neck at work, you can't very well run away. Things don't usually work out for people who choose the fight response either. Some people do, but someone who punches their boss is probably going to have a hard time finding another job.

You can't reach through the line and punch the tech support person on the other end of the phone who is only trying to help. Besides, it's not their fault you waited on hold for forty-five minutes pumping more and more adrenaline as time passed and the frustration built. There is a term for when someone lets the fight response take control of them in traffic: road rage, and it can have dire consequences.

Perceived threats that cannot be escaped or fought off throw the whole system for a loop, especially if the threat is prolonged. Here is an example. Imagine you are driving on a country road with hardly any traffic and someone from the oncoming lane suddenly swerves into your lane and then back into theirs just in the nick of time. You are going to get a pretty serious adrenal response. Those fight-or-flight hormones are going to shoot through your system! This is extreme stress. But just as quickly as it began, the danger is over. Whew, close call. If you don't consciously dwell on the incident, your body will start to feed you endorphins, serotonin, and dopamine, and you begin to feel pretty good. That is how the system is supposed to work.

But if you are in a traffic jam, the story is different. Every few seconds you must hit the brakes so you don't slam into the car in front of you. You also worry about the person behind you, who is probably tailgating. You are not getting as big an adrenal spike as the incident on the country road, but you keep getting little ones. Your body never gets a chance to release the feel-good hormones because you keep getting fed adrenaline. That is how stress builds in your system. If you don't take steps to manage your state, you can damage both your body and mind.

Unlike the excited state of a good thrill, there is no release in a chronically stressed state. Whether the stress is a real or imagined danger, if it is sustained too long, the body stops producing endorphins and serotonin and overproduces cortisol. As I said earlier, cortisol is produced in the adrenal gland with adrenaline. One of its purposes is to reduce inflammation so your body can carry on fighting or escaping.

The problem with this is inflammation is primarily how your immune system works. Cortisol suppresses the immune system, and you need your immune system to fight off disease. Also, if cortisol builds up in the system for too long, it begins to break down muscle and bone tissue. It's good to have a boost of cortisol now and then, but too much for too long is a bad thing.

Noradrenaline is not good for you in excessive amounts either. As I said earlier, noradrenaline narrows the blood vessels, increasing blood pressure to pump fresh blood to the places that need it. If you are stressed, you don't need the blood pumped faster, but the norepinephrine increases the blood pressure anyway. If that is prolonged, and especially if it is in combination with high cholesterol, it can damage blood vessels and lead to a heart attack or stroke. This is why the first thing most doctors recommend to people with high blood pressure is to reduce stress levels.

The fight-or-flight condition causes muscle tension. Remember, the body is ready for physical combat or making a run for it. Chronic stress causes muscles to remain contracted. This can cause stress headaches and migraines and contribute to many musculoskeletal disorders.

Some stress is good for you. Some of us perform best when there is some stress. When you were in school, if you waited to start working on an assignment until you thought you were in danger of not completing it in time, you may be one of those people. If you are, don't worry. I'm right there with you. However, if you live your life this way, the stress will begin to build, and sometimes the quality of the work suffers, because you are scrambling to get it done and don't have time to properly refine your work.

A level above stress is anxiety, an intense feeling of worry. That beautiful prefrontal cortex is normally a wonderful thing. It is what separates humans from animals. You can remember the past and hopefully learn from it. You can visualize many possible futures, which can help you define goals and the action steps to achieve them. Unfortunately, you can just as easily remember past failures and imagine all kinds of nasty negative possibilities. That can create anxiety unless you keep it in check.

This acute stress response system works perfectly in the animal kingdom where they don't have higher brains to overthink and worry about things. If a wolf goes after a deer, the deer gets a serious adrenal response. It's a life-and-death situation. If the deer escapes and the wolf goes away, the parasympathetic nervous system takes over again, and the deer goes back to grazing. They live totally in the moment. The deer doesn't worry about the wolves that might be in the woods. Yes, if it gets sensory information, like the sound or smell of a wolf, it will go back on alert. But generally, if there is not a threat the deer can detect, it stays in the relaxed rest-and-digest state and concentrates on eating grass or laying down and taking a nap.

In humans, concern about the possibility of a certain outcome can produce an adrenal response, and that is anxiety. Some anxiousness is normal, particularly if you must perform. It doesn't matter if it is in a sport, onstage, or during communication. Most things outside your comfort zone will produce a little anxiety. This becomes a problem when it is excessive. Frequent panic attacks, constant nervousness, apprehension about the future, and obsessive behavior are all signs that anxiety has become a mental disorder.

Unlike the hypothetical deer, if you were chased by a wolf and got away, you would remember it for a very long time. You might worry about the wolf or wolves you can't see that might be lurking just beyond the light of your campfire. If you thought about it too much, you might experience anxiety, feeling the fear of the chase all over again long after the wolf has moved on in search of easier game.

One of the things that can create anxiety is trauma.[16] Trauma sucks, but unfortunately it is usually a part of life. The longer you live, the more of it you will experience. Trauma, simply stated, is an emotional reaction to a disturbing event. Your adrenal response is activated. Then, if your internal coping mechanism is overwhelmed, you experience trauma. If something bad happened or something scared you to the point you have a hard time processing and integrating the experience, you have been traumatized.

A person can suffer from varying degrees of trauma. Some are relatively small, and others can be utterly devastating. Quite a few things in life can cause trauma, such as an accident, an injury, a scare, or a breakup—especially if it was a surprise or infidelity was involved. Witnessing violence, the loss of a loved one, the loss of a job, any event that causes financial distress, the loss of a beloved pet, and being bullied are all possible causes of trauma.

A person who is traumatized may develop certain symptoms like the inability to sleep, depression, anxiety, dissociation (i.e., feeling numb or disconnected from themselves), the inability to concentrate, forgetfulness, nightmares, avoidance of places or things, irritability, jumpiness, flashbacks, and more. If these symptoms are so bad they cause the person to become dysfunctional, it can be classified as a disorder. Acute stress disorder usually goes away within a couple of weeks if it is addressed properly and the trauma wasn't too severe. The worst version of this is a chronic condition called post-traumatic stress disorder (PTSD), which I will discuss at length in the next chapter.

The last possible negative effect of adrenaline is the risk of addiction. As I mentioned earlier, endorphins are part of the chemical rush your body gets when you have an adrenaline dump, and they have opiate-like qualities. Opiates, including heroin, morphine, and prescription painkillers, are some of the most addictive substances known to humans. The opiate class of drugs binds to the same receptor sites in your nervous system as your body's natural endorphins. If exposed often, your body builds up a tolerance or resistance to chemical stimulations, so a bigger dose is required to get the same high. A junkie hooked on painkillers or heroin who is used to the drug takes more drugs or a stronger dosage.

An adrenaline junkie needs to take a bigger risk or do a more dangerous thing to get the same fix they did before. Believe me, there are plenty of stories of adrenaline junkies who have gone off the deep end and sold all their stuff to feed their addiction, just like any other addict would do to pay for their habit. No matter what, it's always possible to go bigger and take the danger to another level, and that's why extreme risk-taking can be so addictive. You can always dive deeper, go faster, climb higher, or do a more technically difficult stunt that's more dangerous and keeps that thrill going. The key is being aware of this possibility from the beginning and finding a balance between taking risks and becoming completely reckless for the thrill of it.

Dopamine is also a big driver in the craving for adrenaline. It plays a role in addiction but not in the way most people think. You don't notice the craving for dopamine the way you do some of the other chemicals involved in a rush. The way dopamine affects memory and learning is when you crave the action that caused the dopamine release. If a dangerous action created an adrenaline rush that included a dopamine feed, you may feel an urge to perform that action again in the future and perhaps even take it a step further to get more of that good feeling.

You took a chance, and your daring act fired off the amygdala's alarm. You felt the rush. If you come out all right after the alarm bell went off, you must have done something right—or so the brain tells you. If the experience is interpreted as pleasurable, dopamine is fired into the system to crystallize the memory of something good. You will want more of that. Each time you experience the rush, dopamine will make what triggered the good feelings very memorable. Dopamine is a motivator, so when you find an experience pleasurable, you produce dopamine, and that enhances the memory of the experience and the pleasure you derived from it.

Dopamine makes you happy, and it sometimes deeply embeds the memory of the thing you did that made you happy. If you are in a similar situation again, it will help drive you to seek that experience again.

This driver has a biological purpose. Animals and early humans who tried new options and were open to novel experiences had the opportunity to find better sources of food and water. They had a better chance of survival. They also risked leaving the known territory to seek better mates and expand the gene pool.

The problem is humans moved from hunter-gatherers, to farmers, to factory workers, through the technological revolution, then to home office workers. This increase in free time has allowed people to invent all kinds of creative ways to produce the pleasurable feelings that were so imperative to our learning and survival in the beginning. Now people can chase those feelings for the sake of it. This can enrich your life, but also just as easily enslave you to the rush.

There are all kinds of adrenaline addictions. It is not restricted to the world of extreme sports. Most addictions have an adrenal component. Many classic addictions have an element of the adrenaline rush, and dopamine plays a role in crystallizing the experience as something to crave. Addiction, like most other repetitive behaviors, is learned. Dopamine—and the other neurotransmitters involved in a rush—play a big role in the learned behaviors that can become an addiction. Even modern addictions, like compulsively checking your social media feeds, are governed by a dopamine feedback loop.

Someone who appears to have an overabundance of drama in their life may have an adrenaline addiction. They constantly find themselves in toxic relationships. They fight with their friends and family. If this type of thing is a repeated cycle, they may be creating it in their own life—not consciously, but the drama is exciting and creates all the chemicals of an adrenaline rush. If they do not have better strategies and methods for creating the excitement they crave, they may create it negatively or subconsciously put themselves in dangerous situations that will generate it.

Hopefully this gives you a basic understanding of the adrenal response and how these powerful chemicals can affect you. They can be incredibly helpful, pleasurable, and even critical to your survival, but they also can be highly addictive and detrimental if not kept in check.

The next two chapters are about the things that create a surge of adrenaline and how to use them. We look at commonly frightening things and learn how to face fears and even convert them into excitement.

EXERCISE

The exercise for this chapter is to give yourself a quick adrenaline rush. In the words of Eleanor Roosevelt, "Do one thing every day that scares you." At this point I don't want you to face any of your major fears. That isn't for two more chapters. You are just going to give yourself a quick jolt of adrenaline and observe what happens.

The best way to do this is to scare yourself on purpose. If you have a heart condition, you can opt out. Similarly, if you suffer from an anxiety disorder or any other condition that could be affected by this exercise, use caution and good judgment. This is an optional exercise.

The idea is to induce an adrenaline rush and then calm down and return to homeostasis. Afterward, write down some observations about the experience. There are several ways you can do this. The first is the trust fall I mentioned earlier in the chapter.

The second, simpler way you can do by yourself is to watch a jump scare video online. A jump scare is a technique used in horror movies and video games in which a seemingly innocuous scene changes abruptly, startling the viewer. Something scary pops out, or a character suddenly morphs into something horrific. There is usually a loud noise accompanying the change of scene to add to the effect. Something happens to startle you.

Horror movies usually contain a lot of jump scares, but there are plenty of stand-alone jump scare videos on the internet. They are usually about thirty seconds to three minutes long—enough time to lull you into a false sense of security and then, boom, the scare! This method is by far the easiest way to give you that fear jolt. This is the method I recommend for this exercise.

Just type *jump scare videos* into a search engine to find a plethora of results. If you are a horror buff, you have probably already watched plenty of jump scare videos. But you have probably never watched one purposely to observe your own adrenal response, and with so many choices, I am sure you can find some you haven't seen before.

Remember, the purpose is to give yourself a quick shot of adrenaline, observe what happens internally, write it down, then calm down and relax.

Write down any observations:

How alert did you feel after your scare?

As the adrenaline wore off, did you have any feelings of euphoria?

How long did it take you to calm down?

This was just a quick scare, but did you get any inclination to run, freeze, or get angry and want to fight?

What else did you notice during or immediately after your scare?

There are no right or wrong answers. You are observing what happens in your own body when you get that adrenal rush.

_____

_____

_____

_____

_____

_____

_____

_____

_____

_____

Chapter 4:

The Fear That Lies Within

> Named must be your fear before banish it you can.
> — YODA, THE EMPIRE STRIKES BACK

First and foremost, it is important to understand that fear is your friend. Fear is not the enemy. Fear is your ally. Fear is a tool your mind uses for survival. Fear keeps you alive! It's okay to have some fear; it's even healthy. Not having any fear is a mental disorder and one of the more dangerous ones at that.[1] So fear is good when governed properly.

We spent the day rock climbing and rappelling (abseiling). Everyone else was taking a break at the bottom of the cliff except me and one friend, who was probably the most fearless of our group. We were still rappelling because it's so much fun! I was waiting for him to descend before it was my turn. When you first start to rappel, there is an awkward moment changing from horizontal ground to the vertical cliff face. In a standard rappel, you back over the edge and assume an L-shaped position, so your feet are planted on the rock face, but your torso is vertical. Once you have the position correct, it's smooth sailing from there.

As he leaned over the cliff, my friend shook his head, looked up at me, and said, "Man, no matter how many times I do this, I still get scared in this part."

I replied, "Dude, you are climbing over the side of a cliff. You should be a little scared! If it wasn't for the fear, one of us would have accidentally walked off the side of one of these mountains a long time ago."

Going back to chapter 2, if the risk is the chance of loss, fear is concern over the possibility of that loss. Whenever there is the possibility of loss, real or imagined, there is the potential for fear. It is not guaranteed, but the potential is there. Fear is the mental construct you produce when you think about the possibility of something bad happening. It creates an adrenal surge to protect you. That's it. Nothing more.

Building from the last chapter on the adrenal surge, in this chapter I talk about fear—specifically fear that doesn't serve you, or the kind of fear that isn't useful to you anymore, if it ever was. Maybe your fear can be useful, but you have blown it up to a disproportionate level. This is the fear I want to explore, the fear I want you to conquer.

A common mental disorder sometimes caused by a traumatic event is a phobia,[2] or an irrational fear of a specific thing or situation. Sometimes even thinking about the thing is enough to fire an adrenal response. Besides being a fascinating subject, the nomenclature and processes involved in forming phobias are the same for all irrational fears, regardless of whether they are severe enough to be clinically diagnosed as phobias or not. Often when I say *phobia* in this chapter, I mean any fear that isn't important to your self-preservation. This should be useful whether or not you have debilitating fears. Sit back. We are going to dive into this pretty deep.

Almost all of us have a couple of illogical or disproportionate fears. If you don't, you are one of the lucky few. Being afraid of something doesn't necessarily qualify that fear as a phobia. If the thing you fear distresses you significantly enough that it adversely affects your life, it might be a clinical phobia.

People with a true phobia often go to great lengths to avoid the object of their phobia. They miss out on activities they would otherwise engage in for fear of encountering the object or situation. If someone refuses a job offer because they find out the office where they would be working is on one of the upper floors of a tall building, that would be well beyond a natural and rational fear of heights. It would be a true phobia.

The parasympathetic nervous and endocrine systems were developed in an earlier stage of evolution, before humans developed brains that could reason, store memories, and learn at the level we can now. The system works perfectly in animals. As I said in the last chapter, most animals live completely in the moment. They don't remember what happened twenty minutes ago, let alone last year.

But humans have long memories. Our brains are designed to learn and store experience. That is how we have built incredible structures and machines and many of the advances our society now enjoys.

Learning some fear is one of the ways humans stay safe. If a kid touches a hot stove, the hand reflexively draws away from the pain, and they probably won't do that again. The fear of touching a red-hot burner is useful.

The problem is if something bad happens to you, it can be hard to forget. You can imagine things. It comes in handy most of the time, but if you have been traumatized, sometimes you overlearn fear and avoidance of things that can be beneficial or should at least be nonissues. This can get embedded deeply, and sometimes collateral objects and situations are grouped into the things you fear, thus impoverishing your life. Unfortunately, the creative part of the brain can exaggerate the level of danger or even invent threats that aren't there.

As you are about to find out, it doesn't have to be a trauma experienced directly to create an irrational fear. The ways phobias are created fall into three basic categories. They are *classical conditioning, vicarious acquisition*, and *informational/instructional acquisition*. These are the mechanisms for developing irrational fear, regardless of whether it qualifies as a phobia or not.

In classical conditioning, a traumatic event has occurred in a person's life that generated the fear. Falling or almost falling from a high place can create acrophobia, or fear of heights. Being locked in a closet or trunk by an older sibling or the neighborhood bully is a common way claustrophobia, or fear of small spaces, is generated.

You may remember learning about classical conditioning in school with the story of Pavlov's dogs. To refresh your memory, in 1897 Russian scientist Ivan Pavlov did a series of experiments in which he rang a bell, then presented dogs with food. When he presented the dogs with the food, they salivated. Because he rang the bell every time he fed the dogs, they began to associate the ringing of the bell with food. After a while, he could just ring the bell and the dogs salivated, even if there was no food. They were conditioned to associate the bell with food. He said this was a form of learning and created the model of respondent conditioning[3] we now call *classical conditioning* or *Pavlovian conditioning*.

In this model, before the conditioning, the bell was a *neutral stimulus*. The food was an *unconditioned stimulus*. The dogs drooled whenever they saw or smelled the food whether Pavlov did anything or not. After they associated the bell with the food, the bell became a *conditioned stimulus*, and the drooling at the sound of the bell was the *conditioned response*. Hopefully I haven't lost you yet.

What does that have to do with phobias? Phobias and fears, in general, are learned behaviors, and classical conditioning is the most common way they are learned. I go into more detail in a moment, but first here's a story to break up all this science.

Growing up in Florida, I was used to alligators. In my younger years, I spent plenty of time playing around in rivers and lakes. Every now and then, I read about an alligator that had killed someone. I naturally learned how to keep my eyes peeled for a gator sneaking up. I built an intuitive feel for how big an alligator had to be before it would consider me prey and how close I could get to one resting on the riverbank before I made it mad. But I am comfortable being relatively close to most alligators. They are just part of the environment in Florida.

Of course, there is always an exception. There was a time when Narelle and I were hiking along a riverbank outside Tampa, and as the trail dipped next to the edge of the river, we noticed on the opposite bank the largest wild alligator I have ever seen in my life. It was at least fourteen feet (4.2 meters) long.

This thing was more like something from the age of the dinosaurs than any modern reptile I had seen. We stood there watching it for a moment, and the thought crossed my mind that if it got close, it could take either one of us, and there was not a lot we could do to stop it. Sure enough, just as I thought this, the gator started sliding slowly and stealthily into the water toward us.

Narelle freaked out and ran as fast as she could. I suppose it probably didn't help that I mentioned that alligators can outrun people for short distances on land. I was a little nervous myself, so I moved up the trail to higher ground. We had to hike back that same way when we returned. We did not see our dinosaur-size friend anywhere. That spot where the trail dipped down to the water was a perfect spot for an ambush, so we left the trail and broke bush a couple of hundred meters before rejoining the trail at a point with a higher riverbank. A little bit of caution can go a long way.

In our case, our fear was justified, but I knew people who were afraid to walk out on a dock if there was even a small gator in the water. They were extremely nervous even seeing one from a distance. For some reason the natural fear of alligators blew out to a disproportionate level. Narelle was fine after our little scare, and we went back to watching the normal-size alligators on the riverbanks whenever we happened upon them.

Back to Pavlov: it took him ringing the bell and feeding the dogs many times before they were conditioned to salivate with just the bell. A phobia, on the other hand, can be conditioned with just one experience. The reason is evolutionary. If an ancestor went down to the river to get water and was almost grabbed by a crocodile or alligator, they would learn to be afraid from that one incident. Onetime learning increased the chances of continued existence. If they got a second chance, they almost certainly would not have gotten a third. Learning to be afraid of crocs increased their chances of survival and passing on their genes. Unlike most things people learn that require repetition, fear can be learned in an instant!

Going back to Pavlov's model, the attack is the unconditioned stimulus. The fight-or-flight response is the conditioned response. Seeing a croc or alligator is a conditioned stimulus. It takes only one close call to learn to be afraid of crocs or gators. Being somewhat afraid of a large alpha predator capable of killing you isn't a bad thing in certain situations.

It is just *how* afraid, and does the fear show up when it's not useful and unnecessary? Another problem arises in that other neutral stimuli can inadvertently become conditioned stimuli. The river could become a conditioned stimulus. And because the brain is wired to associate and generalize, the fear of crocs could expand to include all reptiles. Fear of the river could extend to all rivers, perhaps even all bodies of water.

If someone views crocodiles in a zoo enclosure, even if they are close, the stimulus should be neutral. But if that person gets a massive fear spike in those situations or from watching a documentary on crocodiles, seeing crocs is a conditioned stimulus. This distinction is important, because to desensitize, sometimes you must be able to separate real danger from a perceived danger generated by association.

Another example is the fear of heights. This is usually the result of a close call involving almost falling from a high place. The close call (or an actual fall) is an unconditioned stimulus. Looking out a window from the twenty-fifth floor of an office building at some point in the future should be no more than a neutral stimulus. But if it causes a panic attack and vertigo, it is a conditioned stimulus, and the panic attack is the conditioned response.

If you are at the edge of a cliff, you should be a little afraid. Put the selfie stick down and walk away from the ledge. However, if you are back from the edge, and there is a secure guardrail between you and the cliff, it should be a neutral stimulus. Being high up is not the danger. Falling from high up is. If you are high up but under conditions that make it impossible to fall, you are in no danger, even if your amygdala says you are.

I hope that makes sense. If not, just understand to separate the danger from the thing feared because they are usually not the same. Some collateral objects and situations can become the thing people fear, even though they are not the thing to fear.

Vicarious acquisition of a phobia is learning to fear something by observing other people being afraid of it. This usually happens in early childhood. If little Johnny sees his mother get terrified every time she sees a bee, he too is likely to develop a fear of bees.

There was once an evolutionary advantage to this. It is good to learn from mistakes. But back in the day, when everyone lived on the edge of life and death, a lot of mistakes were fatal. You might not have had a chance to learn from your mistakes. That is why it was good to learn from other people's mistakes. People observed things happening to others and learned to be afraid, then their children observed them being afraid, and they too learned the fear, and in most cases, this increased their chances of survival.

This type of learned fear has been shown in primates as well.[4] A 1984 experiment showed juvenile rhesus monkeys became more afraid of snakes when they were exposed to the snakes with adults in the troop that showed signs of fear. If the adults were scared, so were the children.

Most of the time when someone has classically conditioned a fear response, they remember exactly the moment that triggered the creation of their phobia. In some instances someone has a phobia, and they don't know why. They can't explain how they got it, because they have no memory of what made them so afraid of a particular thing.

Sometimes this can be attributed to a repressed memory from a traumatic event. In these cases, the memories that generate the phobia are hidden from the conscious mind to protect it. It used to be believed that all unexplained phobias were generated this way. But it's actually quite rare.

The more likely answer when someone doesn't know how they developed an irrational fear is vicarious acquisition; they learned the fear from someone when they were little. A parent, caregiver, or older sibling displayed enough fear to have it rub off on them. There is no memory, because they learned merely by observation of the phobic response in someone else, and that doesn't stand out in someone's memory, especially if they were little. It wasn't even their phobia, at least not originally. They could be afraid of something because of an incident that happened generations ago.

Another experiment, this time with children, showed that kids who viewed pictures of marsupials were frightened of the animals if a picture was paired with a picture of a person with a frightened expression.[5] The marsupials were the quokka and cuscus, which are some of the cutest, cuddliest-looking Aussie animals there are. They aren't creatures that naturally inspire terror. An image of someone scared was not only enough to frighten the kids but also made them attach that fear to something innocuous, even adorable.

The third way to develop a phobia or disproportionate fear is informational or instructional acquisition. This is becoming afraid of something after getting information about it. This can be from watching documentaries, reading about it in books or on the web, seeing newscasts, and even public service announcements meant to educate people about safety concerns.

Newspeople have a saying: "If it bleeds, it leads." This is an inside joke about the well-known fact that news organizations tend to overreport tragedies and things that instill fear in the viewing audience. While it is good to be informed, overconsumption of news can be a good way of creating phobias and a host of other anxiety-related mental disorders. Twenty-four-hour news and social media have probably been the worst creations for mental health in the past hundred years.

The constant bombardment of information about COVID-19 is probably the best example of informational mass phobia generation in recent times. We spent over two years where you couldn't watch TV, listen to the radio, or watch videos on the computer without constant reminders about the importance of social distancing, washing hands, wearing masks, getting vaccinated, and of course the all-important daily body count.

While I won't totally dispute the validity of all that caution, like some of my tinfoil-hat-wearing friends, that constant bombardment of fear-inducing information had a severe psychological cost across a broad range of the population. Talk to people who say they used to be very sociable, and now they are afraid to go out in public. Some folks will have serious problems with intimacy, crowds, obsessive-compulsive behavior, and anxieties they can't explain for many years.

When I was young, I created my own information-acquired phobia accidentally. When I was nine, a cousin came to visit from Ohio. I wasn't an only child, but I felt like one. My brother and sister were older than me. My sister had moved away with her husband in the military, and my brother was incarcerated at the time. It was nice to have someone older to hang out with and mentor me.

This was the summer the blockbuster movie *Jaws*[6] came out. Directed by Steven Spielberg, the film is about a rogue great white shark terrorizing a small beach town. My parents weren't going to take me to an R-rated film, so I begged my cousin. Even though I was probably too young, he finally obliged.

The movie scared the bejesus out of me, but it also started a lifelong fascination with sharks, particularly great whites. I bought books about sharks. I checked out books on sharks from the library. I subscribed to magazines about sharks. I built shark models. I watched every documentary I could about sharks. There was just one problem: most of the information about sharks involved over-sensationalized accounts of attacks. Scary stories about shark attacks sold books and magazines.

Even then I knew *Jaws* was only a movie, but reading firsthand accounts of real shark attacks made my blood curdle. Some of them were more horrific than any movie could depict. The more I read, the more terrified I became. There is something about the prospect of being eaten alive that invokes a primal, visceral fear. Through my research, I inadvertently induced galeophobia in myself. Galeophobia is the fear of sharks.

We lived in a Florida beach town, and one of the main forms of recreation was swimming at the beach. Shark attacks, even fatal ones, where I lived were rare but not unheard of. Although I was intensely fascinated by them, sharks became my biggest fear. For a couple of years while in middle school, I refused to swim at the beach. Although I got over that level of phobia by high school, the fear remained buried in my subconscious, and I had nightmares about being eaten alive by sharks well into my twenties. At one point I believed these dreams were a premonition of my death.

My first encounter with a shark in the wild was when I was seventeen. My brother and I borrowed a small pram sailboat from a friend and were sailing around some barrier islands. We got the keel stuck on a sandbar, so I got out in chest-deep water to push the boat off. I was standing in deep mud, so it was difficult to move. I pushed with all my might, and just as I got the boat free, the wind caught the sail, and it started to take off away from me.

Then my brother yelled, "Scott, get in the boat!" I looked at him and shrugged, wondering why he seemed so freaked out all of a sudden. He pointed past me and yelled at the top of his lungs. "Shark!" I turned and saw the profile of the dorsal fin, the back, and the caudal fin of a blacktip shark.

It wasn't particularly big as sharks go, but it was as big as me, which was enough to make it dangerous. Just as I looked at the fin, the shark turned in my direction and started heading toward me.

I turned, and because I was panicking and not thinking clearly, I tried to run to the boat. I was in only chest-high water, so I was running, but the water produced drag, and I was in ankle-deep mud that bogged me down, so I was running in super slow motion.

The sailboat was getting farther away and the shark closer, so I tried even harder to run, but that didn't help much. Finally, my brother yelled, "Swim! Swim!" I realized that would be a faster form of locomotion, and I pushed off, swimming like my life depended on it, which it might have, for all I knew.

My brother pulled me onto the deck in the nick of time. The shark passed within a couple of feet of the boat and sank below the waves. This incident didn't help my fear of sharks.

That is how I created my own phobia. Still, as much as they terrified me, sharks had a draw I couldn't explain. Because my fear and fascination with sharks were commingled, eventually I took the idea of therapeutic exposure and systematic desensitization to an unnecessarily high level.

Approximately 10 percent of the population has at least one fear that could be considered a clinical phobia, making it one of the most common mental disorders. That doesn't account for all the illogical or disproportionate fears that aren't bad enough to be classed as phobias. Almost all of us have some fear that doesn't make sense and doesn't serve us.

Below is a list of the most common phobias, from least to most common. Large portions of the population have some level of one or more of these fears, even if they aren't at the level that would be considered phobic. Read the list and see if any of these things scare you. Note if any of your fears seem irrational.

TOP TEN MOST COMMON PHOBIAS[7]

10. Mysophobia—the excessive fear of germs and dirt. This causes you to avoid other people and can cause problems with intimacy, obsessive-compulsive handwashing and disinfecting surfaces, and avoidance of public places for fear of infection. It is number ten, but as children who grew up during the COVID-19 pandemic reach adulthood, I expect this phobia to move up the list—perhaps even to the top.

9. Agoraphobia—fear of being in a situation where escape is difficult. This could be crowded places, open spaces, or anywhere you feel exposed. You probably have heard of the most extreme form of this phobia, where people refuse to leave their homes.

8. Social anxiety disorder or social phobia—fear of social situations. This can be a debilitating form of anxiety. Since humans are social creatures, this phobia has a high chance of adversely affecting day-to-day life. Normally a person with social anxiety disorder feels others are judging them, and the phobia often manifests as a form of super self-consciousness. It can make public speaking nearly impossible. It can interfere with making friends and having meaningful social interactions. The simple act of going to a dinner party may cause a panic attack. A casual networking event becomes the stuff of nightmares.

7. Trypanophobia—fear of injections. This causes apprehension about going to the doctor. People with this type of phobia may put off necessary medical appointments. Seeing a needle causes severe distress, and the person may break down or go into fight mode to avoid the injection. Another possibility is they pass out when they see the needle.

6. Astraphobia—fear of thunder and lightning. Someone with this may feel a great deal of distress if it appears inclement weather is moving in. They may avoid outdoor activities, obsess over the weather, and compulsively check the weather app on their phone every couple of minutes. This is a big problem for some people on the Gulf Coast of Florida, because in the summertime there are afternoon thunderstorms almost every day.

5. Cynophobia—fear of dogs. This usually springs from an incident of being bitten or menaced by a ferocious dog during childhood. It is natural to feel some apprehension about an animal when you don't know if it is friendly. However, people with this phobia have a debilitating terror regardless of whether the dog is a rottweiler or a friendly Yorkshire terrier that wants to lick them to death.

Cynophobia can also be exacerbated by the dogs themselves. Dogs can sense fear, and some dogs behave aggressively toward people they know are afraid of them. This in turn increases the fear response and leads to a vicious cycle spiraling out of control.

4. Aerophobia, also known as pteromerhanophia, is fear of flying or air travel. It is estimated that up to 40 percent of the population experiences some anxiety over flying. Those with aerophobia experience it to the extreme. Someone having a panic attack on a plane is no fun for anyone around them either. Some people refuse to fly altogether and travel long distances only by car, train, or bus. This phobia can limit a person's ability to visit distant relatives during a family emergency. It can prevent them from going for a job that requires travel and severely limits their options for vacations. Some people have been prescribed Valium or other narcotics by their doctor to relax them and reduce their fearfulness during a flight.

3. Acrophobia—fear of heights. This is a common phobia. Some fear of great elevations is normal, but if the fear of heights prevents you from doing things you might otherwise do, you may have acrophobia. As I touched on before, acrophobics are thrown into a panicked state when high up, even in situations when they are completely safe. Sometimes even thinking of a high place gives them a dizzy spell and sets off the fight-or-flight response. Like all phobias, there are varying levels of it, and in some of the worst cases, taking one step up a stepstool or ladder is too much.

If you have a small fear of heights, and I invite you to go bungee jumping, and you take a hard pass, you are right there with most people. That's normal. However, if you cancel a lunch date to meet with old friends you were really looking forward to because they decided to have it on a rooftop restaurant, and the prospect of looking over the city skyline while you have a nice meal sends you into a cold sweat, your fear of heights might be more in line with a phobia. That fear of heights affects your quality of life.

2. Ophidiophobia—fear of snakes. Snakes and spiders are both potentially venomous creatures, so a little fear is understandable. There may be some innate evolutionary basis for fear of these creatures. After all, it has been only a century since the invention of antivenom. Before that, you had a better chance of surviving and reproducing if you managed to avoid venomous creatures altogether.

In some parts of the world, constrictors are big enough to prey on humans, so again some fear of snakes is understandable. However, if you are afraid to go to the park or a pet store for fear of seeing a snake, you may have a problem.

Still, I understand the reasons for fear of snakes. They are somewhat alien to us. They are ectotherms (i.e., cold-blooded) and have scales. People who have never held a snake may think they look slimy. They locomote efficiently without legs, and this creeps some people out. There is also a cultural bias against snakes. Throughout history, they have been portrayed as agents of evil. From their depiction in mythology and the Bible to modern-day fantasy and horror, snakes have often been associated with the forces of darkness. This amplifies a natural fear to the phobic level.

1. Arachnophobia—fear of spiders. The most common phobia is the debilitating fear of spiders. Most people have at least some fear of arachnids. Like snakes, spiders have been cast as sinister servants of evil forces in mythology and pop culture. Spiders are also difficult to avoid. Chances are you have a few living in your house, even if you systematically fumigate. Most people are not well versed in spider identification, nor willing to get close enough to positively identify a spider. They often assume an ordinary household spider is one of the dangerous ones. Most arachnids are small enough to hide in tiny cracks and crevasses, so spiders have a high potential to surprise, which can be a big factor in producing fear.

I will talk more about what to do about specific fears and phobias in the next chapter. But first I want to explain more about the biggest fear generator there is. This is the most extreme reaction to trauma, PTSD.[8] The person with PTSD has been exposed to an incredibly traumatic event and may develop a host of symptoms. Symptoms can present immediately or develop insidiously over time, psychologically infecting a person's mind and maybe even physically affecting their body if it gets bad enough. Time on its own does not heal all wounds, as the saying goes.

Because it can develop slowly, Post-Trauma Stress Conditions can easily go undetected. If not treated properly, it can last years or even a lifetime. Violence, witnessing violence, or the threat of violence can all cause trauma response. They are normally serious, like sexual assault, rape, the horrors of war, a shooting, childhood or domestic abuse, armed robbery, physical assault, kidnapping, torture, a natural disaster, an animal attack, or a bad accident.

Traumatic events that create PTSD can also create one or more phobias. Some symptoms also mimic those of a phobia, so sometimes the conditions are hard to differentiate. You could also have both stemming from the same event. To make a distinction, remember two major components of PTSD are hypervigilance and hyperarousal. Knowing them may help you identify the disorder.

Hypervigilance is a constant state of alertness.[9] A person experiencing hypervigilance is always looking for hidden dangers and is ultra-aware of everything going on in the environment. This can lead to obsessive-compulsive behavior, like getting up in the middle of the night to make sure the doors are locked. Hypervigilance can lead to paranoia and confrontational behavior if you assume everyone you meet is a potential threat.

Hypervigilant people have a sensitive startle reflex. Overreacting to sudden noise or movement in the peripheral vision is a sign of hypervigilance. Being startled triggers a fight-or-flight response, and with someone who has trauma-induced stress this response can be intense and possibly violent. Triggering the acute stress response over and over can be exhausting and quickly take a toll mentally and physically.

Hyperarousal is when a person's body suddenly kicks into high alert and fires the fight-or-flight response for no apparent reason.[10] This may be preceded by a flashback of a traumatic event, or it can come out of nowhere. Sometimes adrenaline rushes keep looping, completely wearing out a person. They could come in the middle of the night when they are trying to sleep.

Brain mapping shows that people suffering from PTSD have reduced activity in their prefrontal cortex and an overactive amygdala. Repeated episodes of adrenaline rush don't include the serotonin, endorphins, and dopamine, the initial fight-or-flight response included. This makes it harder to calm down from each rush.

Post-Traumatic Stress can take a person through a wide range of symptoms and lead to other mental health issues. It can make it impossible to be a functional member of society. If it goes untreated it can lead to self-medication with drugs and alcohol, extreme anxiety, and depression.

Some cases of PTSD lead to suicide, so it's a serious condition. The stories are countless of people surviving horrific events and then taking their own lives a few years later. Approximately 5–6 percent of men and 10–12 percent of women will suffer from PTSD in their lifetime.

Along with traditional therapy, adventure therapy and adrenaline sports can be effective in treating PTSD. It may seem counterintuitive to use an adrenaline-producing activity to treat a condition that is in part an overproduction of adrenaline. However, a growing body of evidence suggests adventure settings are just what the doctor ordered. These types of treatments appear to work exceptionally well for veterans. The challenges and camaraderie experienced in a good adventure program can replicate some of the good things about the service and create new ways of thinking while having fun.

The cascade of epinephrine and all its corresponding feel-good hormones from a therapeutic adventure may create a pattern interruption in the looping of thoughts and chemical responses of someone who suffers from hypervigilance and its buddy, hyperarousal.

With an adventurous activity the participant interprets as exciting, they get that adrenaline rush, but it is enjoyable. The amygdala is activated, but so is the nucleus accumbens, flooding the brain with dopamine and serotonin. This allows for new learning at the neurological level. You get the rush in a positive way.

Exercise burns off adrenaline and produces feel-good endorphins, anandamide, and serotonin. This can counteract the wired, tight feeling of PTSD. Because there may be physical risk, a certain level of concentration is required to accomplish the task at hand and avoid injury, therefore necessitating mindfulness. This turns off the constant chatter in the head, allowing for relaxation and possibly even some of the peak experiences I mentioned in the last chapter.

Ultimately, if you want to find those peak experiences, you must step out and take some risks. You must push your boundaries. One of the best things you can do for yourself is interact with things and situations that scare you. Taking inventory of your irrational fears is an important part of self-discovery and a convenient place to find the scary things you can use to challenge yourself. If you want to overcome your fear and do things that scare you, it is best to have some tools in your psychological toolbox to help.

In the next chapter, I will share some effective techniques for dealing with fear. You may be tempted to dismiss these techniques. A couple of people have said, "That works for you, because you are the type of person who goes bungee jumping, hang gliding, and does all kinds of other crazy stuff." This is the part of the book where I reluctantly open up and share some of my neuroses to give you a picture of how I used these techniques at various points to control my fears and anxieties. If I can do it, anyone can. Countless others have used these tools to overcome their fears.

I already told you I had an intense fear of sharks. I also mentioned I have asthma, and although I wasn't diagnosed until 2014, I have probably always had it to some extent. It is a good thing it wasn't properly diagnosed when I was younger, or I would have never been accepted into the military. It has worsened with age.

It started when I was little. Whenever I got a cold, instead of passing in a few days, it would invariably turn into bronchitis. I had deep bronchial coughs that lasted for weeks, sometimes months. I couldn't stay home sick forever, so I had to go to school with a horrible cough. Whenever I had a coughing fit in class, everyone stared at me with that look. It was embarrassing, and I became self-conscious.

Another thing I was self-conscious about was my finger. When I was in kindergarten, there was an accident at school, and the tip of my left middle finger was cut off. The doctors were able to reattach it, but with all the scar tissue, when my nail grew back, it was crooked and clawlike.

As an adult, I realized as far as deformities go, mine is insignificant, and usually no one notices it. However, when I was little, I thought it was the end of the world, and everyone noticed it. Every time I tried to make new friends or played with new kids, inevitably they would notice my finger and scream, "Eeewwwwww! What happened to your finger?" It was something that made me embarrassed and ashamed of my body.

If I wasn't self-conscious enough from my finger and the cough, I also had some serious trouble learning. I was held back in kindergarten. Narelle likes to joke that I failed finger painting. Then my teachers decided I needed to repeat second grade as well. When they held me back the second time, the faculty at my school realized something was going on, so I was given batteries of tests, and they figured out I was dyslexic. Back then they did not have the diagnosis of attention deficit disorder, but it normally goes hand in hand with dyslexia. As an adult I was diagnosed with attention deficit hyperactivity disorder (ADHD).

When I was diagnosed with dyslexia, ironically somehow my intelligence quotient score came back as high. I got to wear two labels: intellectually gifted but learning disabled. I rather like the modern terminology people are beginning to use now: *neurodivergent.* The simple change of language has less of a stigma attached to it. It removes the feelings of inadequacy that the term *disabled* produced and takes away the performance pressure that the gifted label can lead to.

I was pulled out of my normal classes for separate classes for both the learning disabled and the gifted. I did not feel like I fit in with either group. The gifted kids all seemed like academic overachievers, and I rarely was able to focus long enough to complete an assignment. If it was a typical work assignment, I often spent more time staring out the window daydreaming than working.

The harder I tried, the more distracted I became. Everyone else in the gifted class excelled in their schoolwork, and not only did I not excel but sometimes I didn't even perform as average. I didn't feel gifted. In elementary school, before tests I sometimes had panic attacks that set off my asthma.

In addition to the normal times, when I went to special learning disability and enhanced learning program classes, I was occasionally pulled out for further testing, or if my special learning disability teacher wanted to experiment with new teaching methods she had just picked up. It gave me the feeling I was some kind of lab rat.

By the time I reached the fifth grade, my reading comprehension was already at the university level, but my spelling, grammar, and writing composition were still below grade level, and I had already been held back twice. (Yes, writing a book is ridiculously out of my comfort zone.) Like most kids, I just wanted to fit in. Kids of a certain age feel awkward whenever they are singled out as different. Being either gifted or disabled was bad enough, but being considered both was hard to understand how it was possible, let alone get a grip on.

I wanted to blend in and be normal, but I was an outlier, somehow simultaneously on both ends of the scale and forever a prisoner of the double-edged sword: gifted but disabled. By middle school, I was self-conscious to the point that it became full-blown social anxiety. It always seemed like my peers were judging me. When I was around girls, sometimes I froze, unable to speak. Because of the social anxiety, I went through several dark depressions in my adolescence. To this day my wrists bear several faded scars, reminders of teenage experiments in self-harm.

In high school I quickly learned to self-medicate my social anxiety with alcohol. By my senior year, I had developed a drinking problem. This wasn't helped much when I joined the one branch of the US military that was born in a bar. In so many ways the Marine Corps helped me grow and build confidence, but social interaction without alcohol was not one of the skills I learned. Founded in Tun Tavern in 1775, the US Marine Corps has a proud tradition of creating a culture that enables alcoholism. For many years my strategy for dealing with my social phobia was to drink copious amounts of alcohol.

Working aboard cruise ships wasn't conducive to sobriety either. The lifestyle revolved around a nonstop party. When in passenger bars, if I tried to order something nonalcoholic, the waiters would sarcastically ask, "What are you, the designated driver?" before talking me into a drink. The ships had designated crew bars, and a beer or mixed drink was cheaper than a bottle of water. On my first ship, the crew canteen, the ship's equivalent to a general store, was in the crew bar. I tipped well and became friends with the bartender, so no matter how busy he was, if I looked at him, he stopped whoever he was serving to pour me a Jack Daniel's and Coke, my signature drink. This became a problem, because when I went to buy shaving cream or water, in the time it took me to walk through the hatchway and get to the bar, he already had a Jack and Coke poured for me. Then he'd guilt me if I refused to drink it. "It's already poured. You have to drink it now." It worked every time.

I was never a "have to have a drink when I got up in the morning" type of alcoholic, although I knew plenty of them. But in any social situation, I was a serious binge drinker. The force that drove my binge drinking was fear of social situations. Plenty of incidents should have been red flags for my behavior, but I surrounded myself with people who also drank, so I didn't understand I had a problem. Not until I worked aboard what was once considered the most prestigious cruise ship in the world and I had a serious, embarrassing alcohol-related incident. This led to a discomforting hearing at sea. It wasn't one of my proudest moments.

I suppose you want me to tell you what happened, don't you? If you must know, I was found by security passed out and naked in a passenger stairwell. Okay, that's not completely true. I wasn't completely naked. I was wearing a pair of black dress socks. Yes, just the socks. Nothing else. Amazingly I was able to keep my job. That incident was what caused me to realize I had a drinking problem. Even so, it took me a few more years to give it up. To do this, I had to face my fear of social situations without the aid of chemical courage. These days you might catch me with a glass of wine occasionally, but that's about it.

I managed to make it through four years in the Marines without experiencing anything that caused PTSD. I felt lucky to make it out without a lot of the physiological damage so many Marines and soldiers go through.

I wasn't so lucky to live an entire life without trauma, though. Later in life, after an attempted robbery at gunpoint, I developed a severe case of PTSD. Between the robbery, grieving the death of my mother, and having to deal with some other stressors, I began to move toward a complete psychological meltdown.

It began slowly at first, then, over the course of six months, my condition worsened and slowly morphed into Generalized Anxiety Disorder. I was afraid of the world and worried about everything. I was even worried something was out there that I hadn't thought of that I should be afraid of.

I took time off work to be a stay-at-home dad to Zoe while she was little. About the time I planned to return to the world of working adults, my mental health deteriorated to the point where this was impossible. I am sure I would have become a full-blown agoraphobic had it not been for one thing. I wanted to socialize Zoe, my then-toddler. So I spent my days running to educational playgroups and making playdates at city parks, trying to pretend I was holding it together when I wasn't.

The robbery happened in November. By the next spring, I had developed a nervous tremble that lasted most of the time I was awake. Then, as I crumbled into a full-scale nervous breakdown, it turned into a spastic twitch. It looked as if I was suffering from Tourette's syndrome or some sort of neuromuscular disease like Parkinson's.

One day Narelle came home and found me curled up in the fetal position, quaking behind the bed. I wasn't in bed, but in the corner behind the bed. Kind of the opposite of claustrophobia, I wanted to be in as small a space as I could. She could see I needed serious help, and that is what started my long, difficult return to normalcy.

That said, the next chapter is about strategies and techniques for dealing with fears and anxieties. This isn't something I put together arbitrarily after a five-minute internet search. I have dealt with fear and anxiety on a personal level that few people can fathom. All these techniques work. Countless people have benefited from them. You will probably find one that works well in some situations, but in other situations, another technique or combination of techniques will work better.

A couple of these techniques saved my life. I have used them all on my personal journey to sanity and a happy life. I try to emphasize in this book that some of the coolest things I have done were often preceded by a panic attack, most of them by at least a moment of hesitation and self-doubt. In each of these cases, I used one or more of the techniques in the next chapter to work myself up to the experience, and you can too.

Before I get into specific strategies for confronting your fears, I want to instill an important concept: fear can be fun. *Yes, fear can be fun!* I have dealt with the horrible negative fear that eats you alive from the inside out, and one of the keys to getting over that was remembering fear is sometimes fun. Think of fear as a friend. It can be played with.

If something scares you, the fear is processed in the amygdala. If it scares you, and you like it, the experience is also processed in the nucleus accumbens, the last piece of the limbic system and your brain's reward center. If you find an experience rewarding, dopamine levels rise in the core of the nucleus accumbens. If you find the experience aversive, dopamine is instead trapped in the ventromedial shell[11] of the nucleus accumbens.

Initially fear and excitement are physiologically the same. It is your conscious interpretation of the signals that determines if dopamine levels rise and you feel elated, or you hate it and never want to go through it again. This is how two people can sit next to each other on a roller coaster, and when it's over, one wants to get back in line, while the other wants to go home and lie down.

How this mechanism works goes back to my earlier discussions on the adrenaline rush and the survival advantage of learned risk-taking. Picture a tribe of our early ancestors getting ready to hunt a woolly mammoth. Yes, our ancestors really did hunt woolly mammoths.[12] Hunting an animal that weighed six tons and had sharp tusks almost nine feet (three meters) long was scary—especially when your primary weapon was a flint-tipped spear. If the hunting party was successful, a mammoth could feed the tribe for a month. They could preserve leftover meat in the snow for over a year. The fur could be used for clothing and the bones for tools and building materials.

The hunters would have had the full adrenaline rush of a life-and-death struggle. If the hunt was successful, it increased the group's overall chances of survival, so the hunters would be pumped full of dopamine. The fear they felt during the hunt was then converted into excitement, and they were more likely to want to hunt a mammoth again. The next mammoth they faced would still be dangerous, of course. They would still get the adrenaline rush, but they were more likely to view the encounter as an opportunity rather than a straight-up threat.

Note that when you go through the fear spike, your assessment after the fact may be different from what you felt when you were going through the experience. Some of the things you see as the best times of your life after the fact actually sucked pretty bad when they were happening—hence the expression, "One day we will look back at this and laugh." That is one of the weird effects of dopamine.[13] If you have the correct mindset going into the frightening experience, the dopamine feed encodes that memory in the hippocampus as pleasurable. Sometimes this is referred to as type 2 fun. You can find something utterly terrifying in the moment, and when the memory crystallizes, you look back and say, "Wow, that was awesome!"

There are three major factors that determine how something fearful is processed by the nucleus accumbens. This makes the difference between the experience becoming traumatic or triumphant and is how the brain interprets scary situations and decides if the outcome was a negative event to be avoided at all costs or a positive one that leaves you with a good feeling of accomplishment. Let's do it again! This is a reward stimulus like the good feeling after taking down the mammoth.

This second interpretation is the kind you want. Remember, biologically fear and excitement are the same thing. There is a small difference in how they're processed that makes the difference. The three primary factors that define if our brain is going to interpret something frightening as exciting or traumatic are anticipation/surprise, context, and control.

Imagine one night you pull into the driveway after dark, and as you walk to your front door, you see a masked person jump from behind the bushes with a butcher knife. You are going to have one serious adrenaline response! Most of us would probably be traumatized by this, right? Yet in the US people spend an average of $350 million per year on admission to haunted houses and Halloween theme parks to have things exactly like that happen. The differences between the encounter in the driveway that might make you soil yourself and the similar encounter people pay money for are anticipation, context, and control.

First, the person jumping out of the bushes would have surprised you. Second, the context of your own driveway, where nothing like this should happen. Yes, one of your friends might be playing a sick joke, but unless you have concrete sensory data to back that up, you must assume you are in real mortal danger. (This is the same type of friend who would have dropped you in the trust fall exercise.) Third, unless you are well armed and have a quick reaction time, or are just a total badass, you do not have much control over the situation.

On the other hand, the people at the haunted house have forked over good money to have masked assailants with butcher knives jump out at them. Even though they will be surprised many times, they are anticipating the surprises. They are expecting there will be jump scares, so the nucleus accumbens is already primed. The context is they know the butcher knives, although realistic looking, are fake. They know the masked assailants are actors, and nothing is going to hurt them. On the purely mental side, they have told themselves it is fun to be frightened. And they have some measure of control over the experience. They want to be there, and if things get too scary, they can leave. Even in the middle of a haunted house, there are emergency exits for a quick escape.

If you have watched a few of the jump scare videos I suggested in the last chapter, you know you had even more control. You can turn the sound down, shrink the screen, or hit pause any time you like. For a fully immersive experience, turn off the lights in the room, expand the screen to full size, sit close, and crank up the sound. Even though you almost certainly will be startled, you anticipate the scare. You are ready for it, even if you don't know exactly when it's coming. You have anticipation, proper context, and full control. You'll have the adrenaline rush, the endorphins, serotonin, and dopamine—and possibly even a little of the cannabinoids. When it's over, you may even encode the experience as fun. Let's do it again!

If you can manage those three elements, you can have fun with your fears, and in some cases, they can be faced at a high level, and you can come out feeling like you had a great time.

Anticipation is knowing something is going to happen or being aware of the possibility of it. The Scout motto—be prepared—extends into your mental state as well. This is a good reason to do a risk assessment before engaging in a potentially dangerous or frightening activity, so that psychologically you are less likely to be surprised and shocked by things not going exactly as planned.

Context is the interrelated conditions in which something occurs. If I tell you I started letting my daughter walk across a wire bridge suspended thirty feet above the ground when she was five, you might find that scary and even be tempted to call Child Protective Services on me. However, if I put it into a proper context, it might change your mind. She was on a high ropes course that has a high standard for safety. She was wearing a safety harness hooked to a safety line with redundant carabineers. One carabineer can be unhooked from the safety line only when the other is hooked. It is literally impossible to fall off. Knowing all that, you would find it far less scary and hang up on Child Protective Services.

When I started taking her to the rock-climbing gym at about that age, she was a little skittish at first. Then she began to understand the change in context with heights. With Daddy belaying her, she wasn't going to fall far. Suddenly being high up wasn't frightening. It was exciting! With that, her confidence soared. When she gained skill at climbing, she started falling on purpose. She would fall and use her feet against the rock wall to swing in her harness like a pendulum. This didn't make sense to my red-blooded male brain, which can be competitive, especially with myself.

"Zoe, what are you doing? You're not supposed to fall on purpose. You're supposed to see if you can make it all the way to the top!"

She explained herself with a wise simplicity that made me feel like I was the child. "I'm just having fun, Daddy!"

Oh yeah, this was supposed to be fun. I let her swing until one of the gym employees came out of the office and told us off for breaking the rules.

On the other side of surrounding circumstances, changing the context is this example. In 1997 the movie *Titanic*[14] came out to rave reviews. At the time it held the record for the highest-grossing film ever made and set records for the most Oscar nominations. It won a stunning eleven of them, including Best Picture. The movie is a romantic tragedy set against a backdrop of real events—the sinking of a British luxury passenger ship in 1912 on its maiden transatlantic voyage.

Most people loved this movie! I did not. I did not think of it as a romance but more a horror movie, and one I found incredibly frightening. Why? Because the context in which I first watched this movie was different from everybody else's. I first watched *Titanic* on a British luxury passenger ship getting ready to do my first transatlantic crossing. As an added level of irony, when the *Titanic* went down, its parent company, the White Star Line, fell on hard times and was eventually purchased by a rival company, Cunard Line. The cruise line I was working on was that rival company. I watched the award-winning movie like everyone else, but I had a different experience because the context in which I viewed it was different.

As tradition and a sign of respect, whenever the ship crossed the longitude where the *Titanic* sank, the captain would blow one long blast on the ship's horn. If you were in the passenger areas, the sound wasn't too bad, but if you were down in the catacombs of the crew area, especially below the waterline, the sound was incredibly eerie. Without fail, every time I was belowdecks and the horn blasted, the hairs on the back of my neck stood up. Sometimes I pictured one of the drowning scenes in the movie. There was nothing to do but lean into the fear. I was in the middle of the Atlantic Ocean, so I wasn't getting away. Besides, we always took a more southerly route than the *Titanic*, so we weren't going to hit any icebergs. The sinking of the *Titanic* changed the way risk management was handled in the cruise industry. Things got much safer. When I thought about that, the context changed again.

Context can be the difference between something being a perceived danger and a real one. Context may be altered by safety equipment and whatever risk management strategies are in place.

Previous experience colors the context in which you view things. Context can also be changed mentally. Attitude about the situation changes context more than anything else. Willpower makes a difference. A positive mental attitude can turn everything around. Irrational fears will lie to you. They will tell you that you are in danger when you are not. It is your job to separate the real danger from the perceived. Flip the switch in your head, and activate the nucleus accumbens. That will change the context and turn what you see as a threat into a thrill.

The third element is control. A person must believe they have some measure of control over a situation. Perceived lack of control in a stressful experience is the quickest path there is to anxiety and trauma. This is why challenge by choice is so important. If coercion is involved in trying to get someone to face a fear, more damage than good can occur. The person engaging in the activity must do it of their own volition. They must have a choice. They must be aware of their choices as well. If they have choices but can't perceive that they do, it's just as bad as if they have no choice at all.

As a tie-in, here's a scenario from our Halloween theme park. Having lived about an hour and a half away from the theme park capital of the world, and having a wife obsessed with scary movies, I have been to a lot of Halloween-themed events. I have seen various versions of this scenario play out multiple times.

Picture four teenage girls going to our Halloween theme park. Three decide to go, and they talk their other friend into going at the last minute. She doesn't like scary things, but they use a variety of social pressure tactics to convince her to come along against her judgment.

They wait in line for the first haunted house. The other girls are getting excited, but the fourth is getting more and more nervous. She is also beginning to feel less and less in control of her situation. As the line pushes them forward, she doesn't recognize that she could get out of line if she wanted. Only a velvet rope she could easily step over is holding her in line. That, and a force a million times more powerful than the gravity of a black hole to a teenager: peer pressure!

She may forget that she got in the car and plunked down her money for admission with the rest of them. She may be inclined to believe she is not there voluntarily and think, like so many teenagers do, that her friends "made" her come. They didn't zip-tie her hands and throw her in the trunk, but in her mind, they might as well have.

By the time she is halfway through the haunted house and the actor jumps out with the butcher knife, she may hysterically scream and cry, paralyzed with fright. If she mentally loses situational context, she might completely forget it is all just pretend. Having choice and control is not enough if you don't realize it. You must know you have power over the situation. The teenager's hysteria will spiral out of control until the actors break character and escort her out of the building. It isn't the makings of a fun night for her and probably not for her friends either.

The above result is not set in stone. With a couple of tweaks, it could be turned into a fun night for all. If one of her friends earnestly offers to wait outside with her and takes the pressure off, she may decide to brave the haunted house. With other options available, she could realize she has a choice. If she actively works to manage her fear from the beginning, that can set the stage with positive anticipation. If her friends stick with her, are understanding, and offer her encouragement, the positive use of peer pressure can give her breathing room. If they laugh after every scare, she may take the social contextual cues and start laughing with them. With a growing sense of control, she can quickly learn she too can have fun with her fears.

Whenever confronting fears, it is important to keep some measure of control over the situation and, just as important, maintain awareness of that control. This alone can be the difference between a *stretch zone* experience and a full-on trip to the panic zone. Completing the task in the stretch zone can help emphasize an internal locus of control, providing the person believes it was their decision to rise to the challenge. I will talk more about the stretch and panic zones in the next chapter.

You are in control. You make your own decisions about what fears to tackle. Similarly, don't try to force anyone else to wrestle with something they are not ready for.

The three factors are anticipation, context, and control. If all three factors are managed sufficiently, the brain turns the fear into exhilaration. When you tackle a fear using all three factors, you get the adrenal response and then the feel-good hormones. The brain releases dopamine into the nucleus accumbens, encoding a good experience, and this helps build an even stronger internal locus of control. This is how you turn fear into excitement.

EXERCISE

For this chapter you are going to name your fears. List all the things you are afraid of. List as many as you can. They don't all have to be classic fears like snakes, spiders, and public speaking. Things that are deep, complicated, or holding you back in some way should be listed too. For example, if you want to go to school or start your own business and you are afraid to do it for some reason, list it.

Then describe the fear in as much detail as you can. What drives your fear? How do you know when to be afraid? Are there certain steps or phases you go through as the fear ramps up? What happens when you imagine what you are afraid of? Does the fear emanate from a specific place? What pictures go through your head when you are afraid? How do you think it will feel when you are no longer afraid?

_____

_____

_____

_____

_____

_____

_____

_____

_____

I had a well-meaning reviewer state that they thought it was contradictory that I advocated producing an adrenal response followed by advice for reducing panic. They missed the point completely. The whole reason we want to induce the stress response in ourselves on purpose is so we can learn to control it. A properly controlled adrenal response can be a tremendous source of personal power for you to draw from. An uncontrolled adrenal dump will have the opposite effect.

Now that you know the primary elements that shape how you deal with fear and how you process it, in the next chapter I'll look at techniques for controlling fear as it arises. It's time to get ready to start challenging those fears.

Chapter 5:

Finding Courage

> Courage is resistance to fear, mastery of fear—
> not absence of fear.
> — MARK TWAIN

At the beginning of chapter 4, I explained that fear is not the enemy. The thing to remember is that your fear is there to help you. You need it. The key is making sure *you control your fear* and not the other way around. In the chapter, I discussed how fear can potentially be fun. Properly utilizing your fears can be the biggest tool for personal growth. That is what this chapter is about—to help you control your fear and make it your servant.

As I have shown in previous chapters, many fears are based on perceived threats, not real ones. Your senses can deceive you. Humans have developed powerful, creative imaginations. Imagination gives you an amazing ability to solve problems. You can visualize things to find solutions. The trouble is the ability to visualize can also be detrimental if you don't manage it properly. You can vividly imagine anything that could go wrong, no matter how unlikely.

If you have read much or been to many courses in the self-development field, you have probably heard this acronym for fear: **f**alse **e**xpectations **a**ppearing **r**eal. (A variation that is sometimes used is **f**alse **e**vidence **a**ppearing **r**eal.) Much of what people are afraid of hasn't happened and probably won't.

A lot of what humans fear is in the imagination. You get a picture in your mind of one possible outcome, and if that vision is clear enough, you might assume that's what's going to happen, even if it is not likely. But it is just one possible outcome. It's not usually even the most likely outcome. This isn't a new concept. As far back as the days of the Roman Empire, Seneca wrote, "There are more things . . . likely to frighten us than there are to crush us; We suffer more often in imagination than in reality."[1] Seneca knew it was easy to be sucked into a mental place where you perceived a danger that was not there.

Some of my favorite television shows are nature programs, but even nature shows can be over-sensationalized. Many are about how dangerous things can be. "The ten deadliest," "the most venomous," and things of that nature are thrilling, and that's what grabs eyeballs. Since fear and excitement are interlinked, this type of show bumps up ratings.

Usually, five of the ten most venomous or deadliest anything in the world are found here in Australia. We even have a snail with a poisonous stinger that is fatal. Because a lot of nature shows focus on this, many Americans seem to think there is a deadly snake, spider, or octopus around every corner in Australia. I thought I was immune to this sort of thinking, especially since there are a lot of venomous creatures in Florida, and I was used to them. I was so wrong.

Before we moved to Australia, we visited several times. On one of the trips, we stayed at an eco-lodge in the Grampian Mountains. We had just arrived and unpacked, and everybody was relaxing. I needed to go for a walk, so I hit the trail by myself.

I had already seen a tiger snake slither right across my path, so I must have had venomous things on my mind. The tiger snake, sometimes referred to as the Australian cobra because it is technically part of the cobra family, *Elapidae*, clocks in at number seven[2] on the world's most deadly venomous snakes list. Its venom is both a neurotoxin and a hemotoxin, and it's very bad if you are bitten. Tiger snakes can flatten their necks to form a hood, just like their cobra cousins in Asia and Africa. They are also common where we live.

After I saw the snake, I walked through an area covered in thick bush. My arm brushed against a plant, and as it did, something crawled into the back of my shirtsleeve and proceeded across my armpit and onto my back! I freaked out. I was sure a poisonous spider had crawled into my shirt. I am not normally afraid of spiders, but at that moment I was scared out of my mind. I didn't know how venomous a spider it was, but the way it was crawling on my back felt like it was probably in the top ten. I went into panic mode, and for a moment I ran around in circles flailing my arms like a maniac. I am sure it would've been hilarious to watch had anyone been with me.

As I lost control of my faculties, I stumbled and fell backward into a bush. Then I crashed my way out of the bushes with the creepy-crawly thing still clinging to my back. My commotion in the foliage disturbed something else—actually, a lot of something elses! Other animals I could not see were now also crashing through the bush close to me. For some reason, all I could think of was wild boar. So I had a poisonous spider about to sink its fangs into me and a bunch of razorbacks that any second would come charging in and gore me to death. Just great!

I hadn't seen the spider or boar yet, so I finally got enough of a grip on myself to start the problem-solving process. I had to figure out what animals I was in contact with so I could deal with them appropriately. After a couple of deep breaths, I calmed down. I had to take care of the most immediate threat first. I reached around and managed to pull the critter off my back as delicately as I could. It was a risky move perhaps but better than leaving it on my back. I looked at the thing in my hand and realized it was not the deadly venomous arachnid I'd thought it was. It was just an ordinary green grasshopper.

I continued forward into a clearing, and there I saw what animals I had disturbed. They weren't pigs but a large mob of kangaroos that were now hopping in every direction, trying to get away from me. They had been quietly napping in the bushes during the midday heat until my antics scared them into a panic. Both the spider and the boar had been in my head. Imagined fears come to life. False expectations appearing real. This was fear induced by incomplete sensory information and an overactive imagination, combining to create a false perception of danger.

After that incident, I quit watching documentaries about how deadly Australian wildlife is. If a nature show has the words *most deadly* in the title, chances are there are a few representatives from Down Under, and I won't watch because it will make me paranoid. I spend a lot of time in the bush, and I don't need that. Don't get me wrong—it is important to study what dangers Mother Nature might offer in any place you are going to be. However, I want to do it pragmatically, not with overdramatized hype. Stay clearheaded, and don't do what I did and let your imagination get the better of you.

In this chapter I give strategies for overcoming fear. Think of them collectively as a psychological toolbox. You may have to use one or more tools for any given situation. Some tools or combinations will work better in some situations than others. Remember, the goal is not to eliminate all fear but to keep it at a manageable level and work through it.

It has been said in many ways by many people throughout history: courage is not the absence of fear but the ability to do despite fear. So find and confront your fears.

You know many of your fears are not real, or at least they aren't as big a threat as you pictured. Now let's go over one of the biggest concepts in this book—the three primary states of consciousness, known as zones, people operate in.³ Understanding them and learning to shift between them is a major key to managing fear and learning to grow. This is a model created by adventure education pioneer Karl Rohnke, and it has been adopted across a wide range of fields, including psychology, education, and business.

The first state you are probably familiar with is the comfort zone. It is a favorite topic in personal development and performance enhancement programs. Almost every guru in the world mentions it at some point. But what is it exactly, and why would you want to get out of it?

Your comfort zone is not a physical place like your personal space. However, if someone violates your personal space, it could knock you out of your comfort zone quickly. Basically, your comfort zone is an anxiety-neutral state. There is no sense of risk there. This could be your home, your neighborhood, your normal group of friends, the routines you are used to, doing things you already know how to do well. Your comfort zone is everything you are familiar with, the things you are not afraid of, the places where you are content and at ease. The parasympathetic nervous system is in charge here.

When I say to *get out of it*, I am not saying you should never be in your comfort zone. You need it to help you rest and recharge. Sometimes you need routine and certainty if only for a break. This protective environment is a place you can retreat to if things get too hectic, but it should not be the place you spend all or even most of your time.

The more time you spend outside your comfort zone, the bigger it will get. The more things you do outside your comfort zone, the more things will eventually be in it. However, if you spend so much time out of your area of ease that you stress yourself out, retreat to that feeling of safety and then head back out as soon as you are ready.

There is also a danger that if you don't spend any time expanding your comfort zone, it will contract. I experienced this firsthand when I was suffering from PTSD. I found myself doing less and less as my symptoms worsened, which exacerbated my symptoms even more. I was trapped in a cycle of a continually contracting comfort zone.

Since almost everything—even things that had once been routine—was uncomfortable, I found one of the most important first steps was to *get comfortable with being uncomfortable.* The only way to do that was to keep doing uncomfortable things.

The great thing about having Generalized Anxiety Disorder was it was easy to find things outside my comfort zone. It was almost everything. When I walked through the front door, I was out of my comfort zone. I started out slowly overcoming one panic attack at a time, then expanding on each success. The more time you spend doing things that are uncomfortable, the more comfortable you become. When I learned that, a new world opened right where the old one was.

It is useful to visualize the comfort zone as the bull's-eye of a target. There are two more rings on this target that represent the other two states of consciousness. As you step out of that comfort zone, you want to ensure you keep the experience positive. To do that, you need to know about the two other rings on the target outside your comfort zone. These are the *stretch zone* and the *panic zone*. You want to make sure you don't do more harm than good so, let's look at these other two states.

Successfully expanding your comfort zone is doing things outside of it while maintaining a level of control. That means going into the *stretch zone*. The stretch zone is where you feel a little anxious. Some classic signs of anxiousness you can spot within yourself or someone else are a faster heartbeat, quick shallow breathing, nervous sweat, trembling hands, and restless movement. When you go outside your comfort zone, there is usually a sense of risk involved.

What causes you to leave your comfort zone and move into the ring around it? *Fear!* Yes, fear is what you need to get out of your comfort zone—a little fear but not too much. Let me restate that. You need a bit of fear! A bit of fear is good for you. If you activate the acute stress response just enough, you will get into the stretch zone. When you are stretched a little, it can make you perform better at many things than if you were completely relaxed.

Stretch zone experiences are things that scare you. They include giving a speech, meeting new people, taking up a new sport, and trying the ideas in this book. The exercises in this book are designed to put you in your stretch zone. Please do them!

Those feelings of fear are stress. As long as you keep yourself in the stretch zone, that stress is called *eustress*,[4] or good stress. Eustress is healthy and can give you a strong feeling of personal satisfaction and fulfillment.

In the stretch zone, things should feel challenging. They should be hard enough where you have a strong sense of accomplishment when you complete the task. If it is too easy and doesn't cause discomfort, you won't be stretched, and you won't get the same sense of accomplishment. Ideally, you want to find that sweet spot where what you are attempting feels possible but not necessarily likely. Maybe you'll have to dig in and give it your all.

Think of the children's story *The Little Engine That Could*.[5] The little train climbed up the hill saying to herself, "I think I can, I think I can" (even though she wasn't sure she could). When she made it the top she started saying, "I thought I could, I thought I could". That is what you want—things you think you can maybe do but aren't sure until you do. In the stretch zone, there should be some self-doubt. That is part of the process. That is the stretch.

Uncertainty, insecurity, and novelty are feelings that cause you to produce norepinephrine. From what you learned two chapters ago, you know norepinephrine fired into the brain makes you pay attention to what's going on, and dopamine helps you encode things. That is why the fastest and most thorough learning takes place in the stretch zone. The discomfort makes you focus, and that bit of fear consolidates learning.

This is why on university campuses around the world some of the best learning takes place not in the lecture hall but while cramming for a test the night before. Fear of failure or even performing below expectations generates the stress response. Suddenly information that seemed useless and boring a couple of days before at some level now appears important to survival. The extra norepinephrine helps students focus more than normal, and the resulting dopamine helps the learning go in.

When you go into the stretch zone, the one thing to avoid being in too long is the third mental state, the *panic zone*. Again, fear improves your capabilities to a point. Past that, your skills and reasoning ability begin to degrade. This is the panic zone. In the panic zone your heart rate usually beats faster than the optimal 145 beats per minute. Sometimes as high as 200 beats per minute.

A competitive athlete, performer, or person trying to accomplish a difficult task that goes too far into the panic zone for too long is likely to have a performance choke. When someone chokes, not only does it ruin the performance but also it can sap self-confidence after the fact. Trying and failing doesn't necessarily create this negative effect, but if the person fails while in a panic state, they will likely have dopamine trapped in the shell of the nucleus accumbens. This causes the person to accidentally learn an avoidance response on a neurological level. After a choke, sometimes a considerable amount of remedial work needs to be done to restore the confidence level to where it was.

Remember earlier in the book when I said the *fight-or-flight* was actually *fight, flight, or freeze*? It is in the panic zone that you are likely to find your freeze response. When someone is pushed so far into their panic zone they freeze, if they can't break out of it, they are likely to fall apart or shut down. Sometimes people just stop moving and can't do anything at all.

Someone deep in the panic zone may have trouble processing what is happening or dissociate from it. Dissociation is a weird feeling that you are disconnected from yourself. You may feel you are a detached witness to what you are experiencing. You may have a train of thought that seems like it's coming from someone else. It can make rational thought difficult, never mind taking action. I have been there.

The stress you experience in the panic zone is different from the eustress in the stretch zone. In the panic zone, it is distress, and it has the potential to create all the negative effects of fear and anxiety discussed in the previous two chapters. That is why if you feel yourself sliding into the panic zone, it is important to pull out of it as quickly as you can. You can do this with the techniques I am about to share with you, but you need two things before you can start.

First, you need to recognize you are panicking. The second thing is you need to be willing to do something about it. Some people half-heartedly try a single strategy for overcoming panic, and if it doesn't work right away, they panic even more. You need to be willing to keep working on your mind and body until you have overcome the panic and are back in the stretch zone.

To be clear, a panic attack is your adrenal response going unchecked and uncontrolled. The clinical definition is a brief period of extremely intense fear or anxiety based on a perceived threat rather than imminent danger. Even if there is imminent danger, maintaining control of your fear response greatly increases your chances of a positive outcome or at least avoiding a worst-case scenario.

A panic attack has all the classic signs of an adrenal response: rapid heartbeat, quick breathing, nervous sweat, trembling hands, and restless, jerky movement. But there are additional symptoms like nausea, feeling lightheaded or dizzy, sometimes a feeling of doom, shortness of breath, and possible tightness in the chest. (Because some symptoms are similar, thousands of people go to the hospital each year mistaking a panic attack for a heart attack.)

You need to be able to keep functioning, ideally as close to the optimal level as possible, so if you feel yourself sliding into the panic zone, you need to pull out of it. You also want to encode the experience in your brain as a positive one, and getting out of the panic zone is the thing that will help you do that. It is okay to go into the panic zone a little if you can back it into the stretch zone. This chapter gives some effective strategies for taking yourself out of the panic zone or catching yourself before you go into it.

Before I move on, a word of warning. If you go looking for the boundaries of your comfort zone, you might find them in unexpected places. This brings me to my second anxiety attack during my Outward Bound hiking, rock climbing, and backcountry camping trip. On the first day, we hiked to our first campsite under the cover of darkness. We set up camp and cooked dinner by the light of headlamps. This was designed to be a little unsettling but nothing too serious. It was a perfect stretch zone experience by design.

I slept fine, and the next morning one of my tentmates and I were first awake. We started some yoga stretches to loosen our legs for the upcoming hike. Then it hit me: the uncomfortable gurgle in my bowels. It was time. I grabbed the communal roll of toilet paper and the small, collapsible spade. The only toilet around was the one I was going to dig myself.

As I walked into the woods, I suddenly felt humiliated. I didn't know why. No one was going to watch me. I hadn't dug a cat hole since I was in the military, twenty-something years before. I had been camping many times since but always at campgrounds with bathroom facilities. Wow, I had gotten soft over the years. I had spent too much time on the couch watching TV and not enough time in the wilderness roughing it.

After this strange wave of humiliation, out of nowhere came another wave of nervousness and self-doubt, just like when I finished the medical questionnaire. "Who am I to be tromping through the woods and sleeping on the ground? I'm a middle-aged asthmatic with joint problems." Panic swept over me. I started hyperventilating. I had to stop and take a few deep breaths to calm down. Once I got used to the idea, the rest of the trip was fine. I found it funny and fascinating how a little discomfort over an everyday function could be the tip of the iceberg of a lot of other seemingly unrelated insecurities and self-doubts.

Most of us in the Western world take having a porcelain toilet, clean water, indoor plumbing, and electricity for granted. Never mind that great swaths of the population don't have these things that we consider essential. (According to the World Health Organization, 2.3 billion people don't have a toilet, and 892 million go out in the open.[6]) When we in the developed world are denied these things, it can be a bit uncomfortable, even humiliating. For me it was so much so that it set off an anxiety attack.

Once I got over my trepidation about going without a bathroom and electricity, and having to purify my own water, I became comfortable without it. This reminded me to have empathy for the people who live without the things we consider necessities and gave me pause to appreciate some of the other things I take for granted. If you want to discover a way to appreciate something small, force yourself to go without it for a while. Who knows? Maybe just reading about someone taking a dump in the woods made you a little squeamish. If so, perhaps we found an edge.

METHODS FOR COPING WITH FEAR

Remember, going out of your comfort zone means you are dealing with something that is generating fear. It could be a little, it could be a lot, but it is certainly fear. Below are ten of the best strategies for handling fears and anxieties. Each of these techniques is designed to manage your fears using one or more of the primary factors of influence: positive anticipation, proper situational context, and a sense of control. This will keep the experience in the stretch zone, activate the nucleus accumbens, and allow your brain to encode the experience as a positive accomplishment.

Remember, you are not trying to eliminate the fear completely, just keep it down to a manageable level. If there was no fear, it would not be a stretch zone experience. It would be something in your comfort zone. As World War I flying ace Eddie Rickenbacker once said, "Courage is doing what you are afraid to do. There can be no courage unless you are scared."[7]

You cannot always control the external circumstances you are faced with, but the one thing you can control is yourself. Below are the best methods for dealing with fear, stress, and anxiety. Read the list first. Then I will expand on each technique and strategy individually.

1. Breathe.
2. Rationally evaluate the danger level.
3. Monitor and correct your internal dialogue (i.e., self-talk).
4. Break it down.
5. Challenge your fear incrementally.
6. Use visualization.
7. Develop skills.
8. Withdraw and reinsert.
9. Reframe the experience.
10. Get support.

1. Breathe.

It all begins with breath. When it comes to fear, pain, anxiety, and general stress, the best advice I was ever given was to breathe. Just breathe. It seems so straightforward, doesn't it? For some reason whenever people are in pain or exposed to massive amounts of stress, they tend to hold their breath. Some theorize that breath holding is part of the freeze response. Whether or not this is true, breath-holding exacerbates feelings of anxiety. If you are not getting enough oxygen, that alone will fire the adrenal reflex, adding the fear of suffocation to the reasons to go into panic mode.

Sometimes in panic mode people hyperventilate. Hyperventilating is a series of quick, shallow breaths. This overbreathing is restrictive and doesn't regulate air intake into the lungs. That, in turn, causes an imbalance of carbon dioxide in the blood, which can cause the feeling that you are going to pass out, which can create more panic and then trap you in a loop of increasing fear, shallower breathing, and more fear. But extended breath holding is even worse than shallow breathing. Nothing accelerates panic more than holding your breath. The key is recognizing this vicious cycle early and breaking it as soon as possible.

Breathing is normally controlled by the autonomic nervous system, but when your adrenal response is being counterproductive, breathing is one autonomic function with a manual override. It is something that can be taken over consciously.

I was once one of the worst about holding my breath when I was stressed or frightened. It is also something I have to be mindful of when I am having an asthma attack, because difficulty breathing can make me hyperventilate, and it can snowball from there unless I get control of my breath. I still do it sometimes, but now I am geared to recognize breath holding and do something about it.

The first order of breathing is awareness. You might become much more relaxed as you become conscious of your breath. If you are trying to tackle a fear, you should constantly check to see if you are breathing. Breath holding and hyperventilating are usually the first signs a person is about to go into panic mode. If you catch it in the beginning, you can use a controlled response before the stress spirals out of control.

The first time I took my skydiving accelerated free fall test I failed it. I had to do a series of 180- and 360-degree spins while in free fall, then go into a forward dive called tracking. When I spun to the left, for some reason I couldn't stop myself right away. I spun about 1500 degrees before I was finally able to stop. When I got back down on the ground, I asked my instructor what advice he had. He told me that when I was trying to perform a maneuver, I had the tendency to hold my breath and tense up my body.

When I asked what to do about it, he said simply, "You just have to keep breathing deeply, relax, and have fun with it."

"Um, okay, so you want me to achieve a relaxed state just by breathing in addition to performing a complex aerial maneuver while plummeting toward the earth at a hundred and twenty miles per hour?"

"Yes, and remember to have fun with it" was his answer.

I followed his advice and passed easily on the next try. It works with the intensity of free fall, so I am sure controlled breathing can work for just about anybody for almost anything. Step one: keep breathing.

Once you remember to breathe, the next step is to consciously deepen your breathing. Deep breathing brings an incredible amount of calmness to your body. This will back down the adrenal response to a manageable level. It is important to breathe as deeply as possible from the diaphragm. Breathing from your diaphragm is easier than you think.

You can see you are breathing from the diagram if your abdomen is expanding and contracting—in simpler terms, your tummy is going in and out. If it's your chest rising and falling, you are shallow breathing, and you need to work on using the tummy.

Keep doing this until you feel you have control of your breath. Then you are ready for the next step. From there it is a matter of making sure you take longer to exhale than inhale. If it takes you five seconds to inhale, you should spend seven to nine seconds exhaling. The long, slow exhale will help engage the parasympathetic nervous system and calm you down even more. As you begin to feel in control of your breath, if your sinuses are not congested, work on breathing through your nose. This will aid in the calming process.

There are other variations of breath control, such as 7-11 breathing, tactical breathing, and box breathing, made popular by US Navy SEALs. The commonality in each of these breathing techniques is at least as much time is taken on the exhalation as the inhalation. Take a long out-breath. Slow and controlled.

An acute panic or anxiety attack will usually pass once you get your breathing under control. When you can comfortably breathe through your nose slowly and rhythmically, you have full control of your breath.

Controlling your breath is the first step, and it is the key to everything else. Before you try any of the other techniques listed here, always take control of your breathing first. When panicked, normally you must get that down before you can think clearly enough to apply any of the other strategies. Nice deep, controlled breaths should calm you down enough to give you some clarity on how to proceed.

2. Rationally evaluate the danger level.

I can still remember when I was about thirteen and was camping in the mountains with my parents. I had gone on a hike by myself. I was on my way back and still about two miles (3.5 kilometers) away from our campsite when someone fired up a chain saw over the hill I was hiking up. This probably wouldn't have been a big deal, but I spent a great deal of the summer having sleepovers with my best friend, whose parents had just gotten premium cable. We would hang out until his parents went to bed. When we determined they were fast asleep, we'd stay up late into the night watching slasher movies. More than a few depicted a maniac chasing some hapless victim through the woods with a chain saw.

Being alone in the woods and hearing a real chain saw fire up made my heart about leap out of my chest. I did not want to run screaming back the way I had come, so I had to evaluate the situation. I was not in a horror movie, so the logical conclusion was that the rangers were performing routine trail maintenance. I pressed on, slowly sneaking up, hiding behind trees, and sure enough as I crested the hill, I could see two workers cutting up a fallen tree. I sighed in relief and hiked the last bit back to camp.

When your imagination begins to get the better of you, Occam's razor is a useful tool for cutting away false beliefs about your situation. Occam's razor is a philosophical principle that states that if there are competing explanations for the same phenomenon, the one that makes the fewest assumptions is most likely to be correct. In other words, the simplest explanation is most likely the correct one. Trail maintenance makes fewer assumptions than a chain saw–wielding maniac and allowed my rational mind to evaluate my situation instead of being controlled by my knee-jerk, reactionary mind.

Sometimes just telling yourself the worst-case scenario is unlikely can calm you down. Sometimes it helps to do research. The insurance industry has stats on how likely it is that something bad can happen for almost anything you can think of. For instance, the chances of being killed in a hang-gliding accident are about one in 116,000 flights.[8] This is related to risk evaluation in chapter 2. If you know what the actual risk is of something going wrong, and what the best course of action is if it does, it is far easier to use logic to mentally talk yourself down if you start freaking out.

Sometimes it is a good idea to list what might go wrong, starting with the worst-case scenario. Then go through any other fears about a situation. Once you have listed everything, separate real risks from imaginary. Then create a risk management plan and emergency actions for each potential pitfall. This can greatly put your mind at ease. If you have that preplanned course of action, you can't fret about the hypothetical. "Oh my god, what do I do if this happens?" No, you already know *if this happens I do that*! End of story.

3. Monitor and correct your internal dialogue (i.e., self-talk).

Sometimes it helps to talk your way through something. We all talk to ourselves in our minds anyway. Sometimes people are not even aware they are doing it. Become aware of the things you say to yourself. Is what you are saying helping or hurting as far as controlling your fear? Sometimes being mindful enables you to catch yourself before a negative thought snowballs into a mindset.

The biggest danger of not squashing negative thoughts early is the possibility of them becoming a negative thought loop. These thought loops, called rumination in the medical profession, are an endless repetition of negative thoughts that form a reverse mantra. The continued repetition can sap confidence, create indecision, and be a self-fulfilling prophecy of failure. Rumination is usually a major component of depression and anxiety disorders. I can tell you from experience, in the same way laughter is the best medicine, rumination is the worst poison.

If a negative thought pops up, make sure you breathe, then immediately explain to yourself why it isn't true. Give yourself counterexamples. Be encouraging to yourself. Use language to guide your thoughts in the direction you want to go . . . toward your goal. Brainstorm, problem-solve, and create action plans. Do what is necessary to change your focus to the possibility of positive outcomes. Use logic to rationally explain to yourself why negativity is unjustified.

Some forms of positive self-talk are more effective than others. According to a study by Harvard business professor Alison Wood Brooks, people who spoke the sentence "I am excited" before performing an anxiety-producing task like public speaking, singing karaoke in front of strangers, or taking a math test not only felt more confident but also performed much better objectively. Another group who told themselves they felt calm before engaging in the task had no such improvement. She attributed this to *arousal congruency*. This goes back to the fact that fear and excitement are almost identical physiologically.

Relaxed and calm are physiologically the exact opposite of anxious or excited. If you tell yourself you are calm when you are obviously not, your brain will instinctively know you are lying to yourself. That will not be helpful and may even increase the fear response.

According to Brooks, anxiety is characterized by "high arousal, negative appraisal, uncertainty and lack of control."[9] Whereas excitement is also a high arousal state, it is characterized by "positive appraisal and optimism." The arousal, which is another term for adrenaline rush, comes whether or not you give it permission to. Telling yourself the increased heart rate, sweaty palms, and trembling hands are excitement makes it much easier to flip the switch in your mind from fear to enthusiasm.

This amounts to performing psychological aikido or judo on yourself. In martial arts like these, an opponent's force is never challenged directly but deflected and then redirected into something else. As you grapple with your fears, explore other ways you can use your internal dialogue to turn them into something else.

4. Break it down.

Breaking things into manageable steps is the technique to use when your fear takes the form of feeling overwhelmed. If a task seems too daunting, the best thing you can do is reduce it to sizes you can handle. After you break it down, concentrate on the step you are working on. There is no use worrying about what you'll have to do two or three steps down the line. The military uses this a lot. If you focus on the task at hand, this is a way of mindfulness, and if the task is significantly challenging, this may shift you into a flow state.

When on a particularly hard obstacle on a high ropes course like an unstable bridge with stepping logs that rotate, I concentrate on just the next place I have to put my feet or hands. I don't look at the whole obstacle, just the next place I have to be. Move slowly and deliberately. Slow is smooth, and smooth is fast.

This is where lists come in handy. Having ADHD makes this imperative for me. If I don't work off a list, I will interrupt myself to do something else and then interrupt my interruption. Before I know it, I have about fifteen tasks half completed, and I am at a complete loss about what to do next. It is easy to get overwhelmed this way.

When packing for a hike or a family trip, working off a list helps keep me calm. I am not normally the most organized person, so the idea of forgetting something critical weighs heavily. Once I am sure my list has everything on it, I look at one thing at a time. Once I tick that off, I look at the next thing. Before I know it everything is done. This works for daily to-do lists as well. If you have a lot to do, you can be overwhelmed and delay even starting, but if you put all your energy and thought into just one thing on the list, you can get that done and move on to the next with ease. Before you know it, you are done.

5. Challenge your fear incrementally.

You want to make sure you can walk before you decide to run. If you have a serious fear of heights, you don't start challenging it by immediately trying to jump off a bungee tower or launch a hang glider off a cliff. If your first step in trying to get over a fear of clowns is a clown-themed haunted house, you are asking for trouble. The last thing you want to do is traumatize yourself further by doing something you aren't ready for yet.

When I was learning to skydive, I was getting ready for a jump when one of the instructors said he was bumping me from the next load. We had to continue our training on the flight after. A large group had arrived, and they wanted to do a tandem jump together, so all the instructors were needed. When you are not jumping, it is fun just to watch others do it. I sat around the hangar and watched. When they landed, all these eighteen- and nineteen-year-olds had that super excited *man, that was cool* look on their faces. They were all high fiving each other, laughing and carrying on, the adrenaline still pumping through their veins.

Then one of them looked around and said, "Where's Billy?" (Not his real name, I hope.) Billy was nowhere to be found. The plane had landed about the same time they did and taxied up as they realized they were missing one in their group. They were looking around for their friend when the plane door opened and there was Billy, standing in the doorway. He was crying hysterically. From inside the hangar, I could see the tears and snot pouring down his face.

He had gone deep into the panic zone. When it was his time to jump, he had been overcome by fear and couldn't do it. Now he was a nervous wreck, having to deal with what should have been a feeling of triumph but had turned into trauma. I am sure there was an extra level of humiliation, since all his friends had managed to jump, and he hadn't. When I boarded the aircraft getting ready for the flight up to jump altitude, I could see his buddies were still trying to console him.

He obviously had a serious fear of heights, and his friends had talked him into something he wasn't ready for. There was serious peer pressure involved, even if it was unintentional. The worst part about this kind of thing is that the failure is interpreted neurologically as trauma, and it set him back significantly in overcoming his fear of heights.

Yes, there are plenty of examples of people who have gone straight from overly timid to crazy brave in one big leap. However, to avoid the kind of thing that happened to Billy, take it in smaller steps. Give your brain bite-size chunks it can swallow and give it time to digest before you move on to the next step.

You want to do something that scares you but on a level where you can manage the fear. That maximizes your chances of success and minimizes your chances of freezing due to mental overload. Toward the end of the chapter, I give a step-by-step process for how to challenge fears incrementally. Build on successes one manageable step at a time. Keep it challenging but doable. Each challenge you choose is of your own accord. This is what builds confidence and self-assurance. Build those up enough, and it begins to shine through as self-esteem.

6. Use visualization.

This technique saved my life. Most sports training programs include training in creative visualization. Everything from basketball to golf has programs devoted to visualizing success. A huge body of research suggests taking the time to visualize success improves performance significantly, sometimes almost as much as physical practice. If the visualization is combined with physical practice, the cumulative effect can be astounding.

Mentally rehearse successful outcomes. Repeated mental rehearsal familiarizes you with doing it successfully. If you have a memory of having done it, even if that memory was formed by your imagination, it is far less frightening when you do it for real.

To visualize success, close your eyes, breathe, relax, and picture doing the steps involved with what you are trying to do. Imagine yourself doing exactly what needs to be done. If you need to complete a physical task, sometimes it helps to physically go through the motions along with your visualization. If you are afraid of doing something, closing your eyes and picturing yourself successfully doing it repeatedly can have a big impact.

My best example is another skydiving story. I don't think anyone would disagree with the statement that skydiving is an intense sport. And that is when things are going right. Believe it or not, skydivers usually do a lot of visualization exercises. If you go to a busy drop zone on the weekend, you'll find them practicing on the ground what they will do in the air—a lot of times with their eyes closed. They practice docking with each other and separating. Almost any maneuver is visualized thoroughly many times before it is performed for real in the air.

Of all the things done in skydiving, probably nothing is practiced and visualized more than the cutaway procedure. In skydiving you are responsible for saving your life should something go wrong.

Before your first solo jump, you spend a day in ground school learning everything that could go wrong. Then you start practicing and visualizing the cutaway procedure. "What is a cutaway?" you may ask. Most skydivers carry two parachutes—the main one and a reserve backup chute. The cutaway, or breakaway, procedure is performed if your main parachute doesn't open properly and cannot be fixed before you hit the ground. It is the last-ditch effort in a parachute malfunction emergency action plan. It consists of pulling the quick-release handle to eject the main chute, then going back into the proper position for free fall and releasing the reserve or backup parachute. If your main chute malfunctions to the point it is unusable, and you fail to pull this off correctly, it is usually a death sentence.

From the get-go, I practiced the cutaway over and over and over. I closed my eyes and saw myself releasing the main as I physically grabbed the place on my chest where the release handle would be. Then I imagined the handle that opened the reserve as I assumed the arch in my back that puts you in the stable, belly-to-earth position needed for a correct opening. If you are in the wrong position when you deploy your emergency chute, you risk it getting tangled with your body.

Most skydivers practice and visualize the cutaway so many times it's ridiculous. But actual cutaways are rare. Some skydivers with hundreds or even over a thousand jumps wonder if they could do it for real, because they've never had to do it for real. I guess I am just lucky, because I had to do one on jump twenty. Had I not spent so much time visualizing the breakaway as vividly as I could, I am quite certain I would not be here today.

7. Develop skills.

Competence begets confidence. Sometimes people are afraid of things because they haven't developed the necessary skills to deal with them. The cure for that is to figure out how to get better. Build the skills. If you know how to do something but doing it still frightens you, maybe you haven't learned how to do it well enough. Keep building the skills you have and take them to the next level. By the time you have fully mastered the skills, you will probably have already mastered your fear.

When I was in a workshop on developing techniques for overcoming fears, one of my fellow students had a fear of water, or aquaphobia. Everyone was eager to perform our newly learned visualization techniques and test them in the pool. I asked one simple question: "Do you know how to swim?" He didn't, so he had a good reason for being afraid of the deep end. It wasn't an entirely irrational fear. We went through the exercise, but the more important next step was for him to get into a good adult swim program. You're never too old to learn.

I had insight into this because when I was five I had a near-drowning experience. It wasn't a little coughing and spitting up water kind of almost drowning. I had to be resuscitated and was in the hospital for two days.

While at the home of some family friends, I was found at the bottom of a pool. Their quick-thinking Eagle Scout son jumped in, rescued me, and performed CPR, but they didn't know how long I had been down there before I was rescued. While I was unconscious in the hospital my parents sweated out the possibility that oxygen deprivation might have done permanent damage and left me brain-dead.

As soon as I was cleared medically, my parents enrolled me in swim lessons for two reasons: First, if I was ever in that situation again, I would have the skills to save my own life. The second reason was to help prevent me from developing aquaphobia. I had been traumatized and was beginning to show signs of a fear of water. As I mentioned, I lived in a Florida beach town, so it was important to get over a fear of water because there was a lot of it around.

The initial skill learning should be done in a relaxed atmosphere.

Scientists have found that learning in a stress-free environment in the early stages helps people internalize lessons. After a foundation of learning is established, you will need to stress-test the skills.[10] This is done in an incremental way similar to building up a fear tolerance, which I explain in a bit. They can be done together in most cases.

Stress testing is important, especially if what you are learning is a survival or emergency skill or a skill to be applied in some other high-stress environment. Chances are if you use survival skills, it will be under extremely high-stress conditions. If you can't perform the task under stress, the skill is useless. As you are learning, reapplying the skills under stress helps you learn the material thoroughly. The norepinephrine and dopamine generated in the stress test help deepen the learning process and ensure the relevant information is available under stressful conditions in the future.

Since I talked about swimming, a good example to progress to is learning to scuba dive. Initially, everything is learned in a classroom. You learn about hooking up the regulator (i.e., the thing you breathe through) to the air tank and to your buoyancy control device as well as how to wear your gear, methods of computing how long you can be at certain depths, and what to do in case of an emergency. Yes, more emergency action plans.

Then you head to the shallow end of a pool in chest-height water. Everyone puts on their gear and learns to breathe through the regulator. Breathing underwater is counterintuitive, so if anyone panics, they can just stand, take the regulator out, and relax. When they are ready, they put it back in and put their face in the water until they get used to breathing through the regulator.

After everyone is good at that, you practice taking the regulator out and putting it back in underwater as well as clearing your mask while submerged if it is full of water. After everyone gets this, you go to the deep end of the pool and do it all again. Now you are deeper underwater, so it is more challenging. It's also a bit scarier but not too much. It creates a small increase in stress. The beginning of the stretch.

Once everyone is competent at this level, it is time for the final test, which is demonstrating the same skills again but in open water at a depth of forty to sixty feet (twelve to eighteen meters). This creates a higher level of stress. It is literally going deeper into the stretch zone. Taking the regulator out of your mouth and putting it back in at this depth can be anxiety-inducing the first time. Once you do it, it seems easy afterward. Confidence is built through a series of successes.

The fact that I learned to scuba dive was amazing considering my near-drowning incident and the fact I had to work through a fear of sharks. It started because of the foundation I built in the early swim lessons.

As you gain skills, the confidence you build mustn't be overconfidence. In other words, don't get cocky. I have a basic open-water scuba certification. I am not qualified to dive in shipwrecks or caves. These are very dangerous places to dive and require another layer of skills I do not possess. I should remain fearful of diving in such conditions until such a time as I decide to get the relevant certifications, develop the necessary skills, and am properly stress-inoculated.

8. Withdraw and reinsert.

Sometimes the second effort is more powerful than the first. You may need a moment to step away, gather yourself, then go back. I have had to do this on several occasions. I see this often with people who are afraid of heights going zip-lining for the first time. They step back from the edge, psych themselves up, then go for it.

Often it's a good idea to combine this with other strategies like deep breathing and correcting your self-talk. Remind yourself how exciting this is. Another option when you pull back because of fear is to get indignant. Like fear and excitement, anger is a state of arousal. It's congruent to flip the switch and get pissed off about being scared to do something. Anger used correctly can be motivating. Remember, fight is one of your adrenal options. I wouldn't make a habit of using anger every time you are afraid, but occasionally it's what you need to get that second wind.

9. Reframe the experience.

Reframing is the ability to look at the situation from a different perspective and therefore change its meaning. Changing your point of view can have a profound effect. If you look through a camera lens and zoom in and out, it changes the picture. Change the light filter setting, and it changes more. With digital editing, you can crop and add sophisticated special effects, so your final product doesn't look anything like what you started with.

You can do this with your mind as well. Changing perspectives can reshape the context of an event or situation. Renaming a problem as a challenge or opportunity is a simple example of reframing that has caught on in the outdoor and business communities. The change in terminology takes it from being a heavy burden to a more positive thing you can tackle, something you can rise to meet and take care of or use to make things better.

When I was suffering from PTSD, my first breakthrough was reframing my situation by changing the questions I was asking myself from *why* to *how* questions. I had been ruminating with *why* questions, asking, "Why did this happen to me?" This is a question you are never going to answer without purposely directing your thoughts. The other big question was "Why can't I get over this?" This question presupposes failure, and if I kept asking it, I never would have gotten better. These are not questions someone with an internal locus of control would ask.

Instead, I began to ask, "How do I get better?" This presupposes there is a way and I will find it. That reframed the situation. The other question I asked was "How do I make meaning of this?" It was a reframe of the question "Why did this happen to me?" but it put the ball in my court, so I could assign the meaning.

I went through PTSD and crippling anxiety so I could be an example that you can go through trauma, recover, come out of it, and live a happy and productive life. That was a meaning I chose before I overcame the PTSD, so I wasn't sure I could make it come true, but I kept telling myself that, and eventually it became reality.

10. Get support.

The last strategy is as simple as asking for help. Calling my brother-in-law and telling him I was lost in the bush and my phone was about to die required humility. I probably will never live it down, but it got me out of a potentially dangerous situation.

You may need help sometimes with things you don't know how to do. Often pride gets in the way of seeking the help people need. You might know you need help, but you don't want to admit you need it. It's as if admitting you need help is a weakness, but it's not. Asking for help is a sign of good character. Of course, if one of your fears is rejection, you have to tackle that fear and work up enough courage to ask for help.

It may be as simple as asking a friend or colleague who has experience dealing with what you are facing. It may be finding a mentor. If you are genuinely appreciative, many people are willing to give time and energy. Others may want something in return, but if they can help you make progress, it is usually worth it.

This might not apply to you, but sometimes fears and anxieties must be dealt with by professionals. There should be no stigma attached to seeing a mental health professional. Many top-level athletes, business professionals, and movie stars use or have used mental health professionals to overcome fears and get themselves past stuck states. Sometimes counselors and personal life coaches can fill this role, and sometimes it takes a doctor. There is no shame in seeing a doctor to help look after your mental health.

The doctors who handle this kind of thing are clinical psychologists (i.e., psychotherapists) and psychiatrists. A psychologist is someone you can talk with. They usually have a PhD, whereas a psychiatrist is a medical doctor. I have used both, and they bring different things to the table. If a clinical diagnosis is needed or drugs need to be prescribed, a psychiatrist is who you need.

Although they are often trained in psychotherapy as well, I have found psychiatrists tend to think in terms of neurochemistry, and their solutions tend to weigh in the direction of medication.

Still, medication may be needed, especially if fear or anxiety causes a loss of sleep. Being able to sleep is probably the most important aspect of mental health there is. Make sure your doctor listens to you. They have a lot of knowledge, but you are the one in your body. Dosages or types of medications may need to be changed. Doctors need to work with you to get it right.

Psychologists use various forms of talk therapy to help you overcome fears. Psychotherapy is as much an art as it is a science, so different therapists will be effective for different people. Make sure you get one you feel comfortable with, and you should start noticing an improvement by at least the third session.

If you feel your therapist isn't helping, change therapists. Be your own advocate. You want results, not somebody who will act as a sounding board and milk you for money week after week, month after month, year after year. Some therapists are happy to do this, so you need to manage your treatment. Also, it's important to understand the responsibility for change is on you, the client. A good therapist or coach can help facilitate positive change, but they are not performing a magic ritual. Whether or not you use professionals, it is your responsibility to make changes within yourself.

I have found that psychologists trained in neurolinguistic programming (NLP) and/or eye movement desensitization and reprocessing (EMDR) are most effective for me. This is what I used to help me get back on track.

EMDR is a form of therapy in which you recall a traumatic event in your mind while some sort of stimulus is introduced that oscillates the attention back and forth between both halves of the body. Originally this involved the therapist holding a pen or pointer and waving it in front of the client, so their eyes tracked back and forth as they recalled a traumatic memory. It simulates the eye-tracking people do when they are in the rapid eye movement stage of sleep. When I had it done, the therapist had me hold a wand in each hand, and they vibrated one side at a time. The idea is that switching attention from side to side allows you to process memories more effectively, greatly reducing the negative effects of the trauma.

If you don't need psychological help, that's great. Hopefully you never will. But this section is worth reading anyway, since anxiety and trauma are prevalent in our society. Chances are you know someone—or will know someone—with a severe anxiety disorder. Maybe this information will enable you to help someone get the help they need. The older you get, the greater the chance you will experience trauma, so it is good to have ideas in your pocket just in case.

If you have any irrational fear—and most of us do—that isn't bad enough to need a therapist, and you want to handle it yourself, I highly recommend this powerful creative visualization exercise.

I suggest you use this technique on your top three fears as an experiment. When you see how easy and effective it is, you will probably want to try it on all your fears. It is the most useful mental exercise I have found in overcoming fears: the NLP fast phobia cure.

It has been called by other names over the years: the rewind technique, the double dissociation technique, and the visual kinesthetic dissociation technique. No matter what name you use for it, this technique works, and has helped me immeasurably. It isn't new. It's been around for some time.

It can be effective on serious, life-impairing phobias. However, the fear does not have to be as extreme as a phobia. It also works for everyday fears and minor traumas that you spend too much time rehashing in your head. It was created by NLP cofounders Richard Bandler and John Grinder.

For this to work, you need to accept the idea that anxiety and fears, including phobias, are something you do, not something you have. They are behaviors.

The second thing to accept is that fears, including phobias, are learned behaviors. The reaction you have, you learned to have. Phobias and irrational fears are learned in one of the three ways I talked about in the previous chapter: classical conditioning, vicarious acquisition, and informational/instructional acquisition. Sometimes you learned this behavior with a single event you interpreted as traumatic. I was held up at gunpoint by a robber only once, but boy did it influence my psyche. This is onetime learning.

If the fear was learned from a onetime event, it can be unlearned from a onetime event. More aptly, you can learn a behavior that is more useful. That is what makes this such a powerful technique. Something that has been affecting you for years can be wiped away in less than fifteen minutes.

Step one: sit back and get comfortable.

Pick a phobia or something that causes intense fear or anxiety. If you don't have anything you would classify as a phobia, good for you. Pick the thing you are afraid of the most.

Remember the event that caused the trauma in as much detail as possible. If you can't remember the event, remember the first time you experienced the fear. If you can't remember the first time, remember a time when it affected you the most. Remember with as much detail as you can.

Next, imagine you are sitting alone in the center front row of a movie theater. In front of you is a blank screen. You are waiting for the movie to begin. You are perfectly safe and comfortable.

Imagine floating out of your body and back to the projection booth. Now you are watching yourself watch the screen. Remember, you are in control of this experience. You can stop it anytime you want.

Put a still frame of your fear in color on the screen. Run a movie of the fear all the way to the end to a point where you feel safe. Remember, you are watching yourself watch the film. At the end of the movie, freeze the frame into a still.

Next, change the picture to black and white. Then fully associate into the picture. Walk into the screen. Now you are in the movie. You will see what you saw, only without color. Run it backward at triple to eight times the normal speed. As you do this, have circus music or funny cartoon music playing. When you get to the beginning of the movie, freeze the frame again.

Walk out of the picture and sit in your seat again. White out the screen in front of you. Do this several times until you can vividly recall the original experience without any distress. If you can remember the experience without emotional attachment, you have learned a new behavior to replace the fear.

The first time I performed a fast phobia cure outside training was on Narelle. One evening I went to bed early. I was awakened from a dead sleep by the most bloodcurdling scream I have ever heard. I jumped up in a panic! I was certain the only thing that could cause my wife to scream like this was an intruder. When I rounded the corner into the living room, there was my wife, screaming hysterically. She was paralyzed with fear. Sweat was running down her face, and she was trembling.

On the floor in front of her was an inch-long (two-centimeter) spider advancing on her slowly. She couldn't move. The spider got closer little by little, but she could do nothing but let out ear-piercing screams. She was in full freeze response. My wife had arachnophobia. She stood there trembling until I took the spider outside.

The next day we did a fast phobia cure as an experiment, then I completely forgot about it. We went through the exercise only once. About a week later, we happened on an opportunity to test it. We were in the nature section of the state fair, and there was a ranger letting people hold a rather large tarantula. I somehow managed to talk my wife into holding the spider. It wasn't that hard. She seemed more eager to try than I expected, given her reaction a few days before.

The ranger placed a spider that was almost as big as her hand in her palm. Beads of sweat appeared on her forehead as she held it. With her right index finger, she pet its furry abdomen. You could see the tension on her face as she concentrated deeply on touching the spider. Then she started petting the spider, and amazingly she smiled. After that, she was relaxed. I was proud of her for being courageous enough to face her fear. A few weeks earlier, asking her to hold a tarantula would have been as preposterous as asking her to fly to the moon by flapping her arms.

Now, Narelle still doesn't particularly like spiders. I won't say she has lost all of her fear of them. I wouldn't want her to. We live in a country with some of the most dangerous spiders in the world. But now they don't paralyze her with fear. She can function around them and carry on. No more paralysis.

Zoe, on the other hand, never had a fear of spiders. She learned about spiders as a fun thing by playing itsy bitsy spider with me. When she was two, we went for a walk in a local park in Tampa called Lettuce Lake. I liked to take her for walks there when she was that age because the trails were mostly boardwalks with rails, and I could corral her.

One day two university girls were ahead of us on the boardwalk. They had stopped and seemed scared to walk any farther. Overhanging the boardwalk was a large spiderweb with a hand-size banana spider hanging right in the middle of it. The bottom of the web was high enough to duck under, but the girls were too frightened. Zoe walked right between the girls, then pointed up and said, "Itsy bitsy," before walking through. The university students started laughing at themselves and then worked up the courage to go under the web. Zoe had learned a different frame for how she viewed spiders.

Of course, the fact that Zoe is fond of spiders has turned all my getting-rid-of-spider activities directed by Narelle into catch-and-release operations. I have gotten pretty good at removing even the largest huntsman. All I need is a Tupperware dish, a piece of paper, and a stepladder.

Huntsmen are one of Australia's unique spider types. Unlike some other Australian spiders, huntsman bites aren't dangerous to humans, but that doesn't mean they aren't high on the most-feared list. They are big and furry like tarantulas, but unlike tarantulas, which stay on the ground and move slowly, huntsmen are fast, agile, and they don't mind being upside down. Also, if harassed, they tend to jump.

At first, my catch-and-release operations went rather badly—like good-material-for-a-slapstick-comedy bad. Spiders jumped on my head several times and at least once right on my face. I almost fell off the ladder a few times, but I kept at it because I was under the watchful gaze of my little girl, whom I had promised I wouldn't kill any spiders. You know you have mastered your fear of spiders when you can stay balanced precariously on a ladder as an arachnid roughly the size of a three-year-old's hand lands on your face. After the birth of several dozen baby huntsmen in our living room and their safe removal, I had become an old pro. Now Zoe is old enough to take spiders outside herself.

Some people have resigned to live the rest of their lives in debilitating fear of something: spiders, snakes, water, heights—you name it. Thankfully, most of the time, fear isn't as debilitating as an outright phobia. Nonetheless, fear might limit how productive and joyful life can be. Imagine how amazing your life would be if you conquered a few of your fears. Avoidance is never a good long-term strategy. Sooner or later, something will crop up that activates that fear, so you might as well deal with it on your own terms. Fear inoculation is the way to do it.

After running the fast phobia cure a couple of times, you want to test to see how well it worked. This is called **desensitization, exposure therapy, or stress inoculation.** This is how you challenge your fear incrementally. Experience shows that learning to overcome fear is best done first in a relaxed atmosphere, concentrating on the theater of the mind, then stress-testing incrementally in the real world. If this sounds a lot like the process of skill-building I mentioned earlier in the chapter, that is because it is. Learning to manage fear is a skill just like any other, so the same rules apply.

Take it in stages, creating a high probability of success and then building on those successes. To do this with precision, inoculate against fear in four distinct phases or levels. You will need to use only three of these, but the fourth is there if you want to take it to that level.

I have designated these levels with letters to cut down on confusion. After running through a few fast phobia cures, you should be able to test to a level B and be at a comfortable fear level. The four levels of incremental fear inoculation are

A. Mental construct
B. External controlled encounter
C. Immersive encounter
D. Extreme immersive encounter

Keep a handle on how what you do affects your stress levels. If you are tilting toward panic, back off until you have gained control. Stay in control of yourself.

Below are detailed explanations of the incremental levels for facing fears.

Level A: Mental Construct

Think about the object or situation of fear with no anxiety. After performing a fast phobia cure, you should be able to vividly recall or imagine the experience and be comfortable. If not, repeat the fast phobia cure three or four times, then retest. Don't move on to level B until you can visualize your fear comfortably.

Level B: External Controlled Encounter

Normally this means seeing the real thing in a controlled environment. The important aspect of this level is control. You can move closer to the object of your fear or farther back until you have control over your nervous system, for example seeing a live snake or spider from a distance or close-up but behind a glass enclosure. For a fear of heights, a level B test is standing on top of a multilevel parking garage and looking down from behind a wall or being in a tall building and walking up to the windows to look out over the city. Riding to the top of that building in a glass elevator would be level C, since unlike the car park and window, you can't retreat from the edge. You are stuck in the elevator until it gets to the floor you have selected, which gives you less control. After running through several fast phobia cures, you should be able to test to level B and be comfortable. Keep at this until you can relax. As always, remember to breathe.

Being there is your best option. On the other hand, with the development of high-definition point-of-view videography and a catalog of online videos, you can get the feeling of getting up close and personal with many of your fears without having to leave the comfort of your living room or office. Want to spice this up? Use virtual reality goggles. Anything you can do to make your virtual encounter with your fear more realistic while maintaining a sense of control will vastly improve the desensitization process.

Another option for a controlled encounter with animals is a toy. A realistic-looking rubber snake or plastic spider makes a good level-B experiment. Being able to physically handle realistic-looking toys is a step on the path to being able to handle the real thing.

Level C: Immersive Encounter

This involves fully experiencing the thing you fear without going into panic mode. For spiders and snakes, this would be holding a live animal. Level C for flying would be to take a flight. If you can get to level C and function in that environment without panic, that is considered successfully beating your fear. You should be able to test to level C and feel in control. A little discomfort is okay if you can keep it as an overall positive experience, staying in the stretch zone. If you feel your fear creeping up to the panic zone, use any of the strategies from earlier in this chapter to calm yourself down. If you can do this, you have accomplished something, and you should be proud of yourself!

Level D: Extreme Immersive Encounter

As the name implies, level D is gnarly to the max! Level D is beyond what a reasonable person would be expected to do. I would not want anyone to try level D unless they really want to, and they were able to go to level C repeatedly without any anxiety. You should be able to perform a level C task with your perceived fear and be completely comfortable before you consider doing anything at level D.

At this level, the consequences of a worst-case scenario increase exponentially. At the previous levels, we were dealing mostly with perceived danger. At the D level, there may be an element of real danger. It still shouldn't be as high as the perceived danger, but there is real risk.

Another differentiating factor is at this level it might be more difficult to bail out. The withdraw-and-reinsert strategy may be closed off after a certain point. If you are challenging your fear of heights by going to the observation deck of a tall building and start to panic, you can back away from the edge (level B). If you perform a level D task like abseiling down a cliff face, once you back over the ledge, you cannot get back up if you panic. You must keep going down and finish your rappel. At this level, you have less control over the external conditions, so you have to make up for it by controlling your internal world. You have to manage your state.

Good risk management strategies should be used to keep the danger to a minimum, and when possible, enlist professionals to help ensure every precaution is taken. They should ensure mitigation strategies and safety equipment are properly set up.

Level D for heights would be bungee jumping, rock climbing, or skydiving. Caving might be your level D exercise if you were previously claustrophobic. For public speaking, giving a speech in front of a dozen work colleagues or a Toastmasters club would be level C, and level D would be giving a keynote speech in front of hundreds or thousands of people.

For fear of snakes, hold an eight-foot-long (two-and-a-half-meter) boa constrictor and let it wrap around you. Trust me, this is a vastly different experience from holding a little corn snake at the pet store or nature discovery center.

You get the picture. It is not necessary to take anything to level D, but there is something incredibly empowering about taking something you were previously deathly afraid of and facing it at a level most people can't. The more debilitating the phobia was, the greater the accomplishment if you can push the envelope to the extreme!

If you decide to take a level D challenge, the onus is on you. You decide what your challenge is. Again, level D isn't necessary. Challenge by choice.

Only you can decide if and when you are ready, and if something goes wrong, you must accept responsibility. If you succeed, you also get to keep the sense of accomplishment all to yourself!

The last time I went bungee jumping, Zoe decided to do it too. She was only twelve. I made it very clear that if she decided to back out, even at the last second, I would not be disappointed. After all, jumping off a 150-foot tower with a bungee cord attached to you is not something most adults can do. To my surprise she did it! She did it of her own accord with no coaxing from me.

My wife was a different story. There was no way in hell Narelle was going to throw herself off a 50-meter tower. She did, however, meet the challenge at her level. My wife climbed up the steps to the top of the bungee tower. This is no small feat for someone with a fear of heights. Towers that high are made with some flexibility to withstand high winds, so they tend to rock and sway. About three quarters of the way up, the tower started swaying, and I could see the color drain from my wife's face. She stopped her climb, grabbed the handrail, and started deep breathing.

When she had shifted herself out of the panic zone and into the stretch zone, she finished her climb. When she got to the top, she was rewarded with not only an incredible feeling of accomplishment but also an amazing panoramic view of the surrounding mountains, rainforest, and, farther out, the sea. Two level Ds and one high level C. Not a bad day for facing fears.

Do you want a picture of progressively moving up the levels? The best example I can give on all these levels is how I incrementally challenged my fear after suffering PTSD from the robbery. Here is a brief description of how my testing went and what I used at each level.

Level A was getting back to functioning like a normal human being. I had to first stop constantly trembling and having nervous tics. I had to be able to sleep at night without waking up and compulsively checking to make sure all the doors were locked five to six times a night. I had to not jump every time a car backfired. I had to stop having flashbacks and panic attacks. I had to stop looking at every stranger as a potential threat.

This took several sessions of going back through the robbery in my head until I was able to remember it without anxiety. With most things, you can do this yourself, but this was a serious trauma for me, so for this one, my mental constructs were facilitated by a trained therapist. When I could vividly recall and describe the robbery in detail without anxiety, many of my symptoms started to fade away.

For level B I started going to the gun range. It took a little effort to work up the nerve to be around guns. I got a concealed carry permit and armed myself. This was my way of taking the power back.

Level C was being able to go for a walk in my neighborhood at night. I practiced gun disarms with partners, using rubber training guns. This included the gun-to-the-back-of-the-head execution position. This was a big trigger for me, no pun intended.

It wasn't a hypothetical exercise like it was for my training partners. I had experienced the real thing. Even the rubber gun caused flashbacks and panic attacks at first. I remember one training session when I performed like everything was normal, but when I got in my car to go home, I started sobbing uncontrollably in the parking lot. Getting past this level required some extra work to handle a simulated gun put to the back of my head while controlling my breath and heart rate. After doing a few fast phobia cures on myself, this became a lot easier.

Level D was not something planned but something I fell into through circumstance. This needs a Do Not Try at Home disclaimer.

A couple of people thought I had crossed the line from bravery to stupidity, but it was something I had to do. A few years before, fear stemming from an asshole with a gun almost put me in a mental hospital, and I didn't plan on letting myself feel that disempowered again.

My level D was taking my normal walk around the neighborhood at night when there was an active serial killer stalking the subdivision! His modus operandi was to walk up to random people and shoot them at close range, then walk off into the night. I was determined I would not be overcome by fear just because my home turf was the hunting ground of a madman. My night walks were under the backdrop of a very real and deadly threat.

Packing heat myself, I went out to face my fears on a level that far exceeded reasonable and rational, possibly even sane. I had gone through so much to overcome my anxiety. I had let fear of bad guys defeat me once before, and I wasn't about to go back to that place.

The threat wasn't something I could forget about. Every time we turned on the news, our neighborhood was being talked about. Even when the TV was off, it was always at the forefront of the mind because of the constant drone of police helicopters overhead. When I was on my walks, sometimes they shone a spotlight on me from the air for a moment and then continued with their sweep. It was a weird time for my family and it was one hell of an extreme immersive experience. It was an experience I repeated night after night for almost two months.

Hopefully, any exposure therapy you try will not include anything on the level of a serial killer. I will tell you more about that later. For now, let's plan on **desensitizing** your fears.

EXERCISE

Create your own fear exposure therapy program:

- In a notebook, make a list of your top three fears.

- Write a plan to desensitize yourself to each fear. Level A should be the same for every fear: being able to vividly imagine your fear without distress.

- Write down your plan for level B.

- Write down your plan for level C.

You want to expose yourself up to level C for each fear.
Look at the list below to help you plan to test your fears to level C.

A. Mental construct: Mentally bring your fear to light. Perform a fast phobia cure on yourself. Repeat as many times as necessary until you can vividly imagine the thing you fear and remain calm.

B. External encounter: You want to perform this as soon as possible after the fast phobia cure to take advantage of the momentum and build on your success. You should be able to get close to the thing you fear and stay relaxed. If not, back off and perform more fast phobia cures until you can approach and feel comfortable.

C. Immersive Encounter: The sooner you can do this, the better. If you can arrange your immersive experience to be right after your external encounter, that is best. Experience the thing that made you afraid close-up and personal. The fast phobia cure should have reduced any anxiety to a manageable level. Remember to breathe.

If you need to use any other strategies to help you feel comfortable, do so. You should feel comfortable or only slightly distressed. If you feel yourself creeping up to panic, dig in and manage your state, or you may have to withdraw and reinsert once you have calmed down. Level C is where the money is. Take something that causes fear and immerse yourself in it. Once you have done that, you can feel good about it.

Watching yourself successfully overcome big fears makes all the other fears in your life seem like cake. Get in the habit of overcoming fears and insecurities, and the adrenaline and dopamine you get from it will make tackling challenges almost compulsive as opposed to something you procrastinate on or avoid altogether.

Along with the term *internal locus of control*, *self-efficacy* is thrown around a lot in circles of positive psychology. Self-efficacy is belief in your own abilities and your ability to meet challenges.

A high level of self-efficacy increases the chances of success. One of the reasons is if a person with a high level of self-efficacy has determined they do not possess the skills to succeed in a specific endeavor, they believe they can and are more likely to take the necessary steps to acquire and master those skills.

It doesn't mean people are overconfident and think they can do things they can't yet. It means they realize few endeavors are based on raw talent but instead on skills you can learn if willing to put in the time and effort.

If all that seems long-winded, the simpler explanation is that the more hard things you do, the more you realize you can do hard things. With each fear you overcome, you increase your self-efficacy. It's a simple formula. If you want to feel good about yourself, learn to do things that scare you. If you want to feel really good about yourself, do things that scare the shit out of you!

Chapter 6:

Creating the Expeditionary Mindset

I looked down and saw that great conical head rising at me through a cloud of my own blood, and that's when I knew I was in trouble.
— RODNEY FOX, INVENTOR OF THE ANTISHARK CAGE

This chapter is about shifting your consciousness to that of an adventurer. You want to create what is called an expeditionary mindset. You want to take the curious, flexible, creative, and resilient attitude of an explorer.

There are a couple of mental subsets you need to take on board if you want to go expeditionary. First, you need to be prepared for disappointment. You also need the willingness to seize opportunity. These are two key traits of the expeditionary mindset. Just as important is the ability to quickly adapt when the pendulum of circumstance swings between these two possibilities. Let me explain with a story of pushing one of my most serious fears to the edge.

I felt very deflated and defeated. I was cold, tired, starting to feel sick to my stomach, and beginning to get the feeling I had utterly failed in my quest. We were running out of time.

I was sitting on a twenty-five-foot boat we had chartered. We were anchored approximately five miles off the coast of Gansbaai, South Africa.

The afternoon sky had been brilliantly bright, with not a cloud in the sky. Now it was late in the day, and the sun was getting lower. To my starboard were Dyer Island and Geyser Rock, which was home to a colony of about fifty thousand Cape fur seals.

On the port side was a South African man dumping buckets of blood and fish guts into the water. The buckets of gore we were dumping overboard every couple of minutes probably contributed to the nauseous feeling, but I couldn't smell it anymore. We had been at this since nine in the morning, and the overpowering smell had overloaded my olfactory system long ago.

A frigid wind had whipped up from the south. The next landmass, if you traveled due south, was Antarctica, so I do mean frigid. I went inside the cabin to escape the wind, sun, and gory chum. In the cabin I began to think about what had started this adventure so long ago. My cousin had vouched as my guardian to take me to a horror movie I was probably too young to see. That started an intense fascination, almost an obsession with sharks. But coupled with that obsession was a deep primal fear.

At its worst, the fear had kept me from enjoying the beaches where I grew up. Back then, the face of fear that haunted my dreams had hundreds of razor-sharp teeth arranged in rows. Strangely, as I got older, those dreams began to pull me toward my fear, not away from it.

Even when my fear of sharks was at a phobic level, I vowed one day I would see a great white shark up close and live to tell the tale. I put that childhood fantasy away for a while, but the pull grew. Twenty-something years after the young boy was taken to a horror movie about a killer shark, I was on the other side of the world, sitting in a dive boat chasing them. Here I was hoping to scuba dive with a species of shark nicknamed "white death." This was an odd thing to do for someone who at one time didn't want to swim at the beach for fear of sharks.

We were floating in an area famous to anyone who has watched Shark Week on the Discovery Channel. This area is known as Shark Alley, or the great white shark capital of the world. The only problem was the sharks hadn't shown up.

I had gone through a logistical nightmare to arrange the shark dive while in transit on a world cruise on board the *QE2*. A friend from one of my previous ships lived in Cape Town and did some of the initial research on the dive company. She sent me a brochure in the mail with a note that said this seemed like the most reputable shark diving company she could find. Cage diving was not something you wanted to use a disreputable company for, that was for sure.

At first, I planned to go by myself. Then my friend and dive buddy Julie decided to go with me. She started telling people about it, and soon people wanted to join our crazy little expedition. By the time we finished arrangements, more than a dozen people had joined our party. Some of them weren't diving because they were not scuba certified. They tagged along anyway, since white sharks are surface feeders, and they figured they would get a good show and be safer than those of us who wanted to get in the cage.

We were in Cape Town for only two days, so it was now or never. We set out while it was still dark on our second day. Before dawn, a van from the diving company picked up our party at the cruise ship terminal in Cape Town. We drove to Gansbaai two hours away in the early morning light.

Seven hours after setting anchor, I had long since grown used to the smell of blood and fish guts—a mixture referred to as chum. We had been on the water since early morning dumping chum overboard every five minutes. A shark can smell a drop of blood in the water from over two miles away, so this was considered the best way to attract them.

The quandary we were in was the fact that the world's largest predatory fish was apparently very shy. Seven hours of chumming, and we hadn't seen even a fin. I was becoming convinced the sharks would be a no-show. I was now mentally preparing for the disappointment of having to return to the ship empty-handed. I might never get this chance again.

Scattered throughout the narrow strip of False Bay were four other dive boats doing the same thing. Finally, about a half an hour before we had to return to shore, an overly excited voice began talking on the radio. One of the other boats had made contact. The pendulum was about to swing.

They were saying something in Afrikaans. Then that voice said something in English I had been waiting to hear all day. Now, however, that phrase made my blood curdle: "Great white, five-plus meters!" The shark was heading toward us. I headed up on deck as fast as I could, and soon after we spied a sliver of a fin. Then abruptly in front of us, a sixteen-foot great white materialized out of the shadows. It was like some kind of obscure phantom at first, but as it inched its way closer to the surface, the shark took on a more corporeal form.

Things happened fast from there. We threw large chunks of bait overboard to lure the sharks in close. We lowered the cage into the water. We tore off jackets and clothes and struggled to get into our wet suits as fast as we could. A host of emotions played through my head—excitement, fear, anxiousness, anticipation, and the thrill of the ultimate adventure I had dreamed about as a kid. I was super excited but also scared out of my mind. Not only was I going to dive in the water, but also I was about to deep dive to a place in my psyche where my wildest dreams and worst nightmares were one and the same.

The bait was a full-size tuna almost the size of a person, and in a couple of bites it was gone. As I said, white sharks are surface feeders. You can watch all the action from the safety of the boat. They are amazing to watch. The glistening of the light reflected off their enormous bodies as they tore through flesh and bone like a chain saw through shrubbery.

Few things are as awesome as watching an alpha predator feeding! There were two sharks in the water at first, but great whites have a pecking order, and the larger dominant female shark chased the smaller one away before anyone got in the cage.

We watched from the deck for a bit as they prepped the cage. Soon it would be time to enter the water. When we boarded the boat, we had all signed multipage legal waivers almost as thick as a book agreeing that in the event of loss of life or limb, neither we nor our heirs would litigate against the dive operators. Of all the liability waivers I have signed, this was the only one that used the word *dismemberment*. In fact, the word was used multiple times throughout the document—so many times it was almost comical.

When we boarded the boat, one of the first things I noticed was the steel wire of the cage was rather thin. I remember nervously joking it looked much like chicken wire. Great whites have a bite force of over 1.5 metric tons, or four thousand pounds per square inch,[1] and they have as many as three hundred serrated, razor-sharp teeth. I wanted as much steel between me and that maw as I could get. I was further unnerved when during our briefing the dive guide told us that if the sharks wanted to, they could break through the cage. They aren't shark-proof. More like shark-resistant.

There is a scene in *Jaws* where the shark smashes through an antishark cage. I had chalked that up as Hollywood hype. Nope, there was some truth to it. Our dive master informed us they really can but probably wouldn't. (I have since seen video footage of cage breaches shot in the same location with the same kind of cage we dove in.)

According to our dive operators, there are two reasons white sharks normally don't break in. First, they are lazy, and it's just not worth the effort. The bait is a much simpler meal to obtain. Second, the steel creates an electromagnetic field that irritates their sixth sense. Yes, I was about to trust my life to things like energy fields and the slothfulness of a predator roughly the size of a small bus.

We are taught in school there are only five senses—visual, kinesthetic, olfactory, gustatory, and auditory. Sharks have two additional senses. One is the lateral line, which detects vibrations in the water. The other is the one often referred to as the sixth sense. Sharks can sense your aura—not in any supernatural, clairvoyant way but with a real sense organ. Not only is there an electromagnetic field around all living creatures but also certain creatures like sharks and rays have a sense organ to detect it. It is called the ampulla of Lorenzini. These specialized receptors are jelly-filled pores around the shark's snout. They look like freckles close-up.

There was a safety barrier in place, but to say there was no real danger would be a lie. The thickness of the liability wavier and the seriousness of our predive briefing were testaments to that. Wild animals are unpredictable, especially ones that outweigh your car. We had to have faith in things like electromagnetic fields to keep us safe.

After we suited up, we entered the cage in groups of two. I dropped into the water and within seconds began to have a terrible panic attack. It wasn't just that I was in the water with a giant predator that could easily bite me in half. It was also extremely turbulent water. The top of the cage floated on the surface so every wave that hit bumped us around. Although both of these things were factors in my rising panic, neither was what bothered me the most.

What bothered me the most was the fact the water was freezing cold. Most of my diving experience was in the tropical waters of Okinawa, Florida, or the Caribbean. The icy water of the Southern Ocean literally took my breath away, even with a wet suit on. I could handle the shark and the turbulence, but the cold proved too much for me. I started to hyperventilate. I had to get out. I opened the top hatch to the cage and signaled for the dive master to get me up.

I stood on the deck, trembling with cold. I watched the other divers do their dives. I was angry at myself. This was my dream. How could I mess it up? The anger turned into a tool to work up my nerve. The wind was increasing, and the weather was getting worse. The dive instructor said, "There is time for only one more dive because the water is getting too rough to enter and exit the cage safely."

I couldn't believe I was giving in. Fear and discomfort could not be allowed to snatch my dream from me. I dug down and found my resolve. I had come too far not to experience this fully! I would go again. Withdraw and reinsert.

Back in the water I went. This would be the best dive of the day. The shark got closer to the cage than any of the other divers had experienced. Almost as soon as I entered the water, I found myself face to face with the colossal shark! As she swam by, it felt like being passed by a semitruck.

Amazingly for such big animals, they move fluidly. The fact that most of their skeletons are cartilage instead of bone adds to the fluidity of movement. White sharks are comfortable in their own skin and are at one with their environment. Their cartilage skeleton gives sharks an amazing level of flexibility. They can turn on a dime. She made multiple passes, and each time approached from a different direction. To the observer it appeared more like the shark was gliding through the water rather than swimming.

The great white shark is one of the most fascinating and without a doubt the most misunderstood creatures in the sea. The scientific name is *Carcharodon carcharias.* They are called white pointers here in Australia and just white sharks in many other places in the world. The great white shark is the largest predatory fish in the world and one of the few fish adapted to eat Marine mammals. As such, unlike other fish, great whites are semi-warm-blooded. Most fish have an internal temperature equivalent the ambient water temperature but not great whites. To have the speed and maneuverability to chase fast seals in cold water, their muscles heat their blood.

Great whites have cognitive abilities far beyond what was previously thought a fish could have. They employ strategy when hunting and have a social order as opposed to being the lone eating machines they were once thought to be.

More research is showing that great whites don't particularly like the taste of humans. We do not have enough calories to be worth burning the energy to catch. We see more and more videos featuring instances of interaction with white sharks without attacks. Still, they kill people now and again, so the cage is an important safety feature I wouldn't want to be without.

Great whites have natural camouflage. This takes the form of countershading, so if you were to look at a profile of one, the top half of its body are gray, and the bottom half is white. When looking down from above, you see the gray, so it blends in with the shadows. The bottom half of its body is white, so in the daytime, if you looked up at it from below, it would blend in with the sun. To see one slip out of the shadows underneath you, even in a cage, is an incredibly awe-inspiring and frightening feeling! Being in the water with a white shark is certainly humbling.

The shark opened her mouth wide to eat large chunks of bait. When her jaws opened, you could see the muscles ripple. The power was unbelievable.

After passing under the cage rather close, she went out and turned back toward us. For a moment she hovered in the water, staring at us. Their eyes weren't really black as coal, but during the day the pigment of sharks' irises almost matches their pupils, so they look black, and they don't blink. It feels as if they are looking into your soul. For a few seconds, we stared at each other. Then in the next instant, she charged forward toward the cage! The shark moved so fast it was like a torpedo coming in at us.

I grabbed the handles conveniently placed inside the cage for *oh shit* moments such as this, so if she rammed the cage my arms wouldn't flail outside into a waiting maw. She barreled toward us at an ungodly speed. At the last second possible the shark made a quick turn, barely bumping the cage and swimming right over it! This was the most exhilarating experience I had ever had. I could even feel the pressure wave from her tail swish.

I didn't have long to think about it, though. Something was suddenly horribly wrong. The flow of air into our regulators had stopped! Most of the time when you are scuba diving, you carry your air tank on your back.

Because having tanks on our backs would make it difficult to climb in and out of the cage opening, we had long hoses that went to an air tank situated on the boat. When the air cut off, we had no idea what had happened. Since the shark had brushed the cage, I assumed she had accidentally bitten or bumped the air hose and broken it somewhere.

I mentioned earlier a near-drowning incident when I was little. I was traumatized and had occasionally tested my fear of drowning. Well, this was one of the biggest tests of drowning anxiety I ever dealt with. I was now faced with the ultimate triad of all my fears. I had to deal with freezing cold, dangerous shark, and now my childhood nemesis—the very real possibility of drowning.

The cage was about ten feet high on the inside and floated at the surface with the aid of several buoys. It was just big enough to fit two divers, and we went two at a time. Most of the cage was submerged under the waterline. If the surface of the water was calm, approximately a foot (a third of a meter) of the inside would be above the waterline. Unfortunately, we were not in calm water. The Antarctic wind caused four-foot swells.

To take a breath, we had to time it between waves, then hold our breath as the next wave rolled over us. I looked up at the boat. No one seemed to be doing anything like pulling the cage back to the boat to get us out. It looked like all their attention was on the shark. I wasn't even sure they were aware we were without air.

If ever there was a time to lose my faculties to sheer panic, that was it. I was pretty sure if I stayed in the cage much longer, I would mistime one of these waves and start inhaling water. On the other hand, if I tried to open the top of the cage and swim the ten or fifteen feet to the boat, the shark could easily cover the distance to me before I could make it back. Even a test bite to see what I was could be fatal. I was sure this was it.

Then something weird happened. I felt a tingle up my spine, and the whole world took on this unearthly glow. Everything was so much brighter, so much more vivid. All I did for the next minute or so was time my breaths with the swells and just *existed*. I felt calm. It was almost like the height of meditation. It was as if I were part of the sea around me.

Then as abruptly as the airflow had stopped, suddenly there were bubbles from our regulators. The air supply was back on. The shark made another close pass, so we descended to the bottom of the cage to watch, forgetting all about the fact we were worried about drowning.

We watched her feed for a while longer. After a few more passes, the shark turned and swam back into the shadows, disappearing the way she came. They hauled the cage in, and when they pulled me into the boat, I was beginning to show the first signs of hyperthermia. I was shivering uncontrollably. My body was numb from the cold. I couldn't stand on my own. I had to be held up until I could get to a safe spot to sit down and pull off my wet suit.

There had been real danger, but it was not nearly as bad as it had seemed at the time. The reason our air supply had stopped was because the dive operators had forgotten to change tanks between divers. In all the confusion trying to get people in and out of the cage safely, a little thing like air supply had been overlooked. They just happened to notice our air was about to run out as the shark made her close pass. Unable to signal us underwater, they decided to change tanks in the middle of the dive. They had trouble unscrewing the valve, so it took longer than expected.

It was no big deal to the dive operators. Provided nobody actually drowns or loses a limb to a white shark, the dive is considered a success. When it seemed like the shark was going to ram the cage, it was no accident or act of aggression by the shark. The dive operators had thrown another piece of bait to the other side of the cage beyond our sight to give us an added thrill. The shark was going for the bait, but we were in the way.

The reason I share the story is it was one of the coolest things I have ever done, and it had many elements of a good expedition. It was also my level D extreme immersion test for dealing with my fear of sharks, drowning, and cold. At several points I could have thrown in the towel and given up. There was the possibility of having gone through all the work and the sharks being a no-show and bitter disappointment. At two points I had serious panic attacks and used several strategies of fear control from the last chapter to deal with them. To me, these things are what a good expedition is all about. Most of all, it was a dream come true.

After that dive, my fear of sharks disappeared. I still respect them as potentially dangerous predators, but the irrational fear and nightmares are gone. I tested this again later in life when for my birthday Narelle bought me a dive experience in the shark tank at the Florida Aquarium in Tampa.

This time I dove with sand tiger sharks, which are called gray nurse sharks here in Australia. Like many large aquariums, they use sand tigers in the coral reef habitat because they have long, sharp teeth that protrude from their mouths. This gives them a menacing demeanor, which is exciting for aquarium guests. Despite their fearsome appearance, sand tigers are placid, and unless you are a spear fisher with a catch dangling from your hip, they don't normally attack humans. This makes them easy to work with in aquariums.

Because they were nowhere near as dangerous as great whites, I dove without a cage. It was just me and the safety diver surrounded by hundreds of tropical fish, sea turtles, moray eels, a friendly goliath grouper named Gil, and six intimidating seven- to ten-foot-long sharks.

I had a moment of panic at the beginning of the dive, when a large shark did a particularly close pass as it swam by. Then I did the breathing technique and a couple of the other mental strategies from the last chapter. I was able to calm myself completely, dropping my heart rate down to normal resting levels. At this point I even had the wherewithal to pay attention to what was going on outside the tank.

When diving in an aquarium exhibit, you become part of the show. A presenter talks to the public about what is going on in the tank. A small crowd had gathered that included Narelle and then fifteen-month-old Zoe, watching me dive. Zoe was watching all the fish, then she noticed me. She smiled as she recognized me, then it turned into a confused, frowny face. I am sure she thought something to the effect of "I don't think Daddy is supposed to be in there with the fishies."

Obviously, I couldn't verbally reassure my daughter. Even though we could see each other perfectly, we had an inch-thick Plexiglas window and half a million gallons of water between us. I wanted to reassure her before that frown turned into a crying fit. Thinking fast, I did the only thing I could do. I started a game of itsy bitsy spider with her from inside the shark tank. I couldn't sing the song with a regulator in my mouth and surrounded by water, but I did the hand gestures. She copied me, grinning from ear to ear, pausing only when a shark close to her side of the tank swam between us and distracted her.

If it had not been for the intensity of my great white expedition in South Africa, I doubt I could interact with sharks, an animal I had once been afraid of to a phobic level, calmly—so calmly I could share a tender family moment in the midst of it.

Of the few medals I received in the Marines, my favorite is the Armed Forces Expeditionary Medal. Like getting ready for any great expedition, the explanation of how you earn it is ambiguous and gives an air of mystery. Unlike most campaign medals, which name the time and place, the Expeditionary Medal leaves out the location and gives a loose definition on how it is earned.

To have an expeditionary mindset, you must be ready for anything to happen or, just as importantly, not happen. I was stationed in Okinawa, Japan, when the first Gulf War broke out. Iraq invaded Kuwait. We packed our gear, and our weapons systems were serviced. We even got new filters

CREATING THE EXPEDITIONARY MINDSET ••• 167

installed in our gas masks because we were told that the Iraqi leader, Saddam Hussein, was stockpiling chemical weapons and was sure to use them.

We packed and loaded all gear and equipment onto a battleship. Then we left, first for the Philippines for some last-minute training before we were supposedly off to Kuwait. Only it didn't happen for us. While in the Philippines, our platoon was called back to Okinawa. They believed a second war was about to open in Korea, and everybody else was already in the Gulf.

We waited in Okinawa for months on end with our bags packed, but we never went. I transferred back to the States and was stationed in California. When I had six months left of my service contract, there was talk about a war in Somalia.

I watched Marines do an amphibious landing in Somalia on December 9, 1992, on CNN, just like everyone else. "Oh well, I am way too short to get involved in anything like that," I said to myself. A couple of days before Christmas I called my mom to assure her there was no chance I was going.

On Christmas Eve my first sergeant walked up to me and said, "Corporal Mac, do you speak Somali?"

"No, First Sergeant. Why do you ask?"

He jotted something on the clipboard he was carrying. Then he looked at me with these weird, intense eyes that only old salty Marines can muster and said, "Well, you had better learn it." Then he did an about-face and walked away. That's how I found out I was deploying to a war zone. I arrived in Mogadishu, Somalia, on New Year's Day.

Of course, I learned about having an expeditionary mindset in the Marine Corps. If you google the term, most of what comes up is lengthy dissertations in military manuals about being able to have combat units that are quick-reacting, self-contained, and able to go anywhere in the world with little advance notice.

For your purpose here, you want to have an expeditionary mindset without it being misconstrued as having to do with war. In your own expeditions, you want to plan and prepare when you have the chance, but you also want to be self-contained and be able to adapt on the fly with little or no advance notice.

First, I will define *expedition* in simple terms. According to Oxford, an expedition is "a journey undertaken for a particular purpose."

Now, that could be as complicated and dangerous as Ernest Shackleton's early expedition to Antarctica, or it could be as simple as a trip to the supermarket. If you knew me and how much I detest shopping, you would probably agree with my wife, who says I make out like a trip to the supermarket is as big a deal as a Shackleton expedition.

But I'm going to add the second part of the definition, so you have clarity. The second part of the definition is "especially that of exploration or ... research."[2] If you adjust your mindset to fit that definition, possibilities open.

When people talk about exploration, most are referring to a physical place, but exploration could also take you into the depths of your own mind. If you read about famous explorers and adventurers—especially autobiographies and journals—there appears to be a common thread. Famous explorers travel great distances, endure incredible hardships, and put themselves in grievous peril in the name of exploration. But they often learn as much if not more about themselves than the places they travel. And they grow exponentially from it.

That is why quotes such as this one from Sir Edmund Hillary, "It's not the mountains we conquer but ourselves," are so popular. Of all the frontiers, your own limitations and boundaries are what you need to explore most. Sometimes you have to go somewhere and do something different to go within and change something.

Even my foray into mental illness could be considered an expedition. I left myself and went someplace that sucked. I endured all kinds of hardships, learned a lot about myself, and luckily came back. My destination was the return to my old self.

An expedition doesn't have to be that great a distance or perilous. Mini-adventures or micro-expeditions are little trips you can do on a weekend or a day when you don't have the time to gallivant to one of the four corners of the globe. It is the attitude of an explorer that you take with you that makes it an expedition, not the distance or the danger.

You can take an attitude of exploration in your everyday life too. Using this mindset in your day-to-day activities takes away a lot of the stress associated with feeling the need to reach a certain result. The thought that "I am doing this to explore what happens" or "I am doing this for research" can be very freeing. It helps you be less attached to outcomes. This allows you to continue to be flexible and explore other options instead of getting angry, frustrated, or depressed about something not working out the way you thought it would. It is much easier to say, "Well, that didn't work. Let's explore and see if I can do it another way." This can help in your profession, relationships, and health goals. Start small. Start by telling yourself, "I am doing this for the purpose of exploration and research."

"I am just exploring."

"I want to see what happens if I . . ."

"What happens when I do X?"

"I am researching what will happen if I say . . ."

"Let's explore what they will do if I . . ."

"What will it look like if we do this?"

"How will the picture look if I change this?"

"I want to get a feel for what happens when I go ahead and . . ."

If you want to, you can take this attitude all the way to a global chunk size. "Hey, man, I'm just here on this planet living this life for the purpose of exploration and research." It's very freeing! It kind of takes the pressure off, doesn't it?

Ironically, focusing on the process of exploration rather than the desired result increases the chances of success. You have to be unattached to outcomes in an expedition because there is uncertainty. Expeditions are usually into unfamiliar territory. You may have to adjust to things that are unexpected. Even in everyday life the unexpected is bound to happen eventually.

The expeditionary mindset can be the ultimate form of mental flexibility. Expeditionary mental flexibility requires two traits: adaptability and resiliency.

Adaptable: Having the ability to adjust to new conditions

Resilient: Being able to withstand and recover quickly from difficult situations

My training in being adaptable began in the Marines, but I was able to hone it to another level while I was working on cruise ships. The company I worked for was a concessioner that controlled the massage therapists, beauty therapists, fitness instructors, and hairdressers. Because it is challenging managing the logistics of qualified people to do these jobs on ships all over the world, at the time this concessioner had a monopoly on running the spas and beauty salons on almost all the cruise lines.

Employees signed a contract for usually six or eight months, and we were on board ship that entire time. This gave us the luxury of traveling and getting paid for it. There was a price for this, though. During our contract we could be transferred to any ship, on almost any cruise line, in any part of the world with little or no notice. I had to have an attitude of exploration, and I had to be adaptable from day one.

When I accepted my first contract over the phone, I was told I had to get from Tampa to Miami in two days. "There you do the paperwork, and we will fly you to San Juan, and you will catch your ship that day."

I was excited. I repeated, "San Juan. Okay, so I am going to be stationed in the Caribbean." Being from Florida, this was what I wanted: days off on the beach, my comfort zone.

CREATING THE EXPEDITIONARY MINDSET ••• 171

There was silence on the phone for a few seconds and then the British woman started to explain. "Well, not exactly. You will be doing two cruises through the Caribbean, but your ship is repositioning to Alaska for the summer. You will do one eastern Caribbean cruise, one western Caribbean cruise, then through the Panama Canal, South America, and up the west coast of the US and Canada. The rest of the summer, you will be going back and forth between Vancouver, Canada, and Seward, Alaska."

Alaska was colder in the summertime than Tampa was in the winter, so I was apprehensive about spending a whole summer there. But I resigned myself to enjoying the chance of discovery. The next day, I put everything I owned in storage, had all services stopped, broke my apartment lease, and left to explore the last great frontier.

I must admit I loved Alaska. The spa had large bay windows, so I could look out at the scenery as we cruised through the Inside Passage or Glacier Bay. My days off were spent hiking in the woods, visiting waterfalls, or traversing into the ice fields. It was a great time.

Midway through my contract, I was thrown a curveball. I got back to the ship after having the day off in Skagway. That was when I found out I had been transferred. I had two hours to pack and leave. I would be spending the night in Skagway and then taking a small local airline flight to Juneau the next morning. When you work aboard a cruise ship, you get very close to people. Every time I moved ships it was like losing family.

The fact that you are in this little micro-city on the sea compresses time and makes your friendships tight, but the crew is from all over the world, so when you are transferred or a contract ends, you may never see some of those people again. It is hard, but it generates adaptability.

As tough as leaving was, the flight from Skagway to Juneau turned out to be an amazing adventure. We boarded a tiny turboprop. There was me and just six other passengers. Skagway Airport sits right next to the cruise ship terminal, in a narrow canyon with mountains on either side. I have seen the airport on top travel lists as having the most beautiful scenery and being one of the scariest.

The runway was short and ended at the harbor, so there wasn't much room for error on takeoff. The plane coughed and choked as we lifted off the runway, its motor sounding like a little lawn mower engine. We rose into the air unsteadily. There was a lot of turbulence, and in a couple of instances, we lost serious altitude. I didn't think slamming into the side of a mountain would be a good thing, and a water landing might be even worse. We wouldn't last long in that freezing-cold stuff. Slowly and shakily, we continued climbing over the mountains. The Alaskan mountains create all kinds of strange thermals and wind shears, generating nasty instability for anyone flying in a small aircraft.

I thought Alaska was beautiful from the sea and the ground, but from the air it was even more incredible. Then we hit another air pocket and another drop in altitude. We skirted the Inside Passage for the most part, but then we crossed over the Juneau Icefield. As far as the eye could see were miles and miles of ice. Magnificent spires and crevasses were so big and deep you could see them from the air, not that we were all that high above them. This ice field is almost 1,500 square miles and, in places, over four thousand feet thick. It was the source of some of the area's humongous glaciers.

Flying over it was almost like flying over an alien planet. The views were so spectacular I would certainly call it one of the wonders of the world. Had I not had this sudden transfer, I would never have seen Alaska from the air. Much good can come out of what you think is going to be a bad experience. You don't always know it at the time.

My second contract proved even more interesting. The first three months I spent in the Caribbean. Then midway through the contract, the ship was doing a series of French charters, so they transferred us to different ships and brought on an all-French-speaking crew. I thought I was prepared. But at the last minute, my company brought on one of the executives to oversee the transition. They needed a cabin for him, so they transferred me a week early. Again, it was a last-minute decision, so I had only an hour to pack and say goodbye.

I had been on my newly assigned ship for only two weeks. I had barely learned the names of my coworkers and my way around the ship when the powers that be decided they needed me elsewhere. I was again transferred, this time to Europe.

Europe turned out to be even more incredible than Alaska. Each cruise offered a different part of Europe to explore. One cruise might be the Mediterranean, the next England and the Scottish Isles, the next Scandinavia. Another cruise included Russia and the Baltic. Every trip was different.

Being very flexible for my first two contracts gave me the seniority to select my assignment for my third. Having been to so many places already, I picked a world cruise. We circumnavigated the globe. During that contract, I visited dozens of countries. The world cruise allowed me to fulfill my lifelong dream of diving with the great white sharks I spoke about at the beginning of this chapter.

The world cruise is also where I met the woman of my dreams. That is my wonderful wife, who I have now been with for over twenty years. It allowed me to move to another part of the world, Australia—a place many people dream about just visiting, let alone being lucky enough to live in. This all came from an expeditionary mindset and being flexible enough to roll with things as they changed.

An expedition may require intense planning and preparation, and when you think you have all possible variables covered and something totally unexpected happens, it forces you to go to plan B, C, or completely off the cuff and improvise to changing conditions.

Sometimes events completely outside your control waylay your well-made plans. Injury, sickness, weather, parenthood—unexpected phenomena can wreak havoc on your designs, and you must adapt. A grand expedition is a good mirror of life. The unexpected is going to happen. Plans will be waylaid no matter how good they are. Adaptations need to be made. Sometimes an idea must be shelved until the time is right. Take the attitude of an explorer into daily life. Learn to adapt to change, because change is inevitable.

Resiliency is like adaptability but not exactly. The terms are often used interchangeably, but there is a difference. Adaptability is the ability to adjust to new places and changing circumstances. Being resilient, put simply, is the ability to bounce back from bad stuff.

If you are adaptable, you can frame a lot of inconvenience and minor suffering as just part of the fun. Resilience may require you to adapt to new situations, but there is normally some serious pain involved. That pain could be physical, psychological, or both. Difficulty, crises, traumatic experiences, loss, and major life transitions that may require you to redefine yourself as a person are things that require a high level of resiliency.

I know I called resiliency a trait, but the term can be deceptive. *Trait* might leave you to believe it is something you are inherently born with, and that isn't true. Resiliency is a skill set or, if you like, a group of learned behaviors, just like any other skill set. I have also waffled between what I considered very resilient to totally lacking resiliency, and I had to build it back. Your current level of resiliency isn't fixed. It can be strengthened.

THE ART OF UKEMI

One of the best ways to practice resilience is to learn the art of *ukemi*. You have undoubtedly heard the term *rolling with the punches*. Well, ukemi is a physical manifestation of that metaphor. It is a Japanese word that roughly translates as "receiving body." That is, the one who is about to receive a punch, kick, joint lock, arm bar, or throw.

Ukemi is practiced to some degree in all martial arts, but you see it strongly emphasized in aikido, judo, jujitsu, and jutaijutsu. Ukemi is whatever you need to do as the receiver of the technique to take the least amount of damage. You could say ukemi is the preferred form of risk mitigation when it comes to being punched, kicked, or thrown or taking a fall.

You need to safely handle moves originally designed to dislocate joints and break bones. Some techniques, if done at speed, are easily capable of killing or permanently disabling someone who is not skilled in the receiving aspect of the art. Ukemi requires full attention to the moment. You have to concentrate and continue to be in a flexible flow state while in an off-balance, disadvantaged position. As *uke*, you must learn to control yourself, whether in an awkward tilt or being thrown or pinned in what can be an excruciatingly painful manner.

When you begin, you are normally allowed to commando roll out of a throw. Once your ukemi improves to a certain point, things are moved up a notch, and they force you to take what's called a break fall. At this level they no longer let you do a roll. You are thrown while you are being held in some kind of lock, so it is more of a body slam. You have to fall flat, spreading the impact over the whole body instead of one point.

As you train in these techniques, pain tolerance increases. As the physical resilience increases, so does the mental. Being thrown repeatedly is a quick, easy way to get an adrenal rush too. You know you have increased your resilience when you begin to enjoy the pain.

My first experience with this type of martial art was aikido. A friend of mine on the world cruise had trained in it, and so I started studying with him. I found it so fascinating that when I had a fixed address on dry land again, I found a dojo and took it up formally. My sensei was Japanese, and for some reason, I thought that somehow made my training more authentic. It was about a year into my training during a private lesson when he admitted that while he had studied a couple of other martial arts when he was young, he didn't start learning aikido until he moved to America. Originally it was a way of keeping connected to his heritage, but decades later he was still training and teaching.

The art of ukemi is not for just hand-to-hand combat. It can help you bounce back from all kinds of falls, sometimes literally. I tend to be absent-minded, occasionally a bit clumsy, and my threshold for physical risk is relatively high. A bad combination, I know, but luckily I have become very good at falling. Yes, it's a skill I am proud of, and no, it hasn't kept me from ever getting hurt. It is, however, the reason why as of this writing I can still walk after taking a few spills that probably should have permanently disabled me.

Before sitting down to write today, I went for a hike in the rainforest. While walking over a wet, mildewed log, my feet slipped out from under me. I did an instant break fall. Instinctually I leaned slightly to one side so my bum cheek took most of the impact instead of my sacrum and coccyx. I don't even have to think about this anymore. My body knows exactly what to do, which is good, because a lot of times I don't.

Ukemi can be applied physiologically and spiritually too. Many aspects of life can pull you off balance. Some even throw you for a loop and slam you down hard. A year and a half into my aikido training, my father died. I sat by his deathbed with the family and hospice nurse and watched him slip into a coma. I couldn't bear to sit there and watch, helpless. After a couple of hours, I felt like I was going to crawl out of my skin.

Then, in the final hours of his life, I said my last goodbye and went to aikido class. I needed to bring my attention to the moment and forget about my bereavement, if only for an hour. Getting repeatedly body-slammed and in turn doing that to someone else seemed like the only way to do that. I told my sensei what was going on. With the directness and wisdom that only an Asian martial arts teacher can get away with, he said, "At least this is following the natural order of things." Had anyone else told me that, I probably would have found it patronizing, but I found comfort in those words. I could not control the passing of my father, but I could control the way I took the fall.

Resiliency does not mean invulnerability. Resilient people can be screwed up by the things life throws at them too. But the difference is resilient people don't stay screwed up. Some people stay permanently broken from some event that seems rather trivial to those of us outside it. Then there are people who come back from experiences that are unbelievably horrific and remain well adjusted and happy. You can't help but wonder if you could cope anywhere near as well as them. The difference is their level of resiliency.

Both adaptability and resiliency can be improved by taking up the challenge of becoming expeditionary—going places and doing things for the purpose of exploration and research. What you are exploring and where your research takes you are entirely up to you.

The exercise for this chapter is to plan a small expedition. If you are an experienced mountain climber or backpacker and backcountry camper, feel free to plan something huge. You are probably competent far beyond the scope of this book, anyway. But for the rest of us, this doesn't have to be expedition Everest.

For this exercise, I don't want you to plan a trip to Nepal, where you have to get visas for multiple countries, coordinate Sherpas and supply trains, or any of that. I want this to be a simple trip you can plan and execute easily. Something you can do on a weekend.

Pick somewhere you have preferably never been before or possibly someplace you might have been but haven't had a chance to fully explore. It should be something relatively short that you can do in a couple of days. You could do an overnight or even a day trip if you have to, but a couple of days are best.

If you must stay in a hotel, you can, but camping is better. Tent camping is better than taking your recreational vehicle, and primitive camping with a backpack is best. Many state and national parks offer hike-in primitive camping sites not too far a hike from their full hook-up sites. You don't have to hike twenty or thirty miles into the middle of nowhere if you don't want to.

The important thing is that you maintain the mindset of an explorer. Since I started with a rather loose definition of expedition—a journey with a purpose like exploration—if you don't want to rough it, you can technically call a five-star-resort-stay in wine country an expedition. You may have a harder time proving to yourself that you dealt with adversity, which might be a good example of showing adaptability and resilience. "Oh my god, they were out of pinot noir, and we had to drink merlot all weekend!"

Ideally, if you can factor in a small hardship or challenge that pushes you into the stretch zone, that will be most beneficial and make your little getaway feel like an expedition. It shouldn't be anything so far beyond your reach that you fall into the panic zone but a nice little stretch.

Move beyond the familiar. Expand your horizons and explore uncharted territory. Keep in mind once again: an expedition is a journey undertaken for a particular purpose, especially that of exploration or research.

To begin the first stages of your plan, write it out. Do you want your expedition to be a solo or group effort? Both have advantages and unique challenges that are opportunities for growth.

EXERCISE

That is it. The exercise for this chapter is to plan a trip with an expeditionary mindset. In your notebook, write out your plan.

Take the trip. When you return, perform a debriefing. If your trip was a solo endeavor, you can debrief by writing about it in a journal. If it was a group effort, you can talk about it as a group. Ask questions and encourage participation. It is a good idea to get everyone's perspective about how things went.

Did you achieve your goals and objectives? Why or why not?

Did you face any adversities that required adaptability and/or resilience?

Did things go well overall? If they did or didn't, how much of the answer lies in the planning?

What could be done to improve the overall experience?

What is one takeaway? What did you learn?

Chapter 7:

The Power of the Great Outdoors

> There is more in us than we know. If we could be made
> to see it; perhaps, for the rest of our lives we will
> be unwilling to settle for less.
> — Kurt Hahn

Table Rock Base Camp, North Carolina Outward Bound, 19:30

It was the evening of my birthday. Eight of us sat around the floor of a building called the bouldering hut. We used bouldering crash pads as seats. It was a small building, slightly elevated and made mostly of plywood. One side did not have a wall and was open to the forest. The three walls were covered with the plastic climbing holds of rock-climbing gyms. Some parts of the walls were not straight or even vertical. They were weird angles to simulate the outcroppings and ledges that create the ceilings rock climbers climb over or under. This was where Outward Bound instructors practiced their climbing skills when they weren't in the field. I might have been a little delirious, but the strange shapes and angles in the architecture gave the impression it was the home of some creature from a fantasy novel, perhaps the last of a race of ancient rock-wall sprites.

Outside the rain had slackened again. All day it had alternated between a slight drizzle and a torrential downpour. This was Hurricane Matthew.

Inside we used the plastic climbing molds as makeshift hangers for our raincoats. I was missing my wife and daughter, but other than that we were all in great spirits.

After dinner, the instructors made a birthday cake of sorts. Backcountry chocolate lava cake, they called it. The lava part came from the fact that our ethanol camp stove had run out of fuel before the cake had fully solidified. It wasn't fully cooked, but it was good. When you have been living off the grid, your standards tend to lower a bit. Our bellies were full. We were warm, dry, and relatively clean. This was nice considering we had been living in the forest for the previous week and sleeping on the ground in a different location every night.

That morning, just before daybreak, I had my third and final panic attack of the trip. I woke up coughing and struggling to breathe. Sleeping on the cold, damp ground with only a tarp over us to keep back the rain had triggered an asthma attack. My coughing and subsequent struggle to find my emergency inhaler woke everyone up.

My first thought after I caught my breath was *Oh no, I am getting sick.* That was when the panic hit. We still had a whole day of hiking ahead of us. *What was I thinking, coming out to the middle of nowhere?* I was a middle-aged asthmatic with a spare tire and sore . . . wait. My joints didn't hurt anymore.

Then I started worrying about Narelle and Zoe. This was hurricane rain, and the last we heard, the hurricane wasn't supposed to make landfall for a few more days. Had it hit Florida first? The whole time we were in the Pisgah National Forest, we didn't have communication with the outside world. The instructors had been kept in the dark about the weather too. Their only access to tech was the satellite phone for check-ins and emergencies. The weather wasn't bad enough to scrub the expedition, so they didn't know any more than we did.

The instructors tried to ease my fears by saying it was likely a typical mountain storm. I knew it was the hurricane, but it is hard to logically argue you can feel the difference between hurricane rain and a normal storm because you're from Florida.

After I calmed down from my asthma attack, I set into my chores for breaking camp. Everyone else was cooking breakfast or purifying water, and I was trying to untangle the mess I had made of the bear hang rope. I was getting grumpy, when everyone broke out singing "Happy Birthday." It was hilarious and touching. The instructors called into base camp and confirmed it was the outer bands of the hurricane we were feeling, and it had missed Florida. That set my mind at ease—at least about Florida. The fact that my family was safe was the best birthday present ever.

Even though this area of the forest contained a large number of widow-makers, the winds were not supposed to become dangerously high until later in the afternoon. This was our last day of hiking, so it was decided we would press on and hopefully be back to base camp before things got too hairy.

We hiked the rest of the morning and much of the afternoon in a hurricane! Amazingly, my cough and breathing difficulties disappeared completely after about an hour of hiking.

At one point we decided to take a shortcut. The trail zigzagged down the mountain we were on. If we went off the trail, we could cut well over an hour off our hike. Time is important when racing a hurricane. It was wet, steep, and slippery. We knew there would be spills, so we joked that we would have a falling contest. The person with the most dramatic fall would be the winner of . . . well, a moment of glory.

I won. It was the best backward break fall I ever did. We were hiking down a steep and muddy slope. We could barely see the trail that we would intersect below. I slipped and started sliding down the slope. I grabbed a small sapling to stop myself without looking to see if it was sturdy first. I should have looked, because it was a dead tree.

There was a crack as it broke free from rotten roots. Now I was falling down the hill hard and uncontrolled. The only thing I could do was dive for the trunk of another tree and try to wrap my arms around it. My attempt to save myself by virtue of extreme tree hugging didn't work either. Centrifugal force and the weight of my backpack (almost sixty pounds, or twenty-seven kilograms) slung me around to the other side of the tree and ripped me off. I fell backward down the steep side of the hill.

Since I was already horizontal, the only thing I could do was break fall. I landed flat on my pack. Luckily I had packed all the softer things closer to my back. When I hit the ground, I still had a lot of momentum, so somehow I was flipped sideways, and I log-rolled, my backpack and all, the rest of the way down the slope onto the trail below. My ukemi worked. I was shaken up and a little bruised but overall fine.

Our final challenge before reaching base camp was climbing over a high wall with teamwork. When we finished that, we cleaned our gear and settled into a rustic cabin for the night. We went to the bathroom to take hot showers. It was amazing. I was a bit culture-shocked by running water and electricity. We were gone only a week. Some of the courses designed for college kids or troubled youth were six weeks to several months in length. The culture shock of returning to electricity and running water must be immense, let alone the being reimmersed in the world of the internet.

We sat in the bouldering hut at base camp, warm, dry, and clean, did a debriefing, and celebrated our success. Most of the participants had experienced some serious life change, trauma, tragedy, or all three. Perhaps something about it draws people to outdoor wilderness programs. Everyone had unique challenges with the program. Some had a fear of heights when the trail edged toward the side of a cliff. Some struggled with the idea of working as a team. Some struggled to breathe at a higher altitude while carrying a heavy backpack. Oh, wait. That was me. Some did not want to show weakness or admit they needed help. Oh, wait. That was me too.

We talked about what we had accomplished and the personal challenges we had overcome. My first challenge was being medically cleared to participate with asthma. But as Kurt Hahn, founder of Outward Bound, often said, "Your disability is your opportunity."[1]

I had wanted to improve my backcountry skills and get back some of the fitness I'd once had. We had all upped our primitive camping game, purifying river water for our drinking and cooking needs, cooking with camp stoves that could be carried in backpacks, and leaving no trace behind when we left.

It was a week of sensible self-denial. We hiked the mountains with huge packs and rock climbed. The two nights before the hurricane hit, we slept on the summit with just our sleeping bags and no shelter. All in all, it was an incredible experience, and the best thing about it was there were no screens the whole week, no electronic bombardment of the senses the whole time we were out.

My experience with Outward Bound was one of the final steps and the biggest in my recovery from PTSD. Some of it was the training, some of it was the workload, some of it was the bonding and sharing of experiences with others, but the biggest gain was that I was immersed in the wilderness. Nature has an amazing ability to make changes. It has been changing the world for eons, so of course it can be a catalyst to help you make changes within yourself.

The story of the founding of Outward Bound is fascinating. It started out of necessity at the height of World War II. German U-boats were sinking British supply ships at a horrific rate.[2] Thousands of sailors were killed outright when their ships were torpedoed by German subMarines. But hundreds more died of exposure in open lifeboats in the North Atlantic before they could be rescued. On examining the deaths, researchers noticed younger, fitter sailors' survival rate was far lower than the old crusty salts who were presumably much less healthy.

From there Outward Bound was formed to build adaptability, resiliency, and self-confidence in young sailors. These were traits they would need if they had to survive in a lifeboat in the North Atlantic for up to a month. From this, the whole field of outdoor adventure education was born. Since then Outward Bound and many companies and organizations like it have been teaching teens and adults to build inner strength and character through immersion in nature.

Hopefully, you will not need to survive in a lifeboat for days on end, but the life skills learned can be valuable anywhere. There is one thing you need to know before you consider taking a course or sending your kids to one. Although great strides have been made in risk management over the years, the one thing they are not and can never be is completely safe. Lives have been lost, and others have been grievously injured. That is the trade-off. The potential for exponential growth outdoor wilderness programs provide is great, but without the element of risk, they would lose their value.

In our closing ceremony, we talked about the origin of the name Outward Bound, a nautical term for a ship leaving the safety of its harbor and heading for the open seas. We ended with the quote from John A. Shedd: "A ship in harbor is safe, but that is not what ships are built for."[3]

The next day it was time to head back to our respective lives. I was halfway to the airport when I got phone reception and was able to contact Narelle. I was enjoying a burger while watching the news during the layover in Atlanta when my sister called. She sounded frantic. "I have been trying to get ahold of you for two days! Are you okay? There is a hurricane hitting where you are!"

"I'm okay. Calm down. I'm out of North Carolina now."

It wasn't until I watched the news and talked to my sister that I realized the devastation in the state I had just flown out of. Wow, they'd let us hike in that!

No book on adventure would be complete without talking about the great outdoors. After all, most adventurous activities are held outside. In this chapter I talk about how important it is to spend time in nature. It is good for your health. It is good for your happiness and probably the best tool there is for personal growth.

Another great thing about the outdoors is you don't have to do what I did and drop a few thousand dollars on an outdoor adventure course unless you want to. You can reap most of the benefits of Mother Nature for free. Open the door and go outside. Even if you live in an urban environment, there is probably a park you can walk to. There is nothing better than periodic immersion in nature!

Unfortunately, society has become closed off from nature. From the time people wake up in the morning until the time they go to bed, they are plugged into the internet and disconnected from the thing they need most: the great outdoors.

For the majority of human history, people spent most of their time outside—from the early hunter-gathers, who spent only their sleeping hours in caves or primitive shelters, through the agricultural ages, where people were up before dawn to tend crops and take care of livestock. They didn't go inside until dinner. Then the Industrial Revolution happened, and people began to flock to cities to work in factories. This closed people off from nature. Then the internet revolution occurred and with it the shift from factories to offices. Over the past several decades, technology has continued to expand, and now the average person spends more time in front of a screen than outside. With smartphones, even when they are outside, some people are still plugged in to their screens. That isn't healthy.

In his groundbreaking book *Last Child in the Woods*, *New York Times* bestselling author Richard Louv called this disconnect from the natural world a nature-deficit disorder.[4] His book explains some of the reasons society continues to drift apart from nature. It also shows how direct exposure to nature is important for the healthy development of children and is equally

THE POWER OF THE GREAT OUTDOORS ••• 187

important for the ongoing physical and emotional health of children and adults. If you have children or plan on having them, I cannot recommend this book strongly enough. Get it.

One of the main reasons parks and trails are underutilized is fear. For many people who grew up inside on TV and the internet, forests are scary places full of predatory beasts, venomous creepy crawlies, crazed killers, and mutant cannibals.

I can't tell you the number of times I have excitedly told people about a camping trip I was about to embark on, and the first thing they did was hum a few bars of "Dueling Banjos" from the movie *Deliverance*.[5] This movie is over fifty years old, and somehow that jingle has stood the test of time as the anthem for false beliefs people hold that if they venture into the wilderness, they will be raped and murdered by inbred hillbillies. It is not true. Most hillbillies I have met—even the inbred ones—are nice people.

Statistically, you are far safer in the bush than in the city. A recent study showed that on the Appalachian Trail, for every hundred thousand people using the trail, there were .0072 murders.[6] The murder rate in the average city is 7.35 per hundred thousand people. You are 968 times more likely to be murdered in an urban environment than on a trail. Despite that, people have watched too many horror movies depicting the wilderness as a dangerous place, and because they see it on-screen, they believe it.

The other problem is the news. In the rare event something bad happens in the wilderness, it is plastered all over the news. People see it multiple times. Each time you see a piece on the news about something horrific, it registers as a separate event in some part of your mind. Every time a new detail about the same tragedy is revealed, there is another news segment to report it. One event can easily be registered as forty or fifty events in your subconscious if you are following a case. This can greatly magnify your perception of the likelihood of danger if you venture into the wild. For that reason, people think of the forest as a more dangerous place than it is. But the truth is forests are a lot safer than city streets. That's where you should be afraid.

You are more likely to be attacked in the parking lot of your average shopping mall than in the woods. Murders at malls and fast-food restaurants are more common and therefore hardly mentioned in the news. If you are afraid of the great outdoors, this is a chance to use some of the tools for overcoming fear you learned in chapter 5.

I implore you to spend time outside in nature. Most of us intuitively know it is good to be outside. We are more relaxed, more comfortable, and happier. The outdoors is a place for renewal. I hope you frequently experience how good it is for your body and mind to spend time out in nature.

Use the advice my mother gave me as a kid: go outside and play. Even as an adult you can go outside and play. While this is easy if you don't overthink it, sometimes people feel they need a formal process for everything, including immersing themselves in nature. Luckily over the past few decades, several of these have emerged.

Shinrin-yoku, or forest bathing,[7] emerged in Japan in the 1980s. First proposed in 1982 by the Forest Agency of Japan, forest bathing was designed as a form of therapy. Even back in the eighties, burnout from technology coupled with the anxiety produced by living in densely populated cities, Japan was heading toward a mental health crisis. The government came up with forest bathing. It was meant to give residents a way to connect with and a desire to protect the country's forests. Japan began to research the benefits of forest bathing. After some extraordinary results, the rest of the world followed.

Although shinrin-yoku is a relatively modern pastime, people in Japan have known the benefits of immersion in nature since ancient times. The Yamabushi[8] or Shugenja were hermit/warrior monks who practiced the religion of Shugendo, an eclectic mix of esoteric Buddhism, Shintoism, and nature worship. Many people in feudal Japan believed the Yamabushi had mystical powers, some going so far as to say they were *tengu*, or forest spirits that were half bird and half man.

Even to this day Yamabushi train deep in the mountains. They are known to do extreme forms of training in the name of self-discipline and self-improvement. Facing danger and extreme hardship are part of the training. The hardship is not the core of their training, but being one with nature is. One monk I saw interviewed said, "Everyone knows us as ones that hang off cliffs with ropes, walk through burning-hot coals, and stand under icy waterfalls. But the thing we do most is take very long walks on the mountain trails in complete silence." To them, spirituality is hiking along their sacred mountain trails, along rivers, and through forests.

Japan is not the only place the ancients revered walking in nature. The medical benefits of taking a walk outside were touted as far back as Hippocrates. The ancient Greek doctor and philosopher said, "Walking is man's best medicine."[9]

Almost every ancient or Indigenous culture held some belief in the importance of walking in the wilderness as a component of personal and spiritual growth. This includes my adoptive country, where the term *walkabout* comes from.

The sign in the front of the Rainforest Gallery nature walk on the way up to Mount Donna Buang, not far from where I live, reads:

Question: What do many of the biblical characters, knights of the Middle Ages, ancient shamans, and the initiation rites of many Indigenous peoples have in common?

Answer: Time alone in the wilderness.

Originally *walkabout* was used to describe an Australian Aboriginal rite of passage. It was a physical and spiritual journey for Indigenous Australians (First Nations people). This was often the transition to manhood for adolescent boys. They walked into the bush and disappeared. Sometimes these walks took several months or even a year. During this time they lived off the land. Later the definition of *walkabout* was colloquially broadened to any bushwalk or short walk used as an escape from stress. That is still important.

I still remember the first time I hiked up into the Dandenong Ranges. One thing Australia does well is include plenty of green space and walking trails in the suburbs and even urban areas. One day I grabbed a bottle of Gatorade and a couple of bottles of water and decided to walk up into the mountains, which were only a few miles away. I started in the suburbs, which gave way to farmland, then mountain and forest.

The climb was exhausting at first, and every breath seemed to be a struggle. Then I began to get a rhythm. The farther I walked, the easier it became. The birds flew closer. It was as if when I started I was an outsider, something to be feared. Then I began to blend into the background, as if I was becoming part of the natural world around me. I continued upward, pausing only long enough to drink.

I had been hiking for about four hours when the water gave out. The sky began to darken, and I started worrying that I had lost my way. I still felt exhilarated, but I was getting delirious. As I started heading down, a kookaburra landed on a log in front of me. We stared at each other for quite some time. I began to wonder if he had some wisdom to impart. It would have been of little surprise if he opened his beak and started speaking, telling me of the wonders of the bush.

As I continued my descent in the twilight, the wallabies started to come out. Wallabies are the kangaroo's smaller, cuter cousin. They are nocturnal, solitary, and extremely shy. I would walk right by them, and they would sit very still, but if I stopped, I guess they assumed I had sighted them and would hop off. Sometimes I stopped for a few seconds, and invariably a wallaby I hadn't seen would hop off into the bush. They can jump great distances when they want to. One of them looked like he easily cleared ten feet in a hop. I have since grown used to seeing wallabies and kangaroos on my bushwalks, but back then I was totally amazed by them.

I approached the bottom of the mountain. As I did, I heard the screeching of many parrots. I came to a clearing, and there, gathering in the twilight, were hundreds of wild cockatoos. There were fights over space to roost for the evening. I could make out the bright white of the "cockys" silhouetted against the gray background of the trees. It was quite a sight to behold.

I continued past houses as the cockatoos screeched and fought for the best trees to roost in for the night. I didn't know how anyone could live so close to such a racket. Now I do. I wake up to them squawking in my back tree every morning. I haven't used an alarm clock in years.

Finally, I returned to civilization and continued along the road in the dark. When I got back, I had blisters on my feet, and my legs were extremely sore for a couple of days, but it was a good first immersion in the Australian bush.

Whenever you get a chance, take a walk. The more natural the surroundings you walk in, the better. Scottish-American naturalist John Muir, "Father of the National Parks," aptly said, "In every walk in nature one receives far more than he seeks."[10]

Thomas Jefferson, the architect of the American Declaration of Independence and third US president, highly recommended walking in nature to clear your head: "Walking is the very best exercise. Habituate yourself to walk very far."[11]

Of course, there are plenty of ways to enjoy the benefits of the outdoors without having to blister your feet. Nature sketching and journaling are new hobbies for me. Both are a great way to intrinsically combine science and art. Nature journaling also is a great way to practice mindfulness. You can expand your vision as you duplicate a landscape. You can change up and narrow your focus on the fine details as you study a single insect or plant.

You can reap many of the rewards nature offers by finding a clearing, spreading out a blanket, and having a picnic. Sitting on a bench in the park and reading a book or watching the birds can be very beneficial.

My favorite place in the world is the Daintree Rainforest[12] in far north Queensland. I have never felt so at home in a place. The Daintree is the oldest living tropical rainforest in the world and is estimated to date back 120 million years. With its lush tropical landscape, mountains, pristine beaches, and vast biodiversity, the Daintree is awe-inspiring.

Legendary naturalist David Attenborough called the Daintree "the most extraordinary place on Earth."[13] If you are ever in that part of the world, it's worth checking out. Yes, there is a downside. It's hot, wet, and some of the wildlife can kill you if you are not careful. This just adds to the charm of the place, if you ask me.

The Daintree is home to the ultimate apex predator of the reptile world, the saltwater crocodile. Although similar in appearance, salties are far more dangerous than the American alligators I am used to. They are opportunistic hunters and will not hesitate to kill humans. Salties are not restricted to salt water as their name would imply either. They are equally capable of ambushing from a river or any pond big enough to conceal them, as they are from the open ocean. The Daintree is also the home of Cassowaries, considered the world's most dangerous birds. Think of a brightly colored red and blue sharp beaked ostrich with a helmet and a dagger for a toenail and you have a Cassowary. That is just to name a couple of the more hazardous animals.

The Daintree is on the Cape York Peninsula near the top of Australia, and I live in Melbourne, down at the bottom, so I don't get there much. Regardless of whether I am in the Daintree's Cape Tribulation or in the city park down the street from home, my body instinctively knows it's well to be outdoors. Yours probably does too, if you listen to it.

If you need convincing on an intellectual level, I will introduce you to the value of being in the great outdoors. Below are some of the many benefits of being outside and immersed in nature. The reasons to do this are many, but I touch on a few. Keep in mind this list barely scratches the surface of the importance of spending time in nature.

Stress relief. If you are feeling stressed, there is probably nothing more effective than unplugging from technology and getting out in nature. Being out in nature creates a feeling of well-being. One study found that students who stayed in the forest for two nights had a lower resting heart rate and much lower levels of cortisol than a control group that spent that time in the city.[14]

Sometimes even a view of nature through a window can have a calming effect on people working in an office. When stress starts firing off the fight-or-flight response, the best thing to do is pop outside for a few minutes. Get out and walk near some trees.

Restored mental energy. Everyone experiences times when it feels like they have hit the wall. You have been working hard, and you just can't think straight anymore. That is called mental fatigue. The speed of stimulus technology like television, computers, and phones all competing for your attention contribute to this mental fatigue.

Attention restoration theory tells us that natural environments contain "soft fascinations" you can take in without much mental effort. Soft fascinations are things like trees blowing in the wind, rocks, cloud formations, waves, sunsets, and the flow of a gurgling stream. The lack of mental effort while taking in these things allows the mind to rest and rejuvenate.

One paper on attention restoration theory put it this way: "Nature, which is filled with intriguing stimuli, modestly grabs attention in a bottom-up fashion, allowing top-down directed-attention abilities a chance to replenish. Unlike natural environments, urban environments are filled with stimulation that captures attention dramatically and additionally requires directed attention (e.g., to avoid being hit by a car), making them less restorative."[15] Having been almost hit by cars while walking in urban environments on a few occasions, I can attest to the truth of this statement.

Improved concentration/focus. I listed these benefits separately, but they are all interrelated and synergistic. For instance, this and the next benefit are largely due to the last one. I must admit I belong to a segment of the population that experiences this benefit the most. As someone who has dealt with ADHD all my life, I have always intuitively known that going outside and exercising makes a big difference in my ability to concentrate.

Research has found that children with ADHD, when exposed to nature, show vast improvement in symptoms across the board, including a reduction in impulsiveness and hyperactivity.[16] Of course, you don't have to have ADHD to get the benefit, but for people with ADHD, the effects are profound.

Enhanced memory. With the reduction of attention fatigue and improved concentration, it stands to reason memory or retention of information is also improved. University of Michigan students were given a memory test and divided into two groups. Half took a walk in the arboretum, and half took a walk down a city street. They retook the test. The ones who'd walked in the arboretum scored 20 percent higher, and the ones who'd walked down the street had no significant improvement.[17]

Improved mental health. Time outside can improve several types of mental illnesses, but the biggest effects seem to be as an antidepressant and a relief from anxiety. More studies are being done about the effects of the outdoors on depression, and they conclude that time in the forest—especially combined with exercise—significantly reduces depression and anxiety.[18]

Some doctors write prescriptions for time outside. One study found outdoor walks "useful clinically as a supplement to existing treatments"[19] for major depressive disorder. Sunlight helps elevate levels of serotonin and other feel-good hormones. Even when my PTSD was at its worst, a simple walk in the woods could drastically reduce my symptoms. When I was immersed in verdant surroundings, concentrating on walking or watching animals and birds, the tremors that plagued me most of the day went away for a while.

Enhanced creativity.[20] Entrepreneurs, CEOs, and artistic types often tout the benefits of going for a walk when they are feeling stuck on a project or in need of creative inspiration. Steve Jobs, cofounder and former CEO of Apple, was known for this. One of the reasons scientists think walking in nature is good for creativity is it gives the brain a much-needed rest that allows the system to relax, and when we relax we tend to be more creative.

Another reason is that diversity of sensory information helps you be open to new experiences, and that can cause you to start thinking of new possibilities. Of course, creativity isn't just for the creation of art. It is often a necessary component in problem-solving. There is an old saying: you can't solve a problem from inside it. Going outside physically can metaphorically take you outside that problem.

A University of Utah experiment showed that subjects who went backpacking in the wilderness for four days without electronic devices scored 50 percent higher on a creative problem-solving test.[21] The simple truth is, if you want to get creative, get outside.

Vitamin D production. Some foods contain trace amounts of vitamin D, but the best way to get it is when your body produces it itself. It does this when your skin is exposed to sunlight. That is why vitamin D is called the sunshine vitamin. Your bones need it; your blood needs it.

Vitamin D[22] is important for a healthy immune system. For all the hype there used to be about taking vitamin C to fight off colds and respiratory infections, nowadays most doctors tell you having enough vitamin D is more important than vitamin C.

Immune boost. Besides the production of vitamin D, some of the improved functions of the immune system come from the relaxing effect of being out in nature. This engages the parasympathetic nervous system and allows the production of white blood cells and hormones associated with longevity.

Another fascinating effect of being in nature is something trees produce. In 2005 the Japanese government did a study on the effects of forest bathing on the immune system.[23] Phytoncides, chemicals put out by trees, boost the immune system, including increasing the production of human natural killer cells. These are the cells in your body that kill viruses, bacteria, and even cancer cells.

Scientists widely believe that plants and trees produce antimicrobial phytoncides to protect themselves against wood-destroying organisms like fungus and mold. Phytoncides are then dispersed into the air like pollen and the other pheromones plants produce to communicate.

Increased lifespan. Hey, who doesn't want to live a longer life? With all the other health benefits of the great outdoors, you can certainly see how it might improve longevity. Cumulatively these benefits lead to a longer, healthier life. The less green someone's surroundings are, the higher the mortality rate. The more verdant your neighborhood, the longer your life expectancy tends to be.[24]

As well as extending your life, nature can vastly improve your quality of life. Just being outside brings joy to most people. The positive effects of nature on health, mood, and performance stand a good chance of not only prolonging your life but also making that time worthwhile. When it comes to living, both quantity and quality count.

EXERCISE

The exercise for this chapter is a simple procedure in the practice of mindfulness in nature. Go outside for a long walk. A forest or natural setting is preferable. This could even be a beach if it is not crowded.

Don't wear headphones or bring your phone with you if you can safely avoid it. After you have been walking for a considerable while, stop and name five things you see. You can bring a journal and write them down if you want or just say them aloud. Then resume walking, and after some time, stop and notice five things you can hear. After you have done that, continue walking for a while, then stop and name five things you can feel. Do the same with smell and taste. After you have done all the senses, notice what it was like. Were any hard to come up with five different things for?

When people do the walking exercise, most find coming up with five things they see easy because humans tend to rely on the sense of sight. Tasting five things tends to be the hardest.

This exercise is simple but powerful. It helps you get in touch with your senses and makes you focus on the moment. Doing it regularly helps build self-awareness and gets the creative juices flowing.

I have seen versions of it taught in everything from Zen mediation, to self-defense classes, to business management settings. While this exercise might not be as adventurous as some of the more pulse-pounding suggestions in the book, mindful observation is an important aspect of being expeditionary. Focusing on the natural world around you with your senses is a great way to get out of your head and thus another tool in managing fear and anxiety.

If you have children, do this exercise with them. This is especially effective if your kid is a talker, like mine. When we are hiking, she likes to talk, and it is usually about whatever pops into her head, random thoughts, or some drama that happened in school a year ago. When we do the sensory exercise in the bush, it brings her back to the here and now, and she has a much better appreciation for the beauty and wonder all around her. This is a nice way to turn off the internal noise.

I won't call this next one an exercise, but it might be something to try. Since this is a book on being adventurous, here is a tip on an inexpensive way to adrenalize your proverbial walk in the park. Take a walk in the woods at night under the cover of darkness! I know this idea isn't for everybody. You be the judge if this is something you want to try or if it will forever be relegated to your nope list.

Night walking has a host of benefits you don't get from day walking. First, no matter what part of the world you are in, a considerable amount of wildlife is nocturnal. (This is especially true in Australia.) This gives you a chance to see critters you wouldn't normally see in the diurnal world.

You have to rely on your night vision. In the daytime, the eyes use cone cells to see fine detail, but at night your eyes use rods. They don't have as high a resolution as cones and give up the ability to distinguish color, but they make up for it with the ability to see in almost complete darkness.

You take in different details with night vision. Even familiar areas seem new, different, and sometimes strange in the dark. This strangeness will automatically get the norepinephrine pumping, making you more alert. You, like me, might feel more alive outside at night.

In good lighting, humans tend to favor sight. It goes to figure if you reduce the capacity to see, your other senses are heightened. Hearing and olfactory, or smell, tend to be heightened the most. A lot of plants put out more fragrance at night. It is usually quieter, so you can hear subtler noises, like frogs and insects.

Walking at night can be somewhat dangerous. I know this firsthand. If you are going to partake in night walks, there are a few guidelines.

Pick a place that isn't too isolated, like a small park or nature reserve surrounded by homes or at least surrounded by roads or fences so you have boundaries. At night it is easy to get disoriented and lost, even in a location you know well. If you have boundaries surrounding your chosen location, you can get only so lost. The boundaries should be things that stop you or you can tell in the dark you are about to get out of your prescribed walking area but not anything you can fall off or into. Cliffs and large rivers are not things to use as boundaries. The boundary itself should not pose a danger.

Let a couple of trusted friends or family members know where you are going. Call them, text them, or instant message them. Do not post that you are going alone to an isolated place on social media. You may have a stalker and not know it.

Don't break the law. Make sure it is legal. Don't walk on private property you don't have permission to be on. Many public parks close at dusk, so make sure you are allowed to be there.

Bring your phone. Make sure it's fully charged. Know in advance if you have reception everywhere in the park. Don't bring headphones. You need your hearing. Keep your phone for emergencies only. Don't scroll or even look at the screen if you don't have to. If you do, you will destroy your night vision and reduce your situational awareness.

One time I took my phone out to take a picture of a wombat. I accidentally had it set in selfie mode. When I took the picture, I blinded myself with the flash. Because I was walking on uneven ground, I had to wait in that spot for quite a while for my night vision to come back before resuming my hike.

Understand that the nighttime belongs to predators, both animal and human. I recommend being armed. Bring a can of pepper (capsicum) spray, a knife, or even a walking stick, if you know how to use it. You probably won't run into trouble, but it is good to be prepared. A whistle or portable siren is also a good idea.

If you are doing this solo, you are already tempting fate, so know if there is danger about the place that has hit the news. If so, take a pass. Information like a mountain lion spotted in the area or someone raped or robbed there last week is stuff you should know that might make that location off-limits.

Bring a headlamp or flashlight. I prefer to use a headlamp because it allows the use of my hands. I always bring a headlamp on night hikes but rarely use it. It's more for emergencies or if I hear an animal and want to get a good look at it.

Most nocturnal animals have a layer of tissue behind their retinas designed to reflect light back through their eyes a second time. This helps them see better at night, but it gives away well-hidden animals if you shine a light in their general direction. The light reflects off their eyes, making them appear to glow brightly. It is a dead giveaway for an otherwise well-hidden critter.

Make sure your light has fresh batteries. One night while hiking I ran smack into the middle of a mob of kangaroos. I went to turn on my headlamp, and the batteries were dead. There were a couple of intense moments as I waded through the mob in the dark, trying to find and then keep my distance from the alpha male. Male kangaroos are nothing to mess with. They can kickbox better than the best Muay Thai fighters in the world. They also have very sharp claws and have occasionally killed people. For some reason, male roos are more aggressive at night, so I try to stay wary.

If you are going to walk without the light on like I do, you need to give your eyes ten to fifteen minutes to adjust to the low light conditions before you start moving. If you need to use your light or encounter someone with a light, but you want to retain your night vision without having to wait another ten to fifteen minutes, close one eye while the light is on.

If you are not used to walking in darkness, it can be daunting. A night walk can be a real test of your ability to cope with fear. It can be considerably more frightening for women than for men. That's completely understandable. Of course, I didn't say anything about having to do it alone. Feel free to bring a friend or several. The more the merrier, the less the scarier.

Sometimes I take Narelle and Zoe on night walks. We don't always see wildlife at night, but sometimes we are lucky and see owls, tawny frogmouths, bats, and possums. When the gum trees are flowering, sometimes we see flying foxes. These are giant fruit bats with cute faces.

Nighttime can bring out imaginative fears. One night when Zoe was younger, we were walking back to the house after a short bushwalk through the reserve in our neighborhood. As we walked, we talked about supernatural creatures, as you do when walking with a ten-year-old at night. Suddenly above our heads we saw a flash of movement in our peripheral vision. We were startled, but Zoe just about jumped out of her skin, thinking it was a ghost flying overhead. When we looked up, we saw an adorable brushtail possum looking down at us from the telephone line he was using as a high wire to travel around the neighborhood.

When I am by myself most nights, I feel totally in tune with my environment, with no trace of fear. I am completely comfortable. I am totally in the moment. Occasionally, though, it's the opposite. Something doesn't feel right, and I am nervous. That is when I go through my fear management strategies.

Going camping gives you a chance to get in some night walks, since you are already in the wilderness. If you are camping in a prescribed campground, you already have permission to be there. No one can say, "Hey, you are not allowed to be in this park at night," because that is what a campground is for.

As much as I loved the recreational vehicle, I have gone back to tent camping because I like the "roughing it" aspect. Some people have never seen the night sky without the background light pollution of the city. There is nothing quite like staring up at the night sky on a clear night when the only ambient light around is the light from your campfire. If your field vision isn't restricted by trees and mountains, you can see thousands of stars. It is awe-inspiring and humbling.

Day or night, take some time to get out in nature. You will be glad you did. You owe it to yourself. Your mind, body, and soul will thank you.

Chapter 8:

Reigniting the Passion of Childhood Dreams

A guided missile accomplishes its goal by going forward, making errors, and continually correcting them.
— Maxwell Maltz

Remember when you were a kid? Magic was real, and everything seemed possible. Most of us thought we could be anything we wanted when we grew up.

This chapter is about taking back that feeling of being a kid. It's about believing you can do anything even if the adults in the room say you can't. This chapter is about breaking through the limits other people put on you. This chapter is about getting creative and doing the things you have always dreamed about.

Yes, I do live in the real world. There are certain impossibilities. You can't control other people. There are laws of the universe and of physics that cannot be broken. Or can they? Even the concrete laws of physics started being flexible when scientists discovered the quantum universe. The rules can be bent.

If you are still breathing, it's never too late. Perhaps it won't look exactly like what you pictured when you were little, but on some level, in some way, you can make your dreams a reality, even the forgotten ones from when you were a child. This includes the silly ones, the embarrassing ones. I think an early success in this area is why I was able to do some of the amazing things I have done like traveling around the world.

Be Careful What You Wish For

My father was a blue-collar worker. When I was little, my dad came home from work very tired. We had a screened-in front porch, and he liked to unwind after dinner by sitting on the porch and reading the newspaper. I was an energetic kid and used to try to get him to play with me, and, failing that, I would berate him with questions like children often do. It would drive him crazy.

When I was six, I had a little car with a spring-loaded missile launcher on the top. It would be illegal now, because it was the perfect size for putting somebody's eye out. One day I ran out to the porch, jumping up and down until my dad finally looked up from his paper.

"Dad! Dad! I want a car with a missile launcher on the top," I exclaimed.

My dad, kind of annoyed, responded with "You already have one of those. We . . . um, I mean Santa got you one for Christmas."

"No, not a toy one," I retorted excitedly. "A real one when I grow up!"

My dad must have had a bad day and was in no mood for being interrupted from reading his paper by my ridiculous fantasies. He thought this day he would shut me down. He raised his voice and said, "No, you can't have a car with a rocket launcher when you grow up. That's ridiculous! Don't be silly. James Bond isn't real. People don't have cars with missile launchers!"

He thought that would be the end of it. But I didn't understand. There were missile launchers, and there were cars, so why couldn't I have a car with a missile launcher? His dismissiveness filled my young heart with indignant rage. I screamed back in defiance, "When I grow up, I am going to have a car with a missile launcher! You'll see!" Then I ran off as fast as I could before my dad had a chance to punish me for my insolence.

I didn't realize it at the time, but the energy and passion with which I committed this unusual demand to my unconscious mind made it begin working on how to accomplish the task. I didn't even remember the incident in high school. But somewhere in my subconscious, my mind was working toward the goal I set when I was six.

In my junior year of high school, I got my first car. It was a beat-up old Firebird. On my dashboard I mounted a little switch with a sign I bought at a novelty store that said *missile launcher*. Of course, it didn't do anything, but I thought it was cool, and it got some laughs.

Then the seed I planted so long before—well, I had forgotten about it, germinated it, and it blossomed into reality. I didn't think about the childhood incident until I was in the Marines and graduating from the School of Infantry. We were in formation receiving our diplomas. I looked down at mine, and that's when I remembered that event from my childhood, and I realized what I had done. My new Military Occupational Specialty was 0352, Antitank Assault Guided Missileman. That's when I realized my first career choice was created long before, the whim of my six-year-old self.

Now, you could argue that both the TOW[1] weapon system I operated and the Humvee it was mounted on were the property of the US government—and so was I, for that matter. But in effect, I had a car with a missile launcher on top! At the tender age of nineteen, I had achieved something ridiculous. Goal: have a car with a missile launcher on it. Check.

It was this connection that enabled me to do things like figure out how to travel the world with a budget of zero. When people told me, "You can't do that," I simply didn't believe them because I had already done the preposterous and got myself a car with a missile launcher on top.

Yes, if my therapist reads this book, he will probably make a note that I have father issues and spent an unnecessary amount of time and energy proving my dad wrong. My dad had all these pithy sayings that he thought were his way of imparting wisdom. The problem was they came from his model of the world. My model was completely different. One of his favorite sayings when I was a teenager was "If all your friends were jumping off a bridge, would you jump too?"

This one stuck in my mind, even after I had grown up. One day I sent him a picture of me doing a forward rappel from an overpass in Okinawa with a caption that read, "My friends were all jumping off this bridge, so I did too." Yes, I know his saying was my dad's way of trying to protect me from the dangers of peer pressure and groupthink. To my dad the rule was simple: jumping from a bridge meant certain death. However, I was a contrarian and found an exception to the rule, so his analogy didn't apply.

My point is as we grow, we are given rules to live by. Normally they are made to keep us safe and civil with each other, and that is a good thing. But sometimes they are made by people who get off on having some measure of power over others. Even when there is no malice behind them, the problem is usually that the people who espouse the rules have no concept of how or when they can be bent or broken or are simply not applicable.

It is time to break free, *Matrix* style. It's time to say to yourself, "Maybe there really is no box to think outside of." I want you to fulfill a childhood dream as an exercise. It should be ambitious. Feel free to choose something that may even seem to be preposterous. The more audacious the dream, the better—something the adult in you thinks cannot be done. No judgment here—the weirder the better. Maybe it's something so over the top you might be embarrassed to talk about it with other adults.

Of all the exercises in this book, this one is the most important and possibly the most fun. Once you do something you didn't think you could do, maybe even something the adult in you forgot about, your brain will be more open to possibilities in the future.

If the idea of what you want to do is embarrassing, that is so much better.

It's funny how we can be conditioned to be ashamed of our dreams, isn't it? For many, one of the biggest fears that stop people from fulfilling dreams is the fear of what others will think. Who cares? Sometimes the people who ridicule you the most end up admiring your ability to do what you want. You may even inspire others to follow their dreams too.

This exercise has a host of benefits, not the least of which is it sharpens your attentional control. Attentional control, put simply, is your ability to pay attention to and focus on the things that matter. I will take it a step further and say it's the ability to *focus on the things that matter to you*. I don't mean things you *think* should matter but things that mean something to you deeply and personally. Developing attentional control will help you ignore distractions like the critics who try to derail you on your way to reaching your goals. For some of us, the inner critic can be the biggest distracter of all.

Fulfilling the dream doesn't have to be a change of career unless you want it to. It can be a new hobby or side hustle, or perhaps volunteering will fulfill the desire. Maybe it's trying something new. There was a reason you had this dream when you were younger. Perhaps there is a deep reason to connect with it now.

I came up with this exercise a couple of years ago. I did it myself, and it changed my life. I will share my experience after you go through the exercise.

EXERCISE

Pick a childhood dream or ambition. What was something you wanted to do?

- Get out a sheet of paper and get ready to write.
- First, write it out as a headline, just one quick line in big bold letters.
- Next, write a description with as much detail as you can.
- How will you fit your dream into reality? How will you make it possible?
- What did it mean to you when you were young?
- What does or what could it mean to you now?
- Why is it important to you?
- What did thinking about it do for you?
- What would accomplishing that dream do for you now?
- How would it make you feel?
- If you accomplished it, what other areas of your life do you think would be improved?
- Create an action plan.

If you picked something you think is impossible, good. Redefine it until it's possible. Brainstorm and bend the rules if you must. The idea of this exercise is to do something that you may have previously thought of as unrealistic. However, if you have specific criteria to fulfill your dream, you may have to broaden them or generalize them more.

For instance, if your dream was to be starting quarterback in the Super Bowl, and you are over forty, out of shape, and haven't played football since high school, you may have to tweak that dream to make it attainable.

You don't want it to be too easy either. You want to make this difficult but possible. You may have to massage your dream by creating a definition of success you decide on. Make it a task you find challenging but achievable, not so hard you are likely to give up but hard enough the success makes you proud.

On that note, I discourage you from defining your dream as anything that requires a meteoric rise to fame. When the dream is results-driven, like wanting to be famous, often the person is trying to fill an inner need for validation for their ego instead of the enjoyment of doing.

If you keep your dream process driven instead of focusing on some idealized result, you will get more value out of it and have more fun in the process. For example, "I want to learn to play the *blank* and be the best musician I can be" as opposed to "I want to be a rock god with millions of fans frothing at the mouth when they see me." Again, this is your choice, but from everything I see and hear, fame is overrated.

You can certainly turn your passion into a business, and with enough drive, dedication, time, and luck, you could become world class. Plenty of books will tell you to do this, but for this exercise I want you to focus on your dream hedonically. That is, think of it for the sake of pure pleasure, and if you would like to, indulge in a fair amount of self-gratification. Too many people focus on achieving a result and burn themselves out, killing the passion for the thing they once loved.

If you need to redefine your dream so it fits with your life now, do it. Remember to consider how it will affect the ecology of your relationships. I don't want any angry emails from estranged spouses telling me families were abandoned because I told someone to chase their childhood dream.

You are limited by only your own imagination here. Get creative! Also bear in mind I am not above using bizarre technicalities to bend my perception of reality and give myself a win. For instance, when most parents' kids ask them for a pet dragon, they give them an unequivocal *no*. "Dragons are not real! They don't exist, so you can't have one. End of discussion."

Well, not us. We bought Zoe a bearded dragon. Now, I know what you're thinking, but hear me out. If you look him up (under the genus *pagona*) in a herpetology book, it says "bearded dragon," not "bearded lizard," so technically he is a real dragon. After all, if the scientific authorities who specialize in reptiles are willing to put down on paper that he is a dragon, who am I to argue?

Besides, if you look at his triangular head and spiky scales, he certainly looks more like the mythical creature for which he is named than he does a garden variety *anole*. No, he is not forty feet long, and he can't breathe fire, thank goodness. No, he doesn't have wings and can't fly. Lack of wings hasn't stopped him from trying, though. He has been known to get a running start and then dive out of his habitat or sail off the end of the coffee table. He is a bit of a dunderhead, but who knows? Maybe the dragon has a childhood dream of flying.

I used to think people who carried their pampered puppies in designer handbags were weird, but then I learned becoming a beardie owner is kind of like joining a cult. People are crazy about their lizards. My wife subscribes to at least a dozen platforms of people dressing up their dragons in silly costumes. It's insane.

That is life, owning a real live dragon. Make no mistake. Learning

REIGNITING THE PASSION OF CHILDHOOD DREAMS ... 211

to indulge in fantasy is part of the process. This also makes the serious business of setting goals a lot more fun. Goal: to have a pet dragon. Check. Completely impossible or easily achievable—it's totally up to you.

My point is you set the bar for how you define the achievement of the goal. It is your dream. Only you can set the criteria for its fulfillment. You can make it as simple or challenging as you want. Technicalities like using a herpetology book to call our pet lizard a dragon is one example of how to creatively define reality to fit your vision.

What was my childhood dream that seemed silly but became the basis of this exercise? Well, in some ways I am a product of the 1980s. Back then, one of the big fads was a mass fascination with ninjas. There were scores of cheesy ninja movies. A ton of books about ninjas were published, and suddenly every karate teacher and their mom had some sort of ninja connection.

When I was eleven years old, I wanted to be a ninja when I grew up. That was my dream career. I think this is a common dream, but it was particularly prevalent in the 1980s when I was growing up.

In case you don't know what a ninja is: shinobi, as they were called back in the day, were an elite class of warrior in feudal Japan. They started out as defenders of their families and home province and slowly built the reputation of master spies, experts in reconnaissance, infiltration, sabotage, and other methods of guerrilla warfare. Yes, there is not a huge demand for ninjas in the modern job market, but that's what I wanted to be when I grew up.

Without getting deep into the history of ninjas, they essentially filled the role of modern-day Special Forces or secret agents. They are often wrongly depicted in movies as masked, always wearing all black, and being ruthless mercenary assassins.

When I was eleven, I watched every ninja movie and show I could. Much like with my shark obsession, I read books and magazines about them. I sparred with my best friend. I talked about ninjas to my family and friends until they were sick of hearing about them.

Then one day there was an incident at school with some shuriken (star-shaped throwing knives often associated with ninjas). I was suspended from school, and my parents withdrew me from the karate class I was taking at our local community center. I was disheartened and ashamed. And just like that, my dreams of a future career as a ninja were dashed.

Almost four decades later, at an age when most historical ninjas were already dead, I decided to study the ways of Japan's ancient shadow warriors in earnest. I started taking ninjutsu (Bujinkan Budō Taijutsu).[2] I wasn't sure my body would be able to take it when I started. My aikido days had ended with a shoulder operation, and I wasn't sure if it could withstand the strain even years later. But I did it, and training in ninjutsu has been one of the best things I have ever done. It is beneficial in more ways than I can explain.

It helps improve my fitness level, coordination, and cognitive processing. I am getting older, so injuries don't heal as quickly as they used to, but I can do acrobatic things now that I couldn't do in my twenties. I have made practical gains in the ability to defend myself, and that helps my self-confidence.

A considerable amount of spiritual and philosophical training helps me relax in stressful situations. This training has helped immensely in overcoming the ˋ that once plagued my life. I am learning about another culture, the military history of that culture, and even a bit of another language. Last, ninjutsu is super fun. Even when my arm is pinned in an excruciatingly painful joint lock, I am having the time of my life!

Yes, telling people I am training in ninjutsu is embarrassing—or at least it was when I started. When you are eleven and tell people you are a ninja, the adults in the room are like, "Oh, wow, doesn't he have a great imagination!" When you are in your fifties and tell people you train in ninjutsu or heaven forbid call yourself a ninja, normally you get one of two reactions. Some people instinctively pull away, afraid. "What are you—some kind of mercenary assassin?"

The other reaction is they laugh. When I started, I made the mistake of telling coworkers I was taking ninjutsu. They thought this was hilarious and used it to joke about me. Grown men jumped around, chopping and kicking the air, adding the sound effects of a badly choreographed 1970s kung fu movie. One guy threw out his back trying to make fun of me. At first, I found this embarrassing, but now I laugh and play along with them, remembering never to take myself too seriously. I might not be able to sing, but I make very good bad-kung-fu-movie sound effects.

Yes, I have had to tweak my dream to make it a reality. Of course, some say, "You are not a real ninja," and from a certain perspective, they are right. If you want to take the dry, boring, historical way of looking at things, all the real ninja died a long time ago. I do not live in feudal Japan. I am not even remotely Japanese.

It is not a career. When I think about it, if I really wanted a career infiltrating the fortifications of tyrannical warlords, I probably would have stayed in the Marines. Yes, some of this is fantasy. If I ever have reason to use a sword or sickle and chain or any of the other bizarre weapons we train with, not only has something gone drastically wrong in my life but also with the world at large. I mean like zombie apocalypse wrong!

Overall, I treat it like a hobby. Some people build model trains. Some people paint. Some people take classes in interpretive dance. I take ninja classes. It keeps me busy and active. That is enough to fulfill my childhood dream, as I interpret it now. Goal: be a ninja when I grow up. Check.

Who knew the silly dream of an eleven-year-old would be fulfilled? How could I have known I would find it useful in my life as a "grown-up"? I followed my dream and found a way to make it a reality without getting arrested, at least so far. Now it's your turn. What is the first step you must take? Is it research? Do you already know what you need to do? Write down the first actionable step. Then do it. Make the dream a reality. You will be so glad you did!

Fifty Things to Do Before You Die

The childhood dream is a big confidence builder. Once you have the ball rolling on that, it is time to look at other things you have always wanted to do. If you do the ridiculous, the other things don't seem so out there.

Most people have things churning around in their heads that they would like to do someday. Once you pull off the first one, you can get on with fulfilling other dreams, maybe even ones you don't yet know you have. Getting them on paper is more powerful than letting them bounce around your head randomly. That is where the list comes in. It is time to create a list of fifty things you want to do before you die. This is by far the most powerful exercise for crafting the kind of life you want. Creating the list and implementing it will have a profound effect.

You may have heard of this as a bucket list—a list of things you want to do before you kick the bucket. Bucket lists are a popular exercise, so you may have done it before. That doesn't lessen the value of it and doing it again will not hurt. If you have done it before, how many things have you crossed off your list? When was the last time you looked at your list? Do you even know where the list is? Writing and revisiting your bucket list over and over for the rest of your life is worth doing, and if it is combined with some follow-through, it never gets old.

Of course, you need a list to cross things off. But the end goal is not to make the list. It is to do the things on the list. Each thing you check off as completed helps build the confidence to do other things on the list. Flying a jetpack was something on the list that I didn't think was feasible for the longest time. Then I did it. I decided to take up ninjutsu because it was the last thing on my bucket list from when I was a kid. I had checked off the second-to-last thing, which was hang gliding, so I figured if I could do all this other stuff on the list, becoming a ninja might not be as silly as it sounds.

Some things on the list might not seem feasible. If you have it written down and keep revisiting it, looking for a way, you may find one. That way might not be apparent to you now, but if you put it on the list and keep revisiting it, the way will show itself.

"One day I want to visit Australia" was on some of my early lists. I had no idea that not only would I visit but eventually I would move here permanently. You may have no idea how an item on your list may manifest. You might have to put in a lot of deliberate, focused effort, or you might write something down, and that part of your mind outside your conscious awareness may quietly go to work to put you in the right place at the right time.

A lot of people in New Age circles call this manifesting in a supernatural way, and if that makes you feel more spiritual, go for it. But to me this isn't something mystical. It is just you moving forward and course correcting without the task being in the forefront of your mind. It's like the newest technology in guided missiles: fire and forget.

Having said all that, I think it is good to have a nice mix of things that are easy to accomplish and things that are epic, once-in-a-lifetime achievements. You want some things to work toward and some you can do in a spare weekend. Having a few easy things on your list is another way to build on smaller successes.

EXERCISE

Write down your bucket list (at least fifty things to do before you die). Take a sheet of paper or a notebook and write a simple list of things you would like to do. Leave room for a line that says the date you completed each of your items.

Take your favorites, do some research, and write out a plan for accomplishing each one.

Include a timeline. Keep revisiting these items until you have done them.

The Cutaway

One of the biggest things on my bucket list when I was a kid was skydiving. My grandmother on my dad's side owned a large piece of property in the country. Not far away was a commercial drop zone. When I was out playing in the field or climbing trees at her house, every so often I looked up and saw beautiful, brightly colored parachutes floating down in the distance.

It looked like fun, so as a kid I decided one day I would give it a try. Skydiving was the first entry on my first bucket list. I filed away the idea, then that one day came. I had finished a contract on the cruise ship and was resting my arms. That's when in my spare time, I decided to take up the sport. It was on the list and something I had always wanted to try, so I finally told myself to go for it!

Skydiving is such an unusual sport in that it is one of the most counterintuitive things you can do. As Clint Eastwood's character in the movie *Heartbreak Ridge*[3] explains, "Jumping out of a perfectly good aircraft is not a natural act!" For anyone with a fear of heights, this is the ultimate level D for facing it. Even if you are not particularly afraid of heights, there are not many people who don't feel fear the first time they jump out of a plane.

The first time you jump, your nervous system fights against the notion. The part of your brain that is responsible for self-preservation can't see how this is a good idea. After you exit the aircraft, however, the feeling is incredible. No words can capture the rush of free fall. Once you have leveled out and your eyes have oriented to the horizon, it feels more like floating than falling. The only sound you hear is the wind created by your body slicing through the air at terminal velocity. It is a very free feeling, like being supported by a cushion of air.

You can do backflips, spins, and all kinds of other maneuvers by changing the position of your body. Nothing else compares, and that's why it can be addictive. It is the closest sensation to actually flying a person can experience. This is an illusion, of course, since in a proper stable belly-to-earth position, you are falling at the speed of approximately 120 miles (193 kilometers) per hour.

If you are tracking, you are dropping even faster. Tracking involves straightening the legs out of the bent-knee stable arched position and moving the arms down in a supine position, like a dive. This creates a faster fall but also forward movement. When you see the hero of an action movie dive after a bad guy in free fall, that is tracking. That is one of the first things you learn, along with 180- to 360-degree turns.

Normally the ideal altitude for jumping is ten thousand to fourteen thousand feet above ground level. That's three thousand to forty-two hundred meters. Jumping from higher requires an oxygen supply. Jumping from any lower altitude reduces your free-fall time, which is usually about a minute. Sometimes it is necessary to jump from a slightly lower altitude because of cloud cover. You want to avoid jumping through clouds where possible, because clouds can obscure your sight. Flying at 120 to 180 miles per hour is no joke. When you are moving really, really fast, it's important to have a clear vision of where you are going.

When learning to skydive, most people go through what's called an accelerated free fall course.[4] It is called *accelerated* because compared to other types of training, like static line, it is the fastest way to get to free fall. As I mentioned before, the first jump or two are tandem with an instructor physically attached to you. Some people skip the tandems, but it is not recommended. On your next jump, you have two instructors jump with you, but you are not attached to either one. Once you have deployed your parachute, they track away and deploy their own.

After that, you go through progressive steps with one instructor, learning specific objectives with each jump, and somewhere around the eighth to tenth jump, you graduate and are granted the right to solo on your own.

The first jump I did without an instructor attached I was learning canopy control, so they used a radio to guide me into the landing area. My instructor on the other end of the radio mistimed the wind, and I ended up landing in the cow pasture next to the drop zone. I came to a stop only a few feet from the barbed wire fence separating the pasture from the airport.

Once you are below a couple of hundred feet, you can no longer rely on the altimeter attached to your wrist to judge your altitude. You have to eyeball it. Judging your elevation and rate of descent is a skill you acquire by trial and error.

My second solo landing was even more disastrous than the first. I flared too high and sprained my ankle. Flaring consists of pulling on both steering toggles at the same time right before you land. This creates a lift, slows your descent, and creates forward movement. If done at precisely the correct moment, flaring makes for a nice soft landing. Master skydivers make it look easy, performing what's called a swoop. They come in fast and flare at just the right moment. They appear to just casually step from the air to the ground like some kind of medieval sorcerer.

The error side of trial and error is what I did that day. If you flare too high and too fast, it lifts you back up a few feet, then when the lift gives out, you stall and come crashing straight down much harder than if you hadn't bothered to flare at all—something I learned firsthand.

My swollen ankle and foot gave me better appreciation for the skill level acquired by the turf-surfing masters who perform dangerous high-speed hook turns at low altitudes and then flare just above ground level, giving themselves enough lift to skim the ground for several dozen feet before turning it into a walk.

I was not deterred by this setback, and as soon as I could walk without a limp, I returned to my training. As I progressed, I started to feel as if I were between worlds. When you start skydiving, everybody treats you a bit like a tourist. Skydivers are some of the nicest people in the world. They are all friendly, and most of them seem outgoing. Still, conversations are kept superficial with beginners. "How was your jump? Is this cool, or what? Are you going on the next load?"

For me, the *hop and pop* changed things. A hop and pop—officially called a low solo—is a skill test done within a couple of jumps after completing the accelerated free fall course. While carrying the rest of the skydivers to normal jump altitude, you jump out first, before they are even halfway up. You must immediately get stable and deploy your chute. During this jump, there is no instructor with you and no time for panic.

One of the other counterintuitive things about skydiving is that higher elevation is your friend. Most people think the closer to the ground you are, the safer. In skydiving the opposite is true: elevation equals time. The higher you are, the more time to react, think, and figure things out. In skydiving, when you run out of elevation, you run out of time! The low solo is a confidence builder, because it teaches you it is possible to exit the aircraft and deploy your chute immediately when there isn't a lot of time to think things through. Although the low solo isn't difficult, it is a stress test with catastrophic real-world consequences in the event of failure.

I did my hop and pop out the back of a Twin Otter aircraft. I usually hurled myself out the side door of a King Air, Superman style. The Twin Otter had a hydraulic cargo bay door that opened down in the back. I walked to the edge of the cargo bay door, turned around, and faced the rest of the skydivers, who were not yet halfway to their jump altitude. I could see and hear them applaud, hoot, and holler for me while I took a single step back.

The noise of the applause instantly gave way to the screams of the aircraft's engine and the wind. Then there was the strangest sensation—like a brief pause in time and space. When you jump like this, for a split second it feels like you are standing outside the aircraft, not in the least like the aircraft is pulling away from you at over a hundred miles an hour and that you are accelerating toward terminal velocity.

The best analogy for this sensation is a cartoon bit where the coyote or some other villain falls from a cliff. For a couple of seconds they defy gravity, suspended in the air—enough time to hold up a sign or perform some hilarious slapstick maneuver before they plummet toward the ground.

This feeling of being suspended in the air is another illusion like the floating feeling. This illusion is caused by the forward throw and relative wind. When you exit the aircraft, for a fraction of a second you are traveling forward as fast as the aircraft. The adrenaline makes this split second seem longer than it is. When you shift your momentum from flying forward to falling (into the relative wind), it can create the oddest feeling. By this time in my training the arched back and limb positions necessary to pull the rip cord were mostly instinct and muscle memory, so as soon as I was stable, I pulled the cord.

Another perceptional distortion of time and space is caused by deploying the parachute. Time travels at a speed relative to what you are doing. Canopy deployment shock or moving from 120 miles an hour to approximately eighteen, is probably about the biggest relative change in speed you can make and stay in one piece. This, coupled with the temporal distortion caused by adrenaline, makes for a trippy change in the relative speed of time. *Otherworldly* is the best description I can give for the feeling.

Luckily, when you pull the rip cord on a parachute, it doesn't open instantly. A process takes place. A tiny drogue chute pops out first and grabs the wind. That creates drag and pulls out your main parachute. Then a bunch of guidelines and your slider come out. The slider is a rectangular piece of nylon that comes out, separating the lines. It makes sure everything doesn't open so fast it rips. It's called a slider because it slides down the lines to a point just over your head, fully inflating the chute in the process. Only then are you the pilot of a fully open, safe, ram-air canopy.

Anything less than a fully open chute is a malfunction that needs correcting. If a malfunction can't be corrected, the main chute must be jettisoned. Jettisoning the main chute and opening the reserve is a process called the *cutaway*. Although nowadays the cutaway is done with quick-release handles, the term dates to the beginning of skydiving, when the jumper literally had to cut away their main parachute with a knife.

Although the cutaway is probably the most practiced procedure on the ground, few skydivers have had to perform one for real. Some skydivers with over a thousand jumps to their credit have never had to do it and therefore wonder if they really could.

If everything goes correctly, the process of activation to a safe canopy that can be steered and landed with toggles is about four seconds. When you are lower to the ground than you should be, four seconds seems like an eternity.

My low solo went perfectly, and for me it was a rite of passage. After that, a bunch of the drop-zone regulars took me to lunch at a local diner. For the first time, other skydivers besides my instructors bothered to learn my name. I was for the first time invited on small formations. Then I was invited to stay after the airport closed for the campfire party.

Now I finally felt I was part of the crowd. I drank Coronas and listened to their stories. There were stories to debrief the day's jumps. There were stories of jumps past, stories of hardships endured in the name of the sport. There were stories of people who had slipped over the edge and sold everything they owned to pay for more jumps, pawning their possessions just like any other addict to feed their addiction.

In the skydiver world, there is a pecking order. Your status is determined by jump number and license designation. Jumps are counted from the first tandem (jump one) up. The D license holders have at least five hundred jumps to their credit. The Ds always had the most stories to tell. They were the old-timers still alive and still jumping.

There were stories about the fallen—good people who had made a mistake or been unlucky and *burned in*. Sometimes the *burn in* is also called a *bounce*, because a body impacting the ground at terminal

REIGNITING THE PASSION OF CHILDHOOD DREAMS ••• 223

velocity tends to bounce high. Of course, not all deaths are due to parachute malfunctions. Plenty of skydiving deaths are caused by overconfident jumpers hook-turning into the ground at high speed, trying to look cool.

While listening to a story about a bounce, one of my instructors addressed me privately. His face glowed eerily in the firelight. He spoke to me matter-of-factly in a low voice and said, "Scott, if you stay in this sport long enough, you are going to know somebody who dies from it."

Soon the dark thoughts about jumpers bouncing off the earth turned to better times. They told stories of big conventions called boogies, where people flew in from all over the world to participate in or watch competitions. You could jump out of helicopters, hot-air balloons, or sometimes even commercial airliners. You could hang out with other jumpers in mass. There you could have camaraderie with people who understood you. After all, there were only two kinds of people. There were skydivers, and there was everybody else. Except the tandem tourist and the "maybe one day I'll try it" wannabes, everybody else fell into the *whuffo* category.

Whuffo is a colloquial derogatory term used to describe non-skydivers who don't understand the desire to jump out of airplanes. The term comes from the most common question asked of skydivers by neighboring yokels everywhere: "Whuffo you jump out of dem airplanes?"

Family is the worst type of whuffo. My mother was terrified of my skydiving. My father got to the point of telling me not to bring up the sport in front of her anymore. He said if she knew I was going skydiving that day, she would fret about it all day long.

Plenty of advice was doled out to me the night of the party, such as, "You need to quit your job and find one with weekends off. That's when everybody's here; that's when the cool boogies are." They told me it was time to stop renting gear. I needed to buy a custom flight suit, my own altimeter, and a parachute rig preferably with an automatic activation device so I could deploy my chute if a midair collision knocked me unconscious.

That was going to be expensive. I had already burned through a few thousand dollars just getting to where I was. In a year or so, when I had mastered canopy control, I would need to trade my canopy for a much smaller, more maneuverable one, so I could swoop. I had to learn to pack and do a few more jumps, and I would have my A license. There was no turning back then.

Sure, there is always more to learn, like to gain body control, so I could be in on the big formations. There are more license designations, then free-flying and maybe even BASE jumping. My new life plan was in place. Forget about the whuffos of the world; my place was in the sky. This was my chance to join a tribe of people in which I would not be considered the crazy one.

Like airplane pilots, canopy pilots needed to stay current. I had to jump at least once every thirty days, so I didn't lose my edge. I was assured that shouldn't be a problem, since there was nothing else in the world more fun than playing in the sky. Why would anyone want to do anything else with their free time? If I listened my new life was all laid out before me. For these people, skydiving wasn't a hobby. It was a lifestyle.

I left the party. The embers of the fire were slowly dying out. Most everyone had left, but a few people were still milling about, and a few more were passed out in lawn chairs around what was left of the fire. All anybody had talked or thought about at this party was skydiving. It was an all-consuming passion for everyone. Almost everybody there had considerably more money invested in their parachute rigs than in their cars. A land vehicle was there only to get you to the DZ. That and to work, which was a necessary evil needed to pay for jumps and gear. To some skydivers food and housing were less important in the hierarchy of needs than jumps and gear.

These people were full-on adrenaline junkies. Jumping was their life. Would it be mine too? This could be the thing I was looking for. I was coming to a crossroads, but I didn't know it yet. I had always been a dabbler. I was always trading in the mastery of any one sport or hobby for a more varied experience. But this could be different. If I continued down this road, I would be a full-fledged skydiving addict. Skydiving would permeate my being right down to the identity level. I wasn't sure if I wanted to be this devoted to a sport. This brings me to the big scare I alluded to in chapter 5.

Everything was just fine when I jumped out of the airplane. I was still technically a beginner, not new to skydiving, but I certainly was no seasoned pro. It was my twentieth jump. I was soloing. Nothing unusual happened in free fall. I practiced backflips and turns. I tracked for a while and then took in the scenery. You could see hundreds of lakes from up there. Most of the surrounding area was occupied by green cow pastures. The farmland was occasionally broken up by roads. From this height, the cars driving by looked like little Matchbox toys a child would play with. As the scenery slowly grew in my field of vision, I knew it was getting close to time. I thought to check the old altimeter, one last look before opening the chute.

After I deployed my parachute, I looked up and noticed it had not opened fully. Only the middle third was inflated. It was a malfunction I had studied. The slider was up, and the line attaching me to the canopy was twisted. I followed the procedure to clear it by bicycle kicking like a kid, trying to unravel a twisted swing. Then I tried pulling on the risers. It did not clear, and I was losing altitude fast! This was supposed to be a simple, easily fixable malfunction. I had had line twists before, but they had always easily unraveled. This time was different. I kept trying to clear it to no avail.

I had to decide. I could jettison from my main chute, go back into free fall, and hopefully my reserve would deploy correctly. Or I could try to land the halfway-open chute, and maybe I would live. I probably would shatter most of the bones in my body, but I might live.

The problem was I wasn't sure if I knew how to open the reserve. I had practiced it over and over and pictured it in my mind, visualizing it down to every detail, but I had never done it for real. I had practiced so much that the procedure was ingrained in my muscle memory, but I wasn't sure if it was. I was no longer consciously aware I knew how to do it. What if the reserve malfunctioned? Then I would certainly be dead. I second-guessed myself and continued to struggle with the guide wires. If ever there was a time to go into panic mode, this was it. As I lost elevation, I could feel the fear rising through my body.

As I dropped below the two-thousand-feet mark, I knew I had to decide. I was running out of altitude, running out of time. Then a calm, quiet voice spoke in my mind. "It's now or never." Time slowed, and the world took on a strange, familiar glow. I was now in a flow state. I pulled the quick release and arched my back. I reentered free fall! I pulled the reserve cord without a problem. The three seconds after that were clearer in my mind and took up more space in my brain than entire months of my life. Time moved painfully slowly as the reserve opened fully.

With only a few hundred feet to spare, I steered the smaller, faster reserve down and pulled off a 180-degree hook turn just above the ground. It was a dangerous maneuver that was well above my skill level, but I had to turn into the wind quickly for a hard but safe landing.

The incident took less than thirty seconds, yet it seemed like a lifetime and very well could have been the end of one. Sometimes you have the luxury of mulling things over. This wasn't one of those times. Sometimes you must decide and have faith in the execution!

When I landed, I was shaking with adrenaline. A skydiver came up and said, "Man, that was awesome! I have had over a thousand jumps and have never had to go to the reserve. I don't even know if I could."

I was explaining what happened to a couple of people. I hadn't even stopped trembling when one of my instructors pulled me aside. He said, "You need to jump again right now, or the fear of it will have you, and you will never jump again. I'm bumping somebody so you can jump again right away. Go grab another parachute."

I was on the plane in the next load, which took off a few minutes later. The flight up to jump altitude is about ten minutes. On the ride, I had plenty of time to question whether my decision to jump so soon after such a close call was a prudent one. Was I mad? I had just had a brush with death, and I was doing it all over again. When someone told me to go again, I didn't hesitate for a second. How crazy was I? What the hell was I thinking?

It was too late to back out now. The light was on, and the door was open. Bodies were flying out of the doorway. Then it was my turn. As I stepped to the edge of the doorway surveying the ground 14,000 feet below, I realized I was on another edge. I was no longer just trying this out. This was about to become all-consuming. I exited the aircraft and had an almost perfect jump. I felt more in control doing flips, spins, and dives than I ever had! It was fantastic.

That night there was another party. Part of me wanted to stay, but another part needed to leave. That evening, I left the DZ at dusk. As I turned from the airport road onto the main highway, I saw the silhouettes of parachutes floating down in the pink glow of the fading light. They were the sunset load, the last skydive of the day. I was skipping the campfire party even though I had promised one of the riggers I would stay and buy her a beer. I owed her that much at least. She had packed the reserve chute that had saved my life.

I couldn't stay, though. I had to get away. I had to think. I was shaken up by the malfunction. It wasn't just that I was too afraid to jump again. There was something else.

The multiple transitions back and forth from free fall to under canopy were terrifying. But they also created a rush so intense I can describe it only as spiritual. It was like crossing a gateway between this dimension and some other one. I had crossed a threshold that transcended time and space. You are most alive when you feel you might be about to die! As frightening as the breakaway was, deep down, I kind of liked it. On some level, I thought it was the coolest thing that had ever happened to me.

It had catapulted me almost to the point of no return. I was now on the edge of addiction like the next skydiver on deck waiting to grab hold of the doorway of the plane and fling themselves into the void. If I continued jumping, maybe even if I'd stayed for the party, that would be it. I would be a skydiver. Everything else in life would be subordinate to that self-concept. It wouldn't be a hobby or a sport. Skydiving would be my life. The time for dabbling had ended. The door of choice was closing. It was either full immersion or quit completely. To be fair, not everybody who takes up the sport is an addict. Plenty of people somehow manage to balance it with work and family life. I wouldn't have been one of those people. I would have gone full throttle!

To quit had its own price. Without the periodic injection of adrenaline, my ADHD symptoms grew worse. For weeks after I quit, I had the almost constant feeling I can equate only to that of a caged animal. I was already beginning to feel a certain disconnect with the world of whuffos. My friends and family could never understand my compulsion. They just didn't get it. But I had danced in the realm of the sky gods, and I would never again be part of the world of people comfortable with their feet planted firmly on the ground. If I stayed, I could be part of a tribe that understood that all too well. But then I would be a slave to my addiction. Perhaps at the cost of my life.

The shadowy shapes of parachutes floated down behind my field of vision. I made my decision and pressed down the accelerator. It was time to cut away from the world of skydiving.

While I was going through withdrawal from skydiving, I needed another adventure to take my mind off it. One of the other things on my bucket list was to circumnavigate the earth. I had already set myself up to be able to do this. My previous contracts on ships had given me seniority. I could request to go anywhere in the world, so I chose to go around the whole world.

REIGNITING THE PASSION OF CHILDHOOD DREAMS

A month after the cutaway, I was on another airplane. This time instead of a jump plane, it was an airliner to London. A couple of days after that, I went to Southampton to catch the last cruise ship I would work on.

To this day the last entry in my skydiver's log is jump number twenty-one. Even though it was a lifetime ago, and I didn't do it for that long, I still miss it. I still look at the sky and think about it.

Often when I tell the cutaway story, people say, "Wow, I would never do that," or "I was thinking about trying skydiving, but now I don't know."

Occasionally, though, I tell the story to someone who is a skydiver or who knows skydivers or knows me and asks, "Why did you quit?"

I am usually taken aback and feel a little defensive. "What do you mean, why did I quit? Um, because I almost died. What more do you want?" I thought there was some self-righteous humility involved. The big bad Marine admitted he feared something.

But that wasn't it. That might have been why I stopped, but that wasn't why I quit. I didn't stop because I feared jumping. The thing that scared me most was that I wasn't that scared. My stopping could have easily been a brief pause before pushing in deeper.

I was defensive when people asked why I quit, because I had been lying to myself about why I quit. I had been lying to myself for a long time. It was only through the introspection required in writing this book that I figured out the real reason I quit: Narelle. If I hadn't met her when I had, I would have been pulled right back into skydiving as soon as I left the ship.

My not being a skydiver was a condition of my marriage. It wasn't something she was willing to put up with. Narelle lost her father in a car accident when she was twelve. She has had some issues with death and abandonment. Having a husband who threw himself out of airplanes in his spare time wasn't something she could cope with.

Who knows, maybe this is why I am alive today. One thing is for sure: whenever I test my fear tolerance with something crazy, I also test hers. She did know what she was getting into, because she came along on the boat when we went cage diving, and we had just started dating then. We are a good fit. She keeps me in check, and I get her to push her boundaries a little.

My family ensures my periodic cravings for adrenaline don't pull me too close to the edge. This brings me to the other half of the Hunter S. Thompson quote about how only those who have gone over the edge know where it is. The rest of the quote is "The others—the living—are those who pushed their control as far as they felt they could handle it, and then pulled back, or slowed down, or did whatever they had to when it came time to choose between Now and Later. But the edge is still out there."[5]

There is the edge of your comfort zone, and there is the razor's edge of safety, sanity, and life. People who never take a risk may think these lines are right on top of each other, and people for whom big risks are a way of life may be moving so fast the second line blurs. Somewhere between these edges is the sweet spot, where things are interesting.

I still feel the urge to jump out of planes. I just have two things in my life I consider much more important—Narelle and Zoe. With skydiving, I am glad I did it, but I'm glad I stopped as well.

Besides, there are so many other things I want to do. Dreams change over time, and their realities differ from expectations. That is okay too. Try as many things as you can. I keep adding to my list. The sooner you write your bucket list, the sooner you can start crossing things off. Remember, nothing is as ridiculous as it might seem. I once had a car with a missile launcher on top, so there really is no limit.

Chapter 9:

Be a Traveler

> The world is a book, and those who do
> not travel read only a page.
> — SAINT AUGUSTINE

A great conversation starter is the topic of travel. People love to talk about the places they have been or would like to go. When we lived in the United States, when people found out my wife was Australian, they always asked about Australia. If they had been, they would excitedly tell me about their trip Down Under. If they hadn't, they would almost always say, "You know, that is the one place I always wanted to go."

"So why don't you?" I meant it rhetorically, but all too often they had a list of excuses prepared.

Now that I live in Australia, as soon as they hear me speak, strangers want to know all about the United States. Well, except for the people who think I'm Canadian. If they have been to the United States, they want to tell me all about their trip, which I happily listen to. It is good to see people get that excited. Of course, some have never left their island continent. These are usually the ones who tell me that America is the one place they always wanted to go. When I ask them, "So why don't you?" their list of excuses is almost the same as the Americans who say they always wanted to come to Australia.

If you are already an intrepid world traveler, you certainly don't need this chapter. You can probably give me some travel tips. If not, read on. If you have never passed outside your country's borders, you need this chapter!

Although some people feel it more strongly than others, the urge to travel is one of those traits hardwired into your system on a genetic level. For most of human history, we lived as nomads, hunting and gathering for our subsistence.[1]

When the plants stopped producing fruit and the game moved on, our ancestors had to migrate to new places to survive. This is how the novelty-seeking aspect of the dopamine reward system I described in chapter 3 developed. Traveling to places you have never been is rewarding on a biological level. Despite being inconvenient, despite the discomfort and sometimes even genuine hardship, traveling to new places just feels good. It's the dopamine, baby!

Fernweh[2] is a word unique to the German language. There is not a direct translation to English. It is best described as the opposite of homesickness. Fernweh is the longing for faraway places. Fernweh is the reason you see so many German backpackers all over the world. The closest word to fernweh in English is wanderlust, which is also derived from German.

Restless wanderlust hit me at a young age while I was in high school. Less than a year after I graduated, I was living on the Japanese island of Okinawa. Fernweh was my biggest reason for deciding to go into the military. Yeah, there were other reasons, like patriotism, the desire to be of service, wanting to prove myself, and, of course, my subconscious need to play with the grown-up, real-life versions of the toys in my childhood toy box. But my biggest reason for enlistment was to get beyond the borders of my homeland and see some of the world outside.

Once you contract fernweh, it tends to stay in your system. After I left the military, I had to find another way to travel. Working aboard cruise ships became my next way to travel the world. I could see a lot of places and get paid to travel to destinations I never could have afforded on my own.

Get out there and go. I think domestic travel is underrated. Some of my best childhood memories were formed while traveling in the continental United States with my parents. Travel your own country and see as many of its wonders as you can. But don't stop there.

Your home country is a good starting point, but to truly call yourself an adventurer, you must be willing to go beyond borders. Getting out of your comfort zone is pushing past boundaries, and what better metaphorical boundary is there than going outside the geopolitical boundary of your home country? To get the full benefits of being a traveler, you must be willing to go global.

The reasons to travel are countless. Some of the benefits are obvious, and some are subtle changes you will notice in yourself over the course of your journeys and when you return. I couldn't possibly explain them all, but here are a few of the benefits of travel.

You get to see some amazing sights. I have incredible memories of places I have been. From picturesque scenes in Caribbean islands to azure-blue glaciers of Alaska and Norway, I have seen spectacular places and done some incredible things. I have been so close to a baby humpback whale I could smell her breath. I have amazing images of mountain ranges, deserts, forests, and everything in between burned into my brain. Sometimes I wake up thinking of a forgotten place in a part of the world I haven't been to in years, a place I must have been dreaming about. It makes me smile thinking about it.

There are visions of cities the world over. To see pictures of a city in a travel brochure or see it on TV does not capture the essence of walking down the cobbled streets. A city like Venice can't be looked at in a show. It has to be experienced.

Making memories is far better than any picture I have ever taken. They never seem to do the scenery justice. I have been to dozens of countries, and there are cool things to see in just about all of them. But you have to get out there to see them in real life. Traveling to exotic destinations and seeing some of these wonders firsthand is to touch the sublime. It can be so awe-inspiring you can feel insignificant and yet transcendent simultaneously.

Travel leads to open-mindedness. Mark Twain said it best: "Travel is fatal to prejudice, bigotry, and narrow-mindedness, and many of our people need it sorely on these accounts. Broad, wholesome, charitable views of men and things cannot be acquired by vegetating in one little corner of the earth all one's lifetime."[3]

Before we eliminate prejudice in the world, we must find and eliminate prejudices that lie within ourselves. The best way to do that is to experience other cultures, even if for a brief time. I don't know about you, but I don't want my worldview crafted solely by national identity. You can still love your country, and looking at it through the wider lens of a world traveler might help you appreciate some of the aspects about it that you take for granted. It certainly has for me.

It is important to understand other perspectives, but it is just as important to see how much other people are the same as us. The more people from different cultures intermingle in the spirit of friendly cooperation, the less they see each other as an enemy to be feared and persecuted.

On our own territory, our lens to the world is colored by a film of prejudices we can't even perceive. But when you become the outsider, that can shock you into picking up on the subtle cues that things you took for granted as universal truths may be beliefs instilled in you as part of your national identity. The collective conscience of your country shapes your worldview. If you don't travel beyond your borders, you might not ever know that.

Different groups have different levels of tolerance for you trying to impose your cultural beliefs on their turf. When you travel internationally, in some places if you stray from the beaten path even a little, you may quickly learn that cultural sensitivity isn't just good manners; it's a survival skill.

If you travel, you are exposed to different cultures, people, and ideas. You may grow to understand the world works differently from the way you thought it did. You will come home with fresh ideas and new ways of doing things that can improve your life and the lives of those around you.

Most important, if you build relationships with people from other cultures, you will stop thinking in terms of *them* and instead include more people in the *us* category. Whether looking outside your own country or even when you look within, tolerance and empathy are two qualities the world could really use right now.

Travel can be a process of self-discovery. Travel gives you a chance to learn about yourself. Each location and experience will be different, so there is always a chance to learn and grow. You will be operating in the unfamiliar, so even simple day-to-day activities will be stretch-zone experiences. You will have to learn how to effectively problem-solve. You'll sometimes have to work through language barriers. You'll have to adjust to the location. Along the way, you'll build self-confidence, trust in yourself, and trust in the process of traveling.

One day on the world cruise while we were in Hong Kong, I decided to see the Tian Tan Buddha, better known as the big statue of Buddha. It is over 110 feet tall and made from bronze. I had only half the day off. When I set out, I did not realize how far this Buddha was relative to the ship. I had to take a ferry to another island and about four buses, spending over three hours in transit. When I finally got to the monastery, I climbed the 268 steps to the top.

The view was breathtaking. This was an incredible place where I could have spent all day. Unfortunately, I was going to be late for work, and I was even in danger of missing my ship altogether. I had decided to press on to accomplish my objective, even though the trip took three times as long as I had originally estimated. I could visit Buddha for only a few minutes, and I had to run.

I did have plenty of time to meditate on my teeth-clenching journey back to the ship. It was one of those times when a flow state was not with me because I had missed two buses by less than a minute and in one case was running after a bus that was pulling away from the stop. It seemed like the more frustrated I got, the more off my timing became.

It was as if the big Buddha was trying to teach me a lesson in flowing with the situation rather than trying to force the outcome I thought I needed. I managed to work out a few things in my personal life that I had been struggling with for some time.

I was late for work, but my first client was a no-show, and the receptionist covered for me for a few minutes while my next client waited, so it all worked out in the end. It was one of those cases where the lesson was found in the journey, not the destination. All in all, I spent over six hours in transit and about fifteen minutes at the monastery, including the stair climb.

Travel lets you try delicious food. Usually when you travel, you are out and about doing things, so you probably will eat out quite a bit. This will give you plenty of opportunities to try different foods. Eat local cuisine as often as you can. If you are in a city, sometimes there is a temptation to go to fast-food chains because they're familiar and easy. Avoid this if you can. Taste the culture.

The street fair in developing nations has a similar scent. I first tried the unknown mystery meat on a stick in the Philippines. Even though it smelled mouthwatering, it took me a few beers to work up the courage to try it. I found it delicious. Then when I was in Mexico, the smells of the street food were almost the same half a world away. I still needed a couple of beers to try it, but it was equally delicious. Dozens of countries later, I noticed a lot of similarities around the world. Yes, I have had dysentery and a few other gastrointestinal infections. That's just part of the fun. Besides, it's usually the water, not the food.

Travel lets you meet and bond with new people. I know people from all over the world. I have to say I have been very lucky in this area. I met my dream girl, my soulmate, while traveling on the *QE2*. We have been married for over twenty years, and I wouldn't have met her if we weren't both travelers.

You gain a sense of perspective and appreciation. I have found that people who have done a fair amount of traveling tend to be more easygoing. Once you have seen how people live in impoverished nations, your developed-world problems don't seem so bad. The first place I saw real poverty was in the Philippines as a young Marine. I saw things there that brought tears to my eyes. It did, however, give me a tremendous sense of gratitude for where I came from. Seeing the hard life up close and without filters is a great way to learn gratefulness and foster empathy for others. You get real perspective through immersion.

Travel brings history and geography to life. I first learned this in fourth-grade American history. I talked my parents into going to Colonial Williamsburg, Virginia, for our family vacation that summer. This historical section of the city is like a living museum in which many buildings from colonial America have been restored, and costumed craftsmen show how things were made in that period. This made a mark on me as a young boy.

I was always fascinated by medieval times and the knights of old, so I was able to learn about European castles by visiting several of them. I got a better feel for Greek mythology by visiting the Parthenon. I appreciated European history by walking cobblestone streets and visiting prominent landmarks.

My studies of World War II were brought to life by visiting the USS *Arizona* Memorial in Hawaii. On the other side of the world are the peace museum and memorial park in Itoman, the southernmost part of Okinawa. This was the location of the final battle for Okinawa during WWII. Outside the museum are large stone monuments of the fallen. There are some cliffs with incredible views of the sea below. Even the cliffs had a dark history to tell.

As war rears its ugly head once more in Eastern Europe, I think of a couple of cruises I worked in that part of the world. A ship I worked on, the *Crystal Symphony*, was one of the first cruise ships to visit Croatia after the war with Serbia. I had that day off, so I decided to wander the walled city of old Dubrovnik. The city had sustained considerable damage while it was under siege by Serbian forces. Despite the tragedy that had befallen it, Dubrovnik was eager to regain its place as a premier European travel destination. By the time we arrived, much of the restoration had been completed, and life seemed normal. Although every war is a tragedy, it was nice to see that not all wars end in the perpetual disaster of a failed state.

Travel builds character. It is almost impossible to stay in a comfort zone when you are moving through places you have never been before. You get a chance to test your mettle, to find out what you are made of. When things go wrong, like flight cancelations and lost luggage, how will you handle it?

Can you adapt? Or will those kinds of things defeat you? Mental flexibility, adaptability, and resilience are the three things I stress the most in this book. If you do a lot of traveling, all three will be tested, sometimes to an extreme. When you travel, many things are out of your control, and you have to surrender to this fact. You will probably be faced with the unexpected—sometimes to the point of bizarre. Things happen you can't possibly anticipate, like being in a rented recreational vehicle, driving through a remote desert, and getting caught in a freak snowstorm, as we did in our drive across America.

Another time a friend and I were lost in a taxi in Saint Petersburg, Russia. Neither of us spoke Russian, and our driver didn't speak English. As the driver took us to seedier and seedier parts of town, the meter ran up higher and higher until it was into millions of rubles. That's when I learned the one word of Russian I still know to this day: *nyet*, which means no. We eventually found our way. At the time Russia was going through a recession, and the ruble was worth only one thousandth of what it normally is, so our fare ended up being okay. Still, when you see a cab meter that is seven digits long, it makes you nervous.

Sometimes several poor decisions compound to cause serious hassles and stress. I was walking through an international airport, completely exhausted. I had a couple of hours before my flight, so I was wandering around aimlessly. I was sleep-deprived, and without thinking I absentmindedly stopped to pet a dog standing in the middle of the terminal. I didn't even pause to wonder why a dog was standing in the middle of the airport. I just said to myself, "Cute dog," and started petting him. I was so tired I missed the obvious fact this was a working dog I should have probably left alone.

Well, it was a drug-sniffing dog. After giving him a good scratch, I started back on my way. He followed me. I am normally very respectful of cops, but I was exhausted and not thinking straight. When the dog's DEA agent handler came up and started making accusations, I sarcastically quipped back that maybe the dog just liked me more than he liked him. The agent took this personally, and we got off on the wrong foot.

The long and the short of it was that after a two-hour interrogation and humiliating strip search, I was free to go. From there I literally ran through the airport at full speed to catch my flight. It was stressful at the time, but it's something I can look back at and laugh at now. All these weird situations have life lessons built into them and build character.

Exciting things will probably happen. A lot of my adventures took work, like the dive with the great whites. But sometimes I stumbled into something wild, like the time I was wandering through the crowded streets, in a virtual sea of people, in Cochin, India, and found myself face to face with a cobra. On one corner of the street, a large group of people were gathered. I was naturally curious, because as any street performer worth their salt will tell you, "Nothing attracts a crowd like a crowd."

I started to work my way through the crowd, trying to get to the front to see what was going on. I found it surprisingly easy to wind my way through the dense throng of humans. When I got to the front, I found out why. There, right in front of me, was an enormous cobra! He was barely four feet away from me. Indian cobras raise their heads and the upper part of their body to "stand" erect. This cobra stood with his head raised to almost my waist.

His hooded head swayed slightly, and his reptilian eyes stared back at me. The bottom part of his body was coiled up like a rope in a wicker basket on the ground. He was about five feet (1.5 meters) long.

Sitting behind the serpent was the quintessential Indian snake charmer. He looked exactly the way you might expect. He had a long gray beard. A bright orange turban was wrapped around his head. He wore several bead necklaces. He sat cross-legged, and below his raggedy robes, his dirty feet were bare. Next to the charmer was another, smaller wicker basket to throw tips into. He was playing a flutelike instrument made from a gourd called a *pungi*. This was supposed to mesmerize the snake.

The cobra, however, was less than impressed by its master's music. The poor thing just wanted to curl up in its basket and sleep. To keep the show going whenever the cobra dropped its hood or sank into the basket, the charmer poked and prodded the snake with the end of his flute to keep it dancing.

I had learned firsthand the folly of angering a sleepy snake a few years before when a friend of mine's ball python bit me in the face. The snake had fallen asleep inside my shirt and didn't want to come out.

Knowing what it feels like to be bitten by a snake, I stood in front of an increasingly large crowd with an agitated cobra directly in front of me. I tried to take a step back, but the people behind me pushed me forward again, as if they were using me as a human shield. It had been a lot easier to slide my way to the front of the crowd than it would be to shove my way to the back. So there I stood, trapped.

The snake might not have been charmed, but I stood there paralyzed. I was enthralled at the forked tongue flicking out in front of me. It was hypnotic—like staring into a fire. It was a fire that could reach out and burn you if it wanted to.

I had planted my feet firmly, because the last thing I wanted was to be shoved from behind into the personal space of an angry cobra. The charmer gave another irritating poke of the flute, and this time an audible hiss came in response.

The Indian cobra, or spectacled cobra,[4] is one of the top four snakes for fatal snakebites in South Asia. Its venom is a powerful neurotoxin that can paralyze the muscles and cause respiratory shutdown and even cardiac arrest.

I suddenly felt claustrophobic, social anxiety mixed with a sense of real danger. I needed to move. There was no way to work my way back through the swollen crowd behind me, and people were beginning to push even harder against my back. I did the only thing I could. I took a nice deep breath and took a step toward the snake.

Now I was almost on top of it, but I was in front of the crowd. There was a nervous second as I was well within striking distance and probably violating the snake's personal space. I exhaled slowly and executed a Marine drill–style right face using the space between the crowd and the snake to slip away. I could not wait all day for the crowd to disperse, so the only way to get out of danger was to step farther into it.

It just goes to show you that most venomous snakes bite only if threatened or cornered, and they feel they have no choice. This is another of the many strange experiences I have had being a tourist in a foreign land.

How to Travel

Hundreds of books and thousands of websites serve as travel guides and offer all the latest and greatest travel hacks. I want to concentrate on one major aspect: getting yourself to go. As with everything, regardless of barriers in the way, getting yourself to travel starts with the decision to do it. Decide to take an international trip. Once you have decided, the rest is just details.

One of the biggest excuses people make for not traveling is not having enough money. You may have a mortgage, bills, and responsibilities, or you may be a student with a mountain of loans, but none of these should stop you. For even the poorest couch-surfing dirtbag (I was one), if you have the will to travel, there is a way. Trust me, I know.

Everyone's situation is different. Financing may be as simple as saving the necessary funds or not blowing the money you have already saved. Perhaps you must sell assets to finance your trip. Or maybe you don't have any assets. Maybe you live paycheck to paycheck, and the very idea of financing a trip to your dream destination seems preposterous. Oh, ye of little faith. The paycheck-to-paycheck thing is less of a barrier than you might think. In fact, in some ways it could be an advantage.

When I set out to circumnavigate the world, I didn't have much saved. Before that, when I left for the Caribbean and Europe, I had less. Even before that, when I left for Alaska, I suffered from extreme negative net worth. One of the reasons I wanted to work on a cruise ship was I didn't want to have a fixed address or phone number that would allow creditors to call and harass me.

Being broke isn't necessarily a disadvantage to world travel. If you have nothing, you have nothing to lose. That can be freeing. If you have no mortgage to tie you down, do what I did. Throw your stuff in storage and head out into the great big world.

Of course, if you do have a mortgage, there are options there too, like house-swapping with someone overseas. Several websites allow you to connect with people all over the world to do this. Even finding a property manager and renting your home if you plan on extended travel is an option.

Finance your trip by working, if you need to. If you plan on traveling for an extended period, you are probably going to need sources of revenue. Working aboard cruise ships was my vehicle for working while traveling, but it is certainly not the only way. There are a ton of options for travel-related jobs or working overseas.

Besides cost, the other big reason people tend to put off travel is kids. I admit I have used this excuse myself. Having kids should be *more* of a reason to travel. No, I don't mean you should abandon them to fend for themselves while you gallivant around the world, as tempting as that might be. The earlier and more often you expose kids to various parts of the world, the better off they will be. This can be a way of instilling adaptability, resiliency, and appreciation in them before they get a chance to become resistant to those lessons.

Engineering a Dream Trip

The first task is to make sure you have a valid passport. If you don't have one, get your passport. You never know when you are going to have the opportunity to leave the country. If you have never been outside the country and have always dreamed of international travel, this would be a big sign of faith. Show the universe you're ready to travel by having a valid passport. If you have a passport and it's out of date, get it renewed.

Once you have started the ball rolling with the passport, it's time to get out your notebook or journal. Let's start with the basics: *who, what, where, when, how, why*. But let's change the order a little and start with *where*.

Where do you want to go? Is it one destination or several? Be specific. Do you want to go to Peru? Is anywhere in Peru good, or do you want to go to Machu Picchu? Do you want to go to France? France is big. Do you want to go to Paris, tour wine country, or stay somewhere on the French Riviera? Maybe all of the above?

Research thoroughly where you want to travel. This includes what kind of places you will be staying in. Will you be staying in a resort or on a ship? In hostels, hotels, motels, Airbnbs, house shares, campsites, or a combination of these?

You also want to monitor the political climate of your destinations right up to the point that you leave. Nowadays civil unrest is not limited to underdeveloped nations. The world is a volatile place right now. Know what kind of situation you are going into and adjust your plans accordingly.

The country and the region or time you travel can affect your budget. Your budget can affect the quality of your experience depending on your destination.

You may get more value for your dollar in less developed parts of the world. We stayed in a five-star hotel in Thailand for about the same price I paid for a seedy motel in London. I felt perfectly safe in the hotel in Thailand. In London, I thought a couple of the other guests looked a bit stabby.

Who is going? Are you doing this solo, bringing the family, or going with friends? Are you bringing someone special? Sometimes the more the merrier rings true, but sometimes it overcomplicates things and leads to compromises you don't want to make. Know everyone's special requirements and how compatible the goals and objectives of any traveling companions are with your own.

What do you want to do when you are there? List specific things you want to do while you are there. Find out how far each side trip is away from where you will stay. Are you within range for a day trip, or do you need to find additional accommodation? As you do more research about what you want to do, you may need to expand the *where* section.

You may have to jump between *where* and *what* a few times to refine your itinerary. As you do more research, you will want to do more things, and that may require staying at more locations.

When do you want to do this? When *can* you do this? Is this the year, or is this something to plan a year or two out? When is a good time to do this—when's the weather best? What time of year are conditions ideal for what you want to do? What time are conditions worst?

People often ask me, "When is a good time to vacation in Florida?" I usually suggest not going in September. Why? Because of the high probability of hurricanes. Technically hurricane season is June through November, but September is the peak, and that's when it most often gets hit. Trust me, hunkering down during a Category 4 cyclone is not how you want to spend your vacation. Knowing this in advance increases your chances of having a successful, fun trip.

Is it the busy season when you want to go? If it is peak season, it may be crowded. Accommodation may be more expensive and, if you don't book early enough, unavailable. The off-peak season will be less crowded and less expensive, but activities you want to do may be closed. Is it Carnival or some festival when you want to go? Do want to see Carnival or avoid it at all costs?

Why is an often-overlooked question, and it could be the most important one. Why do you want to do this? Is it someplace you thought would be cool to see, or is there a deeper reason? Will taking this trip fulfill a psychological or emotional need? A strong enough *why* can be a powerful driver! When people find a suitable *why*, it often motivates them to do things and go places they previously thought were unattainable. A strong *why* can clear the fog of apathy. Why is this important to you?

How are you going to pull this off? This is the time for brainstorming. How are you going to get there? How are you going to pay for this? How are you going to con a friend or family member into taking care of your pets (if you have any) when you are away?

How long is this going to take? This is the time you need to start drilling down on how much each leg of your journey is going to cost.

You may need to find out if you can get time off work. If not, is that job that important to you anyway? Hey, I'm just asking. There is something immensely satisfying about handing in your resignation, and when they ask why you are leaving, you tell them you are going overseas and don't know when or even if you will be back.

If you are not willing to throw away a career, you may be able to negotiate a working vacation. The fallout from the worldwide pandemic will probably take several more years to complete its cycle. On the bright side, the rest of the world has now learned what professional vagabonds and digital nomads, who advocate the laptop lifestyle, have known for a long time. Most of the work that is done in an office can be done remotely.

If you are in a beautiful locale that you want to explore, you are far less likely to be watching the clock, watching silly videos, or checking your socials when you should be working. You are going to want to get your work done so you have time to explore. If you can work from home for whatever reason, who's to say you can't work from some beach in paradise?

So, back to your plan. Once you have the basic framework of *who*, *what*, *where*, *when*, and *why*, the next step is to get on a marketing list.

Of course, you can do everything from the internet, but I like to have hard copies of brochures and guidebooks. I try to have them spread around like coffee table books, but my wife keeps hiding things (she calls it putting them away).

Get on a mailing list. The occasional reminder of that place you wanted to go and the things you wanted to do will help keep you motivated. It took me two years of getting Outward Bound course catalogs every quarter before I finally signed up for a course. Get on an email list. Regular research on the internet about places you want to go will create a burning desire.

Another thing to be prepared for is sometimes when you decide, the universe throws obstacles in the way. It's as if your resolve is being tested.

My wife and I shared a mutual dream of driving across the United States in a recreational vehicle and stopping at national parks along the way. This is something you need a lot of time to do, which we never seemed to have. Finally, when we decided to move to Australia, it looked like that was going to be the right time. We would have no jobs, no home, and we had to travel to California anyway to fly out of Los Angeles International Airport. We planned a nice long trip across the US. We thought we would sell our house in the fast-moving real estate market and use the money to finance the trip, which we thought would take about two months.

Getting the house fixed up for sale took a little longer than we thought it would. I had expected it to be done in early August, but it was September before we were done. I was doing the final touches on landscaping and getting ready to list the house. Thats when I saw the first news report. Hurricane Irma had intensified to a Category 5 and was weaving a path of destruction through the Caribbean. As the days wore on, it continued to cause catastrophic destruction across island after island and was slowly turning toward Florida. We did not know if we would even have a home to sell, let alone if we would be able to make a cross-country trip. All we could do was hunker down and hope. It made landfall south of us. It was only a Category 1 hurricane when it sideswiped Tampa. There were trees through houses in the neighborhood, but luckily, we were spared.

We finally got the yard cleaned up and the house on the market when something else came up to block our way. Our neighborhood suddenly became the focus of national attention. A serial killer was stalking the subdivision.

September turned into October and then November. It looked like we might not be able to do our road trip after all. Zoe and I had to be in Australia by mid-December as a condition of our visas. We had to decide—wait until the end and fly or do the road trip. Finally we decided to just go for it. We had money saved. I had intended to use it for things like cars and housing once we got to Oz (Australia), but we decided a once-in-a-lifetime trip across America was worth the risk. Right after Thanksgiving, we left. We had to cut our two-month trip down to three weeks. The killer[5] was caught the day we pulled out of our driveway for the last time.

The trip was well worth it, even though we had to cut out more than half of our planned destinations. I put in a few days driving more than sixteen hours. But we needed this. It was more than a vacation. It was a migration. Each mile behind us was a tiny psychological shift from what we were leaving to where we were going. While traveling in a modern recreational vehicle with electricity, propane gas range, and running water isn't exactly like traveling in a horse-drawn covered wagon like the early settlers did, there was some sort of connection to that experience. It touched some older part of us.

We stopped at a few campgrounds in the Smoky Mountains. Then we headed to Big Bend National Park on the Texas–Mexico border. An article in *Outside Magazine* described the park as "dangerous as hell,"[6] so of course we had to go there. Big Bend, named for the large curve in the Rio Grande, is the most isolated national park in the lower forty-eight states. It comprises over eight hundred thousand acres of the Chihuahuan Desert and Chisos Mountains. This was where we were snowed in. Zoe's first time in real snow was in the middle of the desert. We have a picture of her making snow angels with cacti in the background. After the snowstorm, the next day was clear, and we could see the snowcapped mountain peaks. Their immensity was humbling. We saw roadrunners and coyotes.

After Big Bend, we traveled to Carlsbad Caverns in New Mexico, the Grand Canyon, the Painted Desert, the Petrified Forest, and a lot of little places in between. I signed real estate documents electronically on my phone when we had a connection. Finally, we met up with some friends who had just moved to California. We closed (settled) on the house at the kitchen table at our friends' house in California the day before we left the United States. Then I traded the camper for a rental car, and we hightailed it to the airport, past notorious California bushfires. Then we were gone to the other side of the world.

My point is if you get the chance, go! The conditions may not be perfect; the timing will never be right. Weird stuff is going to come up and get in the way, but you should still prioritize travel. Find a way to go. Hopefully you won't experience hurricanes and serial killers, but if you do, don't let that stop you.

EXERCISE

Plan an Epic Trip:

Who?

Where?

What?

When?

Why?

Once you have a plan, you just have to execute it. What good is a plan without following through with it? Remember to have a great time.

_____

_____

_____

_____

_____

_____

_____

_____

Chapter 10:

Living with Urgency

> Life can only be understood backwards,
> but it must be lived forwards.
> — Søren Kierkegaard

The Attack of the African Sniper Wasp

Florida has an abundance of four things: sunshine, heat, humidity, and insects. Growing up there, you get to know bugs. One of the more interesting insects to observe is the mud dauber.[1] Mud daubers, sometimes called dirt daubers, are a type of wasp. Their name comes from the nest-building technique female mud daubers use. They dig in the dirt or sand and collect it in their mandibles. They then secrete saliva and add it to the dirt or sand. This turns into mud, which they use to create their nest. The female wasp then captures spiders and brings them to the nest to feed her larvae. They are not aggressive as wasps go, so you can watch them from close range without worrying about being stung.

As a child curious about the natural world, I often watched mud daubers do their work. As they dug, the daubers kicked up a big plume of sand, like a rooster's tail. Then they took their collected mud to their nest site, usually in the corner of a building. They built tubes for their larvae and connected them into fascinating structures. When the mud dried, it was like cement. Sometimes they built masterpieces of architecture, combining different colors of soil and clay. As a kid, when I went out to play, I could always tell if the mud daubers were at work by the six-inch-high plumes of dirt or sand they kicked up when they dug.

In January 1993 I wasn't in Florida anymore. I was in a place so different from the Western society I was used to, it might as well have been a different world. I had been taken from my home base in Southern California and thrown onto the horn of Africa with less than a week's notice. I was now in a country where only a month before anarchy had reigned supreme. My new home was the balcony of the airport terminal of Mogadishu International Airport, Somalia.

As I said in an earlier chapter, my team arrived on New Year's Day, 1993. When we arrived, there wasn't much left of the terminal. Before the war, giant plate glass windows had faced the street, which was only about fifty meters away. Doors and windows also faced the runway. Now the windows were giant holes in the side of the building. The bottoms of the windows were low enough to step through. If you didn't want to bother with that, you could walk through the doorway. There weren't doors anymore.

There were some chairs in the lower part of the terminal waiting area. These were left behind only because they were bolted to the floor. There were several rows of them, like old wooden movie theater seats. Everything else in the building had long since been looted. The large windows that opened toward the street were a major security issue. There was a wall around the airport, but huge gaps were open in it, presumably from artillery. Where we were, at a significant section of the wall between the terminal and the city, was complete rubble. Since this section was blown away, the only protections separating us from the city were a couple of thin spools of concertina wire.

At first we decided to set up our cots in an adjoining side room on the first floor. After further inspection of the room, we noticed the far wall was riddled with bullet holes. Any sniper would have a clear shot at us through the window. We would be sitting ducks.

We walked upstairs to the second floor. Then we walked onto the balcony overlooking the runway. This looked like the safest spot in the place, so we decided to bunk there. There was a roof overhang on the balcony, so in the rare event of rain, we would be partially undercover.

The only disadvantage to this location was that when jets taxied down the runway, the place they turned around was in line with us, so we were hit with the exhaust. The blast acted like a powerful, hot, smelly, noisy, annoying wind. We weren't so close that it was dangerous, but when you are in 110 degrees Fahrenheit (42 degrees Celsius)–plus heat, getting blasted with even hotter wind was not a lot of fun. Still, it was the safest place to be in the airport terminal, so we decided to suck it up.

There were many planes, not just fighter jets but military transports and even commercial airliners that had been chartered to bring troops in quickly. I had arrived in one of these chartered planes, and I described the rest of my first day in the beginning of chapter 3.

The airport was the staging area for the United Nations force. Tents, armored vehicles, and people were spread out all over the place. The grounds of the airport were a makeshift bustling city, separate from the city of Mogadishu that surrounded it. There were people in uniforms from all over the world. I often thought it looked like an international Boy Scout jamboree, except everyone had guns.

For the most part, my days were boring. I spent a lot of the day cleaning my rifle, writing letters, reading my book, and taking my turn on guard. My friends had taken to the game of spades, but playing cards never interested me much. Sometimes we went to the beach to break up the monotony. The beach was a quarter mile from the other side of the runway. We dove off the cliffs into the perfectly blue Indian Ocean. Of course, one of us stayed up on the rocks, guarding the rifles and looking for insurgents who might have snuck into the airport or for the sharks that apparently infested these waters.

The lookout was also there to make sure we didn't swim too far from the rocks. Another danger in the water was amphibious vehicles and hovercraft that used the beach to land. Getting run over by one of them would not be fun.

Our balcony overlooked the tarmac, so anyone who arrived by plane had to walk directly underneath us into the terminal before departing, usually by convoy to wherever they were going in the city. Most of these were military personnel, but I was surprised at how many reporters and intelligence agents also went through our building.

I no longer had the missile launcher. My mission required only an M-16 rifle. As I said, for the most part, life was boring. But every day at some point it was time to go for a drive. My sole purpose in Somalia was these drives. Our captain was a liaison to the Marine command at what was left of the American Embassy. Our unit controlled all Marines coming into and going out of the country, so our captain had to go to the embassy every day to transfer information on a hard disk with the colonel in charge there.

I and the three other guys in my section had one purpose: we were the security team for this drive from Mogadishu International Airport to the embassy and back every day. I and another guy had tactical driver's licenses, so we traded off driving. One of us drove while the other rode in the back of the truck with the others as security. Most of the time, I drove. If I wasn't driving, my sole purpose was to watch for ambushes and improvised explosive devises (IEDs). An IED is a bomb designed to be hidden, disguised as debris or some other innocent object either in or alongside the road.

When it was my turn to drive, I reluctantly traded my M-16 rifle for my captain's 9 mm pistol, since it is hard to accurately fire a rifle and drive at the same time. Most of the units traveled in large convoys. We were five guys in an open-air truck variant of a Humvee. If I were a Somali warlord, I would have picked us as a soft target.

Before we drove into the city, there was usually a line of vehicles queued up. The guards opened the gate for only one vehicle at a time. We would be relaxed, casually joking until we pulled up to the front gate. That signaled our turn to be released into the Mogadishu mayhem. Then it was all business.

The gate slowly opened as we loaded a magazine into our weapons and each chambered a bullet. From that moment on, everyone except the driver had his index finger on the trigger and his thumbs resting comfortably on the safety switch. When we rolled out of the gate into the city, my body came alive! I got a strange hyperawareness that comes from an adrenaline surge. The hairs on the back of my neck always stood up as soon as we were through the gate. Then we drove our Humvee into the chaos in the streets of war-torn Somalia.

As we drove, our eyes constantly scanned for anything out of the ordinary. There were only two rules for the driver: don't throw anybody out of the vehicle, and don't get stuck in traffic. The three in the back had no seat belts, so it was easy to lose them if you slammed to a stop or accelerated too fast. Driving on the wrong side of the road, the footpath, and even into marketplaces was fair game as long as you didn't get pinned in one spot. Being trapped in a traffic jam made us sitting ducks for any insurgents who wanted to make a name for themselves by killing a few Marines.

There weren't any concrete rules to the road. On my first drive, I thought to myself, "Wow, this place could really use some cops." Then I had the horrible realization that the closest thing to law enforcement was us. We were part of an international police force. The one advantage of this was when you had five guys in your truck with guns drawn, someone was usually polite and let you merge into the roundabout. Okay, if the traffic congestion was unusually heavy sometimes, you had to point rifles at people to remind them to be polite.

Most of the public transportation had been destroyed in the hostilities, so buses were few and far between. For the ones that worked, there would not only be a ridiculous number of people cramped inside but also at least a dozen people standing on the bumpers or hanging off the windows.

There were pedestrians, motorcycles, minibuses, military vehicles from a dozen countries, and all kinds of makeshift vehicles on the road. Occasionally livestock moved on the street and got in the way. Giant potholes were all over the place, and most of the roads were dirt. There were no traffic lights, and very few road signs hadn't been looted, so traffic accidents and fatalities were common. Even a stubborn ox on the road was a disaster waiting to happen. Clearing an accident could take hours—plenty of time to ambush a military vehicle stuck in traffic. If things got too crazy, we took an alternate route by the infamous soccer field. There was less traffic there, but the area was known as Sniper's Alley for a reason, so we avoided it if possible.

Some days everything seemed relatively calm, and other days you could feel a tension in the air. We aborted a couple of trips a few miles in because our captain had an uneasy feeling.

As nerve-racking as our drive was, it was also the usual highlight of my day. It was exciting, at least. It gave me the chance to feel I was doing something. Here's a bit of exploration. We also went to the port a few times to get supplies, which was different from our embassy runs. I was able to see what once seemed like a vibrant city. Now there was rubble everywhere. There was no glass in any windows. Everything had been destroyed or looted. Many houses didn't have doors—just cloth up in the doorway. The people were incredibly skinny, and the food had been flowing for several weeks at this point. I wondered how horrible conditions were before we arrived.

The drive between the airport and the embassy was approximately nine miles (fourteen kilometers). As we approached, we had to drive several blocks along the embassy wall before we hit the gate. The concrete wall was over twelve feet (four meters) high. Topping this were spools of razor wire, and cemented to the top of the wall were shards of broken glass soda bottles. Anyone who tried to scale that wall was in for a hard time. It certainly looked a lot more secure than the perimeter at the airport. A few hundred yards away was a burned-out multistory apartment building.

The open area of the embassy grounds was covered with tents that served as a command post for the Marines. Several units operated out of here as well. If you weren't shaded by a tent, you were standing in the sand, exposed. It was over a hundred degrees Fahrenheit where we were at the airport, but at least there was a sea breeze sometimes. Here at the embassy, there was no circulation of air. It was just hot and still. Because the air was still, flies constantly buzzed around and annoyed us. The embassy grounds had an abundance of four things—sunshine, heat, humidity, and insects, just like home.

We usually found some friends from other units to talk to while waiting for the captain. Once the captain was done with his business, we did the reverse drive to the airport. One day my friends and I were waiting for the captain to finish his meeting with the colonel. We were leaning against this waist-high wall. No one was talking.

The heat had a way of making you drift off into daydreams. I was lost in thought when suddenly, about ten feet in front of me, I noticed a plume of sand kick up. "Oh wow," I thought. "They have mud daubers here in Africa." Why wouldn't they? It was hot and buggy, just like Florida. I turned to the side to tell my friends about the cool bug I'd seen, but they were gone. They must have walked off while I was lost in thought.

That's when I saw another plume of sand—this time only five feet in front of me. At five feet I should have seen the wasp kicking up the sand, but there wasn't one. Suddenly I got a sinking feeling in my gut. These weren't insects kicking up the sand. They were bullets! I was the target of a sniper, and he was walking rounds in on me! "Walking in" is a technique snipers and artillery gunners use. Assuming the first shot doesn't hit its target, the sniper or a spotter, if they have one, looks at the point of impact and adjusts the next shot. That means if the bullets are not striking to the right or left of the target, they can walk the bullets in. If they have a scope or decent rear sight, they adjust the elevation knob. If not, they aim a little higher.

It took so long (two bullets) for me to figure out what was happening because my would-be assassin must have been using some kind of makeshift silencer. By this point in my life, I had seen a lot of bullet impacts, but they were always accompanied by the loud report of a rifle.

After that second impact, my adrenaline levels shot up. The next couple of seconds slowed to a crawl. The world took on a strange quality that was both very vivid and sharp yet somehow surreal at the same time. In one fluid motion, I moved from in front of the wall around the side, into a covered position behind the wall, unshouldering my rifle at the same time. As I moved, a third round struck at the very spot my feet had just been. I slammed a magazine into my rifle and pulled back the bolt.

I peered over the wall. The shots had obviously come from the apartment building, but in the windows I could see only darkness. No muzzle flash. No Somali peering out at me. It could have come from any number of darkened, blown-out windows. Now he knew I was onto him, the sniper wouldn't show himself. There was no way to return fire. The whole thing had transpired in a couple of seconds.

I told my captain, and he thought it was a big enough deal that I should tell the colonel. When I reported the incident, the colonel looked at me with one of those old salty Marine looks and said, "Son, we take sniper fire here every day." Then he gave me a sly half smile and said, "Lucky for you and me, they're not very good shots." And that was that.

When I had the time to think about it, I began to ponder the brevity of life. I had already almost been killed several times, but that was the first time anyone had tried to murder me, at least that I knew of.

The sniper incident made me realize something. It is easy to die. I expected something to happen on the road. The embassy was where I thought I was the safest. That moment created an appreciation of life and an understanding that our time is short. You can go just when you think you are out of harm's way.

About a week later, two Cobra gunships dusted off from the airport. (Cobra gunships are heavily armed attack helicopters.) We could hear their twenty-millimeter Gatling guns coming from the direction of the embassy. The shooting lasted an unusually long time. The next time we went to the embassy, the apartment building was gone. You couldn't even see the rubble from behind the embassy wall. I guess the colonel had finally had enough of snipers trying to take out his men.

Less than a year later, the US and the UN abandoned their attempt to save Somalia, leaving it to fall back into anarchy. The country and the conflict there would probably have been completely forgotten if it were not for the 2001 Ridley Scott movie *Black Hawk Down*.[2] The movie chronicles the tragic events that ultimately led to the withdrawal from Somalia. The Somalis have been engaged in various levels of civil war ever since. Life is hard and very short there. Seeing it made me understand how lucky I was to be born where I was. I like to revisit this gratitude whenever things are not going exactly as I want. Seeing places like that close-up can give perspective when you are caught up in your personal, developed-world problems.

My time in Somalia was short and not nearly as intense as the experiences of others I knew over there. I can say I was there and got the merit badge. My brushes with death were nothing compared to many of the horrors my fellow Marines and many soldiers endured, especially over the twenty years of constant war in Iraq and Afghanistan.

I tip my hat to all who serve. Some of them never come home, and some leave parts of their bodies and sometimes their minds on the battlefield. I have heard warriors say they felt the need to live to the fullest to honor the friends they lost. To me, that is profound. We live deeply because we are still able to. We have the choice, whereas others no longer do.

People love to repost motivational memes, and back when people worked in offices, you'd see posters in their cubicles about how you should "Live each day as if it's your last"—so much that the saying has become a cliché devoid of value.

Besides being a cliché, the other problem I have with the saying is it creates the apathy it is trying to break. Think about it. If everyone went around every day like it was their last one on Earth, nobody would go to work. I think a more precise statement is to live with urgency!

If you are convinced the end is here, it's too easy to take up a nihilistic "what's the point?" attitude. It's the uncertainty that makes life compelling. Today might be my last day on Earth, but probably not, so I can at least make it interesting.

You may have less time than you think, but you may have more. Either way, in the end it probably won't be enough. One thing is for certain. If you keep saying, "One day I'll . . ." long enough, the statement will eventually become, "I would have. I could have. I should have." Choose to live with urgency. The best statement is "Today, I'll . . ."

These days, unfortunately you don't have to be in a war zone for a sniper's bullet to find you. Criminals and lunatics are all too common. Besides that, there are a million ways to go. An accident, an undiagnosed disease, or a condition can claim you.

The world is volatile. We are living in uncertain times. Life can change quickly. That is why maintaining a sense of urgency is important.

Being an asthma sufferer has often put the fatality of life at the forefront of my mind. Asthma sucks sometimes. I can go from normal to a coughing fit with the feeling of suffocating in a short span. But the value of this is I realize life is fragile, and it helps keep me from getting caught up with little dramas that don't mean anything. The asthma also reminds me that I must live now, while I can.

Strenuous exercise is one of the biggest triggers that can set off an asthma attack. In a bizarre paradox, the treatment most recommended by doctors for strengthening the lungs and circulatory system for asthma sufferers is strenuous exercise. This has greatly contributed to my overall philosophy that something that might kill you might also be the thing that keeps you alive. Paradox and irony are the spice of life. They don't always make things good, but they do keep them interesting. *Amor fati*: love thy fate.

In 2012 my mother passed away. Somehow her doctors missed finding her cancer, even after two MRIs. By the time they figured it out, the cancer had metastasized throughout her body and brain. There was no time for gallivanting around the world, ticking boxes on her bucket list. She was confined to a wheelchair within days. A few days later, she slipped into a coma and then was gone. The time between prognosis and death was two weeks to the day.

I didn't know it at the time, but I was going to need a level of physiological ukemi I did not yet possess. I had a rough time with my mom's death. My mother was the benevolent matriarch of the family. She was the glue that held our family together. This was also a change in identity for me. After my dad died, we still had my mom. But after she died, I could no longer say I was somebody's son.

This was also the time when my asthma was at its worst. It is in times of grief or suffering that people are weakest. That is when something else nasty happens.

One night that November, I went for my nightly walk. I was still grieving. I was also somewhat stressed about all the work involved in handling my mom's estate. I was slightly delirious from a powerful cocktail of antibiotics and prednisone for my bronchitis. Most of the time I am pretty situationally aware, but not this night.

I was on my way home when a car approached from behind. It stopped at the stop sign behind me for too long. The driver cut the headlights, and I got an uneasy feeling. But then they turned the headlights back on, so I told myself I was being paranoid. Then the car pulled up next to me. Were they going to ask for directions?

The passenger got out in attack mode. I was clueless. I thought I was in a fight, not an armed assault. My ego took control. Was this kid trying to jump me? Instead of running, like I should have, I closed the distance on him, arms up and ready to throw a punch, and he ran. "That's what I thought! Thinking better of jumping me, aren't you?" I said to myself. But my feeling of toughness was short lived.

He ran only far enough to clear enough distance to pull the handgun from his waistband. "Give me the money," he said as he aimed the gun at my face. I was still clueless. I just stood there, dumbfounded. The fact I was in a stickup didn't even register. This was the adrenal freeze I described in the chapter on fight, flight, or freeze. My brain stopped working properly. I didn't understand what he had said, nor had the gun that was clearly visible registered in my conscious mind. Somewhere in the fog of my brain was an internal voice that was my own but somehow not. The voice was whispering, "This can't really be happening. This isn't real."

I was having such a hard time wrapping my head around the reality I was facing, and all I could do was stammer out an indignant, "What?" in response to my assailant's demand for money.

"I said give me the fucking money!" he screamed.

This is finally what woke me from my delirium. Now the gun barrel I was staring down became crystal clear, and I consciously realized this was bad.

At this point I decided to act. I hadn't started ninjutsu training yet. But I did have two years of training in aikido, which ended with a shoulder surgery. I had disarmed people with rubber-training pistols dozens of times. I decided to try to take the gun away.

Now, this is the part of the story where I would love to say I executed a perfect *kotegaeshi* wristlock, threw my attacker to the ground, took away the gun, and was my own hero. But that's not what happened.

I shifted my weight to my front foot, preparing to spin and grab the gun. As I said in chapter 3, too much adrenaline reduces motor control and coordination. This was far from the smooth precision movement it had been in aikido class. My movement was jerky and telegraphed my intention. My assailant was far more of an astute observer than I thought. My disjointed movement was easy for him to read and respond to.

Although I had taken away plenty of training pistols, I had never tried to take a live weapon from a real mugger. He had obviously robbed more people than thugs I had disarmed, so he was better at this dance than I was. As soon as I shifted my weight to my front, he took a giant step back, almost a leap. If my life wasn't in danger, it would have been comical how far back he stepped. Now he still had an almost point-blank shot, but for me, trying to snatch the gun, the distance might as well have been across the street.

There was that other annoying, disconnected voice in my head giving commentary. The voice seemed like a separate stream of consciousness. It was a lot calmer than I felt and in an inquisitive kind of way was saying, "Strange, this kind of thing never happened to Steven Seagal in the movies. He always managed to take the gun away."

My normal stream of consciousness was panicked. All I could think was to ask myself the question of whether I would see my wife and daughter again. Some people say when they have a near-death experience their life flashes before their eyes. Well, I didn't have a flashback. I had more of a flash-forward. If I died there on that spot, my Zoe, who was only two at the time, would not know her father. I would just be a picture in the family album. She wouldn't even remember me. I had a vision of my two-year-old as a troubled teen with no father figure in her life. That is what scared me the most!

I needed to survive these next couple of minutes. There was nothing I could do now but settle into my role as victim and try to keep him calm enough he didn't do anything rash. The only tool I had left was the sound of my voice. He once again impatiently demanded money. The only problem with capitulation was I didn't have any money to give him. Luckily, I hadn't brought my wallet with me, although I didn't think it was so lucky at the time. I figured there was a good chance he might shoot me just for spite.

My hands were out, palms at about chest level up at this point. I raised them higher, more submissive. Even though my heart felt like it was going to burst through my chest, I spoke calmly. "Look, man, I don't have any money. I am just out for a walk. You have all the power. Trust me. If I had some money, you could have it. All I have is car keys."

He wasn't happy. "What? Are you kidding me?" he yelled, as if he thought it was rude I hadn't thought to bring any cash for him to steal. "If you are lying, I will beat you with this!" he screamed, waving the gun. On the one hand, the idea of a pistol-whipping wasn't appealing. People have died or suffered permanent brain damage from that. I decided if he did start beating me, if I had my wits after the first blow, I would fight back. It would be no good to avoid a bullet if I let my skull get caved in by the handle of the gun and ended up a permanent vegetable. On the other hand, if he was threatening me with a beating, he probably wasn't 100 percent committed to shooting me.

At this point he told me to get on my knees and put my hands on my head. I kneeled and felt the muzzle of the gun pressed against the back of my skull. Then I heard that other voice in my head: "You know, when the news reports someone was killed execution style, this is the position they are in."

"Not helping," I mentally chided myself.

He riffled through my pockets with one hand while the other held the gun. I felt so violated, so vulnerable. He took my keys, then he and his driver, whom I never got a look at, were gone.

I was alive! Physically, the only damage I sustained was a scrape on my knee. But psychologically I was maimed badly. The PTSD started slowly, building gradually over the course of about six months until it manifested throughout my body and mind as crippling anxiety and full-body tremors.

My return to sanity was a long road, with plenty of ups and downs. I had to figure things out as I went. I had to learn what helped and what didn't. The first step was pulling myself out of hyperarousal by learning to control my breathing.

The reason I had been traumatized by the mere threat of someone shooting me, compared to in Somalia, when someone was really trying to kill me, were the elements of surprise, context, and a sense of control I spoke about earlier in the book. Although the sniper initially caught me off guard, in the bigger context I was in a war zone. Not only was that kind of stuff expected, but I was kind of surprised no one had tried to kill me before. I felt in full control because I had cover, and I was well armed. I had a rifle, 180 rounds of ammunition, and several platoons of battle-ready Marines at my back. Had the sniper continued shooting, he would have been in more danger than I was.

With the robbery, I was taken off guard, unarmed, not in full health, and already psychologically on the back foot after the loss of my mom. Contextually I was in my own neighborhood, which I'd previously thought was safe but wasn't. I had no control over the situation. My life was totally in the hands of the bad guy. It was the perfect recipe for PTSD. I also had a wife and child to think of. Initially, the implications of leaving them behind may have contributed to the trauma. But they also gave me my biggest reasons for deciding to put in the necessary effort to get better.

It took more than two years and a lot of work before I felt like my old self again. But I was alive. I had a second chance. Every day after that was a gift. In fact, it was the greatest gift of all time. I was able to be there for my family and see the young person my toddler became. I was there to read stories, give hugs, protect from scary monsters, and hopefully impart some hard-won wisdom.

I won't say anything like "It happened for a reason," or "I am glad for it." It did, however, instill a sense of urgency to live like never before. I can honestly say I now experience a quality of life at least as good as it was before the robbery, if not better. I know that not everyone who suffers from anxiety-based mental disorders recovers, but I am living proof it can be done. I won't even say I never experience anxiety anymore. I do occasionally but I manage it well now.

One thing people who have near-death experiences get is hyperawareness that their time is limited. This can put things into perspective and help people get their priorities right. Those priorities might be starting that business you always wanted to start, taking that epic once-in-a-lifetime trip, or simply remembering to tell someone you love them and give them a hug. Use the time you have left, no matter how long that might be.

One thing that has given me the time to finally finish this book is that during the revision phase, I ruptured my Achilles tendon—I snapped it clean in half. This gave me plenty of time to sit around and write. Writing also helped me forget about the pain to some degree. How did I manage to rip the strongest tendon in the human body, you ask? Well, you remember how I think I'm a ninja?

The ninja warrior[3] obstacle course / game show has become incredibly popular around the world. There is a different version for each of the countries in which it airs. Here in Oz, we have *Australian Ninja Warrior*, and in the States the show is, of course, *American Ninja Warrior*. Because of the show's popularity, there are gyms that specialize in Ninja Warrior obstacle courses popping up everywhere.

I took Zoe to one of these Ninja Warrior parks for her birthday. Not being a parent content to watch, I had to participate too. We were almost ready to go home when I decided to take one last run up the warped wall.

If you don't know what that is, it is a curved ramp like a quarter pipe for skateboarding that transitions into a vertical wall. You have to get enough momentum up the ramp to take a couple of steps up the vertical part of the wall to where you can grab the top ledge and pull yourself onto a balcony. I had just passed a ninjutsu test in which I had to run up a tree. (Yes, you read that right: running straight up a vertical surface is a skill called *shoten-no-jutsu*.) I figured a wall with a nice ramp for transitioning to vertical would be a piece of cake.

I was on my second run. As I was running up the wall, I heard a loud pop and felt excruciating pain in my leg. I instantly lost power and slid down the ramp on my bottom. I knew what I had done right away, and from there it was a trip to the emergency room. I was in a cast, then a boot for over three months.

Just like that, all the things I loved doing, including walking in the woods, were taken away. I had to spend a lot of time doing the one thing I find most challenging: sitting still. There was a lesson in that experience for me.

My recovery was long and difficult. I had to learn how to walk again. However, I am thankful it was even a possibility. The rehab to get to running, jumping, and some of the other crazy things I like to do was even more difficult. I am thankful for this, though. One day something may happen that I won't be able to recover from. This has really given me an appreciation of the little things I used to take for granted, like the simple act of walking.

I know one day something may happen that takes away my mobility for good. I know several people now who have been struck by progressive neurological diseases who I think are way too young for something like that. It's unfair and unpredictable. But it is a fact of life. These things happen.

The threat of being incapacitated or permanently disabled should be as big a motivator as the possibility of death. Life can change in an instant. Do what you can while you can. That is probably the one thing that will create a sense of urgency to do the things you always dreamed about. Ponder the fact that, whether by permanent incapacitation or death, one day you won't be able to do the things you want to. This can create a positive form of impatience. You know one day the choice will no longer be yours.

The stoics of ancient Greece and Rome believed it was important to meditate on your mortality. *Memento mori*[4] is a Latin phrase that means *remember, you will die*. It was not meant to be morbid or depressing. It was meant to remind us to have humility, that life is short, to cherish the important things, and to enjoy life, despite inevitable hardships. There is no getting out of death for any of us.

Spending time contemplating your mortality is probably the best thing you can do to create a sense of urgency, priority, and perspective in your life. *Maranasati*[5] is the Buddhist practice of meditating on death. Some monasteries go so far as having skeletons in the meditation halls, so the monks are mindful of the impermanence of life.

I don't have a whole skeleton, but I do have a small ceramic skull on the windowsill of my home dojo for when I meditate. I think I bought it as a Halloween decoration, but now I keep it up all year round to remind myself life is fleeting. This is one of those counterintuitive paradoxes, but going into my own mind and reminding myself that death is always out there waiting for me greatly reduces any anxiety about my inevitable demise. It is freeing. It is when you hide from death that it becomes frightening.

None of us will truly understand how short life is until we reach the end of it. That is why it is so important to live it to the fullest. On that note, there is one final exercise in this book. But first I want to make sure you have done the list of fifty things to do before you die. If you haven't already done that one, do it now. This list is important; look at it often. Do things on the list!

EXERCISE

Okay, the last exercise is to write your own eulogy. As I am sure you already know, a eulogy is a speech about someone who has died, usually a tribute to the dearly departed. Eulogies are usually written for others, but for the purpose of this exercise, you are going to write your own.

First, imagine you are going to die in the distant future. You can be creative with this. It gives you plenty of time to envision your ideal self. How do you ideally want to be remembered? What do you want people to say about you when you are gone? What kind of person do you want to have been? What do you want to have accomplished? Will you have left a legacy? What did people most admire about you? What was your most memorable attribute? What did people like about you? What character traits did you embody so much that people would remember them as fundamental to you? What was your career like? Where did you live? Did you travel much? Did you have any interesting hobbies? If people could sum you up in one word, what would it be? Remember, this is your ideal self, having died many years in the future.

Next, you will make it more confrontational. Write another eulogy for yourself, assuming you will die tomorrow. Use the same framework. Look back on your life and think of what you have accomplished so far. You can answer the same questions as the above paragraph and only include things up to now.

The first eulogy allowed for some creativity in how you want to be remembered if you have plenty of time to make improvements and accomplish things. With this second eulogy, I want you to be brutally honest with yourself. How will you be remembered if this is the end?

Now compare the two eulogies. Where are the differences? Is there a big contrast between the two as far as how you want to be viewed as a person and how you think you are viewed now? Are there lots of things on the first list that aren't on the second? Are there things on the first list you should be working toward that you haven't started yet?

If you have done this exercise, it should give you considerable clarity. This should help crystallize what is important to you. Comparing the two lists can build urgency on a deep level.

The last exercise will be, for most of us, the hardest in this book. It's the one that may take a lifetime to complete. The last exercise is to close the gap between the first and second eulogy. The third exercise is to become as much like the person in your idealized eulogy as you can be before someone has to give the real one.

Since death is the topic of this chapter, I would like to give you one final quote from Roman emperor Marcus Aurelius: "It is not death that a man should fear, but he should fear never beginning to live."[6]

Well, here we are at the end. As often as you can, get out there and get out of your comfort zone, face your fears, and do cool stuff. Do lots of cool stuff! Also, remember the best piece of advice anyone ever gave me: breathe deeply, relax, and have fun with it.

Endnotes

Chapter 1

1. Yvon Chouinard, *Let My People Go Surfing: The Education of a Reluctant Businessman* (Penguin USA, 2005).
2. *Intercept Expeditions for Struggling Teens & Young Adults*, Outward Bound, https://www.outwardbound.org/intercept/what-is-intercept/.
3. Marcus Aurelius, *Meditations*, E-Bookarama. Kindle Edition.
4. Richard Branson, *Losing My Virginity: The Autobiography* (Adult Original Trade, 2005).
5. Dutton and Aron, *Misattribution of Arousal* (bridge study), "Some evidence for heightened sexual attraction under conditions of high anxiety," *Journal of Personality and Social Psychology* (1974) https://sanlab.psych.ucla.edu/wp-content/uploads/sites/31/2016/03/Dutton-Aron-1974-arousal.pdf, accessed August 6, 2024.
6. Cindy M. Meston, PhD and Penny F. Frohlich, MA, "Love at First Fright: Partner Salience Moderates Roller-Coaster-Induced Excitation Transfer," *Archives of Sexual Behavior*, vol. 32 no. 6, December 2003, https://doi.org/10.1023/a:1026037527455 (Accessed August 6, 2024).

Chapter 2

1. "Risk," Wikipedia, https://en.wikipedia.org/wiki/Risk, accessed August 3, 2024.
2. Brian Sobel, *The Fighting Pattons* (Indiana University Press, 2013).

3. Aron Ralston, *Between a Rock and a Hard Place* (Atria Books, 2004).

4. Dick Prouty, Jane Panicucci, Rufus Collinson, eds., *Adventure Education Theory and Applications* (Project Adventure, Human Kinetics 2007).

5. "Bear spray," Wikipedia, https://en.wikipedia.org/wiki/Bear spray, accessed August 3, 2024.

6. Amanda Ripley, *The Unthinkable: Who Survives When Disaster Strikes and Why* (Harmony 2009), Kindle.

7. *Human Ecology Theory, The Family As A System*, https://family.jrank.org/pages/820/Human-Ecology-Theory-Family-System.html, accessed August 3, 2024.

8. "Risk tolerance," *American Dictionary of Psychology* (updated April 2018), https://dictionary.apa.org/risk-tolerance, accessed August 3, 2024.

9. "Hypothermia . . . in the Summer?" First Edition, First Aid Training Inc, https://calgaryfirstaidtraining.ca/2022/08/29/hypothermia-in-the-summer/, accessed August 6, 2024.

10. Werner Herzog, *Grizzly Man* (documentary film), Lionsgate Films, 2005. https://www.imdb.com/title/tt0427312/ Accessed Jan 9, 2025.

Chapter 3

1. Joshua A. Waxenbaum, **Vamsi Reddy,** and Matthew Varacallo, *Anatomy, Autonomic Nervous System* (updated Jul 2023), StatPearls Publishing, https://www.ncbi.nlm.nih.gov/books/NBK539845/, accessed August 4, 2024.

2. "Flight or Fight," Wikipedia, https://en.wikipedia.org/wiki/Fight-or-flight_response, accessed August 4, 2024.

3. Alex Korb, Ph.D. "Predictable Fear: Why the brain likes haunted houses," *Psychology Today* (Oct 2014), https://www.psychologytoday.com/us/blog/prefrontal-nudity/201410/predictable-fear, accessed August 4, 2024.

4. Howard E. LeWine, MD, *Understanding the Stress Response*, Harvard Health Publishing (April 2024), https://www.health.harvard.edu/staying-healthy/understanding-the-stress-response, accessed August 4, 2024.

5. Misha Ketchell, ed., "It feels instantaneous, but how long does it really take to think a thought," *The Conversation* (June 2015), https://theconversation.com/it-feels-instantaneous-but-how-long-does-it-really-take-to-think-a-thought-42392, accessed August 4, 2024.

6. Loh, H. H., Tseng, L. F., Wei, E., and Li, C. H., *Beta-endorphin is a potent analgesic agent*, (1976). Proceedings of the National Academy of Sciences of the United States of America, 73(8), 2895–2898. https://doi.org/10.1073/pnas.73.8.2895, accessed August 4, 2024.

7. "Anandamide," Wikipedia, https://en.wikipedia.org/wiki/Anandamide#Obesity_and_liver_disease, accessed August 4, 2024.

8. Mihaly Csikszentmihalyi, *FLOW: The Psychology of Optimal Experience* (Harper and Row, 1990).

9. Christopher Bergland, "Superfluidity and the Transcendent Ecstasy of Extreme Sports," *Psychology Today* (May 2017), https://www.psychologytoday.com/us/blog/the-athletes-way/201705/superfluidity-and-the-transcendent-ecstasy-extreme-sports, accessed August 4, 2024.

10. Kendra Cherry, MSEd., "Peak Experiences in Psychology," *Very Well Mind* (August 2023), https://www.verywellmind.com/what-are-peak-experiences-2795268, accessed August 4, 2024.

11. Steven Kotler, *The Rise of Superman: Decoding the Science of Ultimate Human Performance* (New Harvest, 2015), Kindle.

12. Brett Martin, "Extreme Oxford Sports," *Vanity Fair* (February 2004), https://www.vanityfair.com/style/2004/02/

oxford-university-dangerous-sports-club, accessed August 4, 2024.

13. "History of Surfing," Wikipedia, https://en.wikipedia.org/wiki/History_of_surfing, accessed August 4, 2024.

14. Dalya Alberge, "It feels like I'm choking'—actors reveal crippling effects of stage fright," *The Guardian* (Mar 2020), https://www.theguardian.com/society/2020/mar/01/new-study-reveals-crippling-effects-stage-fright, accessed August 4, 2024.

15. Dave Grossman and Loren W. Christensen, *On Combat, The Psychology and Physiology of Deadly Conflict in War and in Peace* (PPCT Research Publications, 2004).

16. Jayne Leonard, medically reviewed by Timothy J. Legg, PhD, PsyD, "What is trauma? What to know," *Medical News Today* (June 2020), https://www.medicalnewstoday.com/articles/trauma, accessed August 4, 2024.

Chapter 4

1. Laura Sanders, "Rare Brain Disorder Prevents All Fear," *Wired* (Dec 2010), https://www.wired.com/2010/12/fear-brain-amygdala/, accessed August 4, 2024.

2. "Phobia," Wikipedia, https://en.wikipedia.org/wiki/Phobia, accessed August 4, 2024.

3. Lee W Daffin Jr, PhD, *Principles of Learning and Behavior*, Washington State University, (June 2021), Creative Commons, https://opentext.wsu.edu/principles-of-learning-and-behavior/chapter/module-4-respondent-conditioning/, accessed August 4, 2024.

4. Susan Mineka, Mark Davidson, Michael Cook, and Richard Keir, "Observational Conditioning of Snake Fear in Rhesus Monkeys," *University of Wisconsin-Madison, Journal of Abnormal Psychology* (1984), vol. 93, no. 4, 355–372, American Psychological Association. Inc, https://communities.pacificu.edu/addisonbrown/wp-content/

uploads/sites/1536/2023/02/Mineka-Davidson-Cook-Keir-1984.-Observational-conditioning-of-snake-fear-in-Rhesus-monkeys.pdf, accessed August 5, 2024.

5. Gemma Reynolds, Andy P. Fields, and Chris Askew, "Learning to fear a second-order stimulus following vicarious learning," *Cognition and Emotion*, 31(3) (2015): 572–579, https://doi.org/10.1080/02699931.2015.1116978, accessed August 5, 2024.

6. Steven Spielberg, *Jaws*, Universal Pictures, https://en.wikipedia.org/wiki/Jaws_(film).

7. Kendra Cherry, medically reviewed by Steven Gans, MD, "10 of the Most Common Phobias," *Very Well Mind* (updated June 2024), https://www.verywellmind.com/most-common-phobias-4136563, accessed August 5, 2024.

8. WebMD editorial contributors, medically reviewed by Zilpah Sheikh, MD, "PTSD Posttraumatic Stress Disorder (PTSD)," WebMD (July 2024), https://www.webmd.com/mental-health/post-traumatic-stress-disorder, accessed August 5, 2024.

9. WebMD editorial contributors, medically reviewed by Smitha Bhandari, MD, "What Is Hypervigilance?" WebMD (February 2024), https://www.webmd.com/mental-health/what-is-hypervigilance.

10. WebMD editorial contributors, medically reviewed by Smitha Bhandari, MD, "What Is Hyperarousal in PTSD?" WebMD, (July 2023), https://www.webmd.com/mental-health/what-is-hyperarousal-in-ptsd, accessed August 5, 2024.

11. Verharen JPH, Zhu Y, and Lammel S, "Aversion hot spots in the dopamine system," *Current Opinion in Neurobiology*, (Oct 2020), https://pubmed.ncbi.nlm.nih.gov/32146296/, accessed August 5, 2024.

12. Peter Preskar, "How to Catch a Woolly Mammoth: Cavemen hunted six-ton, three-meter-tall mammoths," *Medium*

(Oct 2020), https://short-history.com/woolly-mammoth-f857e073f4f1, accessed August 5, 2024.

13. Arash Javanbakht and Linda Saab, "What Happens in the Brain When We Feel Fear, And why some of us just can't get enough of it," *The Conversation, Smithsonian Magazine* (October 2017), https://www.smithsonianmag.com/science-nature/what-happens-brain-feel-fear-180966992/, accessed August 5, 2024.

14. James Cameron, *Titanic* (1997 film), Paramount Pictures, 20th Century Fox International, Wikipedia, https://en.wikipedia.org/wiki/Titanic_(1997_film), accessed August 5, 2024.

Chapter 5

1. Seneca, Robin Campbell (Translator, Introduction), *Letters from a Stoic* (Penguin Classics, 2015).

2. Jeanna Bryner and Tia Ghose, "13 of the most venomous snakes on the planet," *Live Science*, (last updated June 2024), https://www.livescience.com/deadliest-snakes.html, accessed August 5, 2024.

3. Emma Heaps, "Karl Rohnke Comfort zone, Stretch zone Panic zone Model," *Training Industry* (November 2017), https://trainingindustry.com/articles/performance-management/comfort-stretch-and-dont-panic/, accessed August 6, 2024.

4. "Eustress," Wikipedia, https://en.wikipedia.org/wiki/Eustress, accessed August 5, 2024.

5. Watty Piper, *The Little Engine That Could* (Platt & Monk, 1930).

6. "2.1 billion people lack safe drinking water at home, more than twice as many lack safe sanitation," World Health Organization (2017), https://www.who.int/news/item/12-07-2017-2-1-billion-people-lack-safe-drinking-water-at-home-

more-than-twice-as-many-lack-safe-sanitation, accessed Jan 5, 202r.

7. Lloyd Cory, *Quote unquote* (Victor Books, 1977).
8. Hilary Henly, "Extreme Sports, Extreme Underwriting?" Reinsurance Group of America (June 2018), https://www.rgare.com/knowledge-center/article/extreme-sports-extreme-underwriting, accessed August 5, 2024.
9. Alison Wood Brooks, "Get Excited: Reappraising pre-performance anxiety as excitement," *Journal of Experimental Psychology*, American Psychological Association (2013), https://www.apa.org/pubs/journals/releases/xge-a0035325.pdf, accessed August 5, 2024.
10. Craig Weller, "Stress Inoculation Training in Tactical Strength and Conditioning," *TSAC Report*, National Strength and Conditioning Association (April 2013), https://www.nsca.com/education/articles/tsac-report/stress-inoculation-training-in-tactical-strength-and-conditioning/, accessed August 5, 2024.

Chapter 6

1. Emilio Brown, "White Sharks Bite Force," *AZ Animals* (June 2024), https://a-z-animals.com/animals/great-white-shark/facts/great-white-shark-bite-force/, accessed August 5, 2024.
2. "Expedition," *Dictionary.com*, https://www.dictionary.com/browse/expedition, accessed August 5, 2024.

Chapter 7

1. "Your disability is your opportunity," kurthahn.org, https://www.kurthahn.org/wp-content/uploads/2017/02/2017-obt1960.pdf, accessed August 5, 2024.
2. *Outward Bound Story*, Outward Bound, https://www.outwardbound.org/about-us/history/, accessed August 5, 2024.

3. John A. Shedd, *Salt from My Attic*, (The Mosher Press, 1928)
4. Richard Louv, *Last Child in the Woods: Saving Our Children from Nature-Deficit Disorder* (Algonquin Books, 2006).
5. James Dickey and John Boorman, *Deliverance*, Warner Brothers Pictures (July 1972), https://www.imdb.com/title/tt0068473/, accessed August 5, 2024.
6. Clay Bonnyman Evans, "Examining the Real Numbers Behind Violent Instances on the Appalachian Trail," *The Trek* (May 2019), https://thetrek.co/appalachian-trail/examining-real-numbers-behind-violent-instances-appalachian-trail/, accessed August 5, 2024.
7. "Forest Bathing in Japan (Shinrin-yoku)," *Japan Travel*, https://www.japan.travel/en/guide/forest-bathing/, accessed August 5, 2024.
8. "Exploring Syncretism and Shugendo in the Tohoku Yamabushi and Shikoku Pilgrimage," *Japan Travel* (Sept 2021), https://www.japan.travel/en/japan-magazine/2109_exploring-syncretism-and-shugendo-tohoku-yamabushi-and-shikoku/, accessed August 5, 2024.
9. "Walking is man's best medicine," Hippocrates Quotes, BrainyQuote.com, BrainyMedia Inc, (2024), https://www.brainyquote.com/quotes/hippocrates_380084, accessed July 29, 2024.
10. John Muir, *Steep Trails* (Boston: Houghton, Mifflin, 1918).
11. "Walking is the very best possible exercise. Habituate yourself to walk very far," Thomas Jefferson Quotes, BrainyQuote.com, BrainyMedia Inc (2024), https://www.brainyquote.com/quotes/thomas_jefferson_109180, accessed July 28, 2024.
12. "Daintree Rainforest," Wikipedia, https://en.wikipedia.org/wiki/Daintree_Rainforest, accessed August 6, 2024.
13. "A forest so spectacular, Sir David Attenborough called it the most extraordinary place on Earth," Australia.com, https://www.australia.com/en-us/places/cairns-and-surrounds/

guide-to-the-daintree-rainforest.html, accessed August 6, 2024.

14. Miyazaki Y, Lee J, Park BJ, Tsunetsugu Y, Matsunaga K, and Nihon Eiseigaku Zasshi, "Preventive Medical Effects of Nature Therapy," Pub Med, https://pubmed.ncbi.nlm.nih.gov/21996763/, accessed August 6, 2024/

15. Marc G. Berman, John Jonides, and Stephen Kaplan, "The Cognitive Benefits of Interacting With Nature," *Psychological Science* (2008), https://doi.org/10.1111/j.1467-9280.2008.02225.x, accessed August 6, 2024.

16. Andrea Faber Taylor and Frances E. Kuo, "Children With Attention Deficits Concentrate Better After Walk in the Park," *Journal of Attention Disorders* (March 2009), https://doi.org/10.1177/1087054708323000, accessed August 6, 2024.

17. Lauren F Friedman and Kevin Loria, "This Might Be the Easiest Way to Boost Concentration and Memory," *Business Insider* (July 2014), https://www.businessinsider.com/boost-concentration-and-memory-by-going-outside-2014-8, accessed August 6, 2024.

18. Marc G. Berman, Ethan Kross, Katherine M. Krpan, Mary K. Askren, Aleah Burson, Patricia J. Deldin, Stephen Kaplan, Lindsey Sherdell, Ian H. Gotlib, and John Jonides, "Interacting with Nature Improves Cognition and Affect for Individuals with Depression," *Journal of Affective Disorders* vol. 140:3 (Nov 2012), https://www.ncbi.nlm.nih.gov/pmc/articles/PMC3393816/, accessed August 6, 2024.

19. Cassidy Randall, "Spend More Time Outside—Doctor's Orders," *Glamour* (July 2019), https://www.glamour.com/story/park-prescriptions-are-gaining-steam-as-a-mainstream-medical-treatment, accessed August 6, 2024.

20. Cordele Glass, "Creativity And The Natural Outdoors," *Positive Psychology News* (Jan 2020), https://positivepsychologynews.com/news/cordele-glass/2020012440097, accessed August 6, 2024.

21. University of Utah, "Nature nurtures creativity after four days of hiking," *ScienceDaily*, accessed August 5, 2024. https://www.sciencedaily.com/releases/2012/12/121212204826.htm

22. Rathish Nair and Arun Maseeh, "Vitamin D: The Sunshine Vitamin," *Journal of Pharmacology and Pharmacotherapeutics* vol. 3:2 (Apr 2012), https://www.ncbi.nlm.nih.gov/pmc/articles/PMC3356951/, accessed August 6, 2024.

23. Qing Li, "Effect of forest bathing trips on human immune function," *Environ Health Prev Med*, (published online March 2009), https://environhealthprevmed.biomedcentral.com/counter/pdf/10.1007/s12199-008-0068-3.pdf, accessed August 6, 2024.

24. Chelsea Harvey, "Why living around nature could make you live longer," *Washington Post* (Apr 2016), https://www.washingtonpost.com/news/energy-environment/wp/2016/04/19/why-living-around-nature-could-make-you-live-longer, accessed August 6, 2024.

Chapter 8

1. "BGM-71 TOW," Wikipedia, https://en.wikipedia.org/wiki/BGM-71_TOW, accessed August 6, 2024.

2. "Bujinkan," Wikipedia, https://en.wikipedia.org/wiki/Bujinkan, accessed August 6, 2024.

3. Clint Eastwood, *Heartbreak Ridge* (1986), Warner Brothers, https://www.imdb.com/title/tt0091187/?ref_=tt_mv_close, accessed August 6, 2024.

4. "Accelerated Freefall," United States Parachute Association (USPA), https://uspa.org/Make-A-Skydive/Your-First-Jump/Choose-A-Method, accessed August 6, 2024.

5. Hunter S. Thompson, *Hell's Angels: A Strange and Terrible Saga* (Random House, 1967).

Chapter 9

1. "State of nature: how modern humans lived as nomads for 99 percent of our history," *The Independent* (February 2009), https://www.independent.co.uk/news/world/world-history/state-of-nature-how-modern-humans-lived-as-nomads-for-99-per-cent-of-our-history-1604967.html, accessed August 6, 2024.
2. "Fernweh," Wiktionary, https://en.wiktionary.org/wiki/Fernweh, accessed August 6, 2024.
3. Mark Twain, *The Innocents Abroad The New Pilgrim's Progress* (H. H. Bancroft and Company and American Publishing Company, 1869).
4. "Indian cobra," Wikipedia, https://en.wikipedia.org/wiki/Indian_cobra, accessed August 6, 2024.
5. "Seminole Heights serial killer," Wikipedia, https://en.wikipedia.org/wiki/Seminole_Heights_serial_killer, accessed August 6, 2024.
6. Graham Averill, "The Ultimate Big Bend National Park Travel Guide," *Outside Magazine* (February 2020), https://www.outsideonline.com/adventure-travel/national-parks/big-bend-national-park-travel-guide/, accessed August 6, 2024.

Chapter 10

1. "Mud dauber," Wikipedia, https://en.wikipedia.org/wiki/Mud dauber. Accessed Jan 5, 2025
2. *Black Hawk Down* (2001), directed by Ridley Scott, https://www.imdb.com/title/tt0265086/, accessed August 6, 2024.
3. "Ninja Warrior," American/Australian Wikipedia, https://en.wikipedia.org/wiki/American_Ninja_Warrior, https://en.wikipedia.org/wiki/Australian_Ninja_Warrior, accessed August 6, 2024.

4. "What Is Memento Mori?" Daily Stoic, https://dailystoic.com/what-is-memento-mori/, accessed August 6, 2024.

5. Jo Nash, PhD, scientifically reviewed by William Smith, PhD, "Maranasati Meditation: How to Practice Mindfulness of Death," Positivepsychology.com (Oct 2021) https://positivepsychology.com/maranasati-meditation/, accessed August 6, 2024.

6. Marcus Aurelius, *Meditations*, E-Bookarama, Kindle.

Scott MacWherter

Just three days after graduating high school, Scott enlisted in the US Marine Corps, kickstarting an adventurous lifestyle that would shape his future.

After his military days, he worked on luxury cruise ships, traveling to more than 45 countries, cementing his love for discovery and cultural exploration — indeed, he dated an Australian girl, then married her.

A random traumatic experience of being robbed at gunpoint gave him crippling PTSD, but he immersed himself in therapy and intensive training in fear and anxiety management. His recovery included an outdoor wilderness adventure course that taught him the transformative power of adventure — as a tool for personal growth and healing.

Later on, while most people just dream of these types of trips, Scott rented an RV, and drove across the USA, seeking new experiences and connections. And finally, he moved his wife and daughter to his wife's original hometown of Melbourne, Australia, where he continues to embrace life's adventures and inspire others with his story of resilience and discovery.

Please visit:
makeitalifeofadventure.com

www.ingramcontent.com/pod-product-compliance
Lightning Source LLC
Chambersburg PA
CBHW072149070526
44585CB00015B/1057